WASHINGTON
AND
THE REVOLUTIONISTS

WASHINGTON
AND
THE REVOLUTIONISTS

A CHARACTERIZATION OF
RECOVERY POLICIES AND OF THE PEOPLE
WHO ARE GIVING THEM EFFECT

BY

ROGER W. BABSON

Essay Index Reprint Series

BOOKS FOR LIBRARIES PRESS
FREEPORT, NEW YORK

STANDARD BOOK NUMBER:
8369-1642-5

LIBRARY OF CONGRESS CATALOG CARD NUMBER:
76-111812

PRINTED IN THE UNITED STATES OF AMERICA

Dedicated

to

FRANCES PERKINS
Secretary of Labor

CONTENTS

PREFACE

AFTER the close of the World War—during which time I served as Director General of Information and Education for the Labor Administration—I wrote a volume on *Washington and the World War*, centering it about the first Secretary of Labor, William D. Wilson. Eight years later I wrote a second volume on *Washington and the Prosperity Era*, centering it about the second Secretary of Labor, James J. Davis. During the Hoover administration I wrote a third volume, entitled *Washington and the Depression* centering it about the third Secretary of Labor, William N. Doak. Now, during the Roosevelt administration, I have written another volume, which is the fourth of the series, and is entitled *Washington and the Revolutionists*. Here it is.

If you can imagine a bridge connecting two islands— one called Capitalism and the other Socialism—we certainly are now in the center of that bridge. This book treats of that revolutionary bridge; but unlike other writers, this book is not propaganda either for the bridge or for either island. I frankly say, moreover, that those on this bridge can either turn about very quickly and go back to the *laissez-faire* system, or can continue to cross the bridge to the enchanted island. It is possible that the national election of 1936 will be a Republican landslide. It is equally possible that we shall become much more revolutionary and witness tremendous social, business, and investment changes during the next ten years.

Future events come from the reactions of present personalities. To direct one's business and investments properly, it is essential to understand the real aims of the people who are now in charge. They should not be judged by temporary acts of expediency, nor even by their mistakes, but rather by the big goals which they have in mind.

In this book I have tried honestly and fearlessly to present these goals. I trust that both my conservative friends and the President's Cabinet will forgive me if some lines seem too familiar or facetious. Frankly, I believe these revolutionists are working honestly and in the right direction. Naturally they are not all perfect individuals any more than are you and I.

Permit me to acknowledge obligations to members of my organization and others who have aided in collecting the data. I especially extend thanks to Mr. Theodore G. Joslin, Mr. Clarence N. Stone, Mr. Creighton J. Hill, and Mr. H. Clyde Baldwin. I also could give a list of numerous able and conscientious Washington newspaper men and women as well as magazine writers who have given me suggestions.

ROGER W. BABSON

Wellesley, Mass.
November 1, 1933.

WASHINGTON
AND
THE REVOLUTIONISTS

CHAPTER I

WHAT IS THE REVOLUTION?

EVER since the days of the World War when I was working with the Secretary of Labor, it has been my good fortune to know the active people in Washington, including Presidents Wilson, Coolidge, Harding and Hoover. I might also include most of the Cabinet members and important department heads during these years. So far as my personal knowledge goes they were honest men tending to their jobs, although certain revelations concerning the Harding Cabinet caused me to lose faith for a while. It is true that some of these men were interested in their jobs primarily as a job, or—as in the case of some Cabinet members—as an honor. Some merely went through the motions, performing such duties as were forced upon them but without any special effort or enthusiasm.

The above criticism, however, does not apply solely to government employes. The same might be said of executives and employes of corporations in general. There are exceptions, of course, and these exceptions are those who ultimately rise to the top irrespective of where they start. As a rule, however, only those with a financial interest in a company have an abnormal ambition to get to the office before it opens and stay after it closes. If the same energy and enthusiasm which we see in most private businesses is lacking in governmental service, this is only human. Most government employes are either political appointments, holding their position by pull rather than by merit, or else civil service employes who feel that they will not be discharged except under unusual circumstances. The executives and heads of departments are unable to plan any such long-pull programs as are necessary for doing satisfactory work. This, however, is not the fault of the individuals. They measure up as well, if not better, than the run of the mill in industry. The difficulty is due to the circumstances under which they are employed rather than to their own individual character and qualities. Men and women are actuated by the same motives whether in Washington, New York or Chicago.

Having become so used to this general working attitude, I was somewhat at sea when reaching Washington in April, 1933. When the Roosevelt administration came in on March 4, I was in the South. It, therefore, had been in power for a few weeks when I reached Washington. As usual I went around and saw my old friends among the department heads, as most of them were still at their desks. I also met personally seven of the President's new Cabinet. Some of these I had been acquainted with for several years. Frankly, for the first time in my life I did not feel at home in Washington. This was not due to the fact that it was a Democratic administration; my own work in Washington during the war was under a Democratic administration. I was unable to explain what it was that troubled me.

Even men whom I had known for years and with whom I had had many dealings treated me differently than they had before. I wondered whether I or they had changed; or whether there was something which I could not understand. There certainly was in Washington an atmosphere that was strange to me. It may have been that I had changed since the old days and had become more conservative. I tried to analyze myself and ascertain what was the difficulty. Finally I came to the conclusion, after talking with many others, that Washington had changed and that these officials had changed with it. Then it began to dawn upon me that the nation was in the midst of a revolution and that these friends of mine were the revolutionists!

WHAT CAUSED THE CHANGE?

In the case of certain men like Secretary Ickes there really had been no change. These men had always been "Progressives" and this was really their first opportunity at the bat. They naturally influenced their associates. The real reason for this change was apparently the influence of Franklin D. Roosevelt. During recent years I have personally not been acquainted with the President, but I knew him well during war times when he was Assistant Secretary of the Navy. On a given day each week there was a group meeting of assistant secretaries of the various departments and I often attended this meeting as representing the Department of Labor. Whatever may be said now for or against the President, let me say that at those meetings he and Professor Felix Frankfurter, who served as chairman, were then, as now, the exponents of the "New Deal."

Mr. Roosevelt in those days always took the part of

the under dog and, furthermore, he did it graciously, kindly, and in a conservative manner. He then never lost his temper or even his smile. Also, when we got into a disagreement, he was the real pacifier of the group. Whatever may be said of his present policies, I can vouch that they are real and come from his heart. They are not assumed for political purposes. It has been his personality that has influenced the group in Washington. First beginning with the Cabinet members, thence down to the department heads and through them to all workers. Of course there are exceptions. A good many workers still have their fingers crossed and wonder what this revolution is all about. Others are skeptical and feel that the new condition cannot last. But all recognize that there has been a great change, that a new atmosphere exists in Washington, however long it is to last.

What is this revolution? What is the change that has taken place in Washington? Why is it more difficult to do business in Washington today? Why do not the business man and the banker feel at home when visiting the departments? Why do so many of the acts at Washington seem inconsistent? Why have certain principles of economics been ignored?

I can answer all these questions with the one statement: *These people in the Roosevelt administration feel that they are appointed by God to redistribute wealth. They are not acting from a political angle or any other selfish angle. They conscientiously believe that the great majority of people in this country are not getting a square deal and have not for many years.*

They further believe that it is not only best for the great majority of people, but for those who have property, to have a bloodless revolution instead of waiting for a bloody revolution some years hence. Business men who go to Washington fully understanding this attitude get on easily; those who go there with the old attitude are up against a stone wall.

This is the real reason underlying the strenuous opposition made to the Roosevelt nomination. The great mass of conservative Democrats, as well as Republicans, felt that Roosevelt's talk about a new deal was merely preelection stuff which would soon be forgotten. They felt that a political platform was identical with a street-car platform, of use merely to get aboard. So many aspirants for political office had gone forth before election with similar promises which they had entirely forgotten after election, most political leaders were not disturbed by the promises of Franklin D. Roosevelt. Governor Smith, Mr. Raskob and others, however, knew Frank. They had learned that he was basically for the underdog and that most of what he said in preelection time came from his heart. Franklin's revolutionary ideas were the real reason that split the Roosevelt family. This is what Theodore the Great's relative had in mind when saying, "Franklin and his wife are not of our class." It is true that Theodore swung the big stick and at times rapped the capitalistic group very hard; nevertheless, Theodore never forgot that he belonged to this group himself. Franklin from his earliest days took an interest in the other group. Furthermore, the attitude of the aristocrats of the family toward him and his wife made them both more radical and less interested in the aristocratic group.

Franklin D. Roosevelt's own family were the first to call him a revolutionist and it is only natural that he gathered "revolutionists" around him and has been influenced largely by their advices. Let me here remind you that the President of the United States has no more hours a day than you and I have. He must take the same amount of time for sleep and eating. Yet, he has a hundred times as many calls on his time as we have. We know how difficult it is for us to go off by ourselves for quiet thought and constructive research. How much more difficult it must be for the President of the United States! This all means that he must depend upon the advices of others.

Every President must leave it to others to study and derive conclusions. The acts of all Presidents are ninety per cent a reflection of the thoughts of those who surround them. Franklin D. Roosevelt believes that there should be a more equal distribution of the earnings of our nation. He believes that the debt structure is too heavy for the earning capacity. His primary object is to redistribute more equally this earning capacity. Only when you realize this can you understand the reason for the many strange things now being done at Washington. Furthermore, when you do understand the President's goal many of the so-called inconsistencies disappear and the reasons for those heretofore unexplainable actions appear clear.[1]

SPECIFIC INCONSISTENCIES EXPLAINED

Let me explain a few of the glaring things which seem to bother business men and others. The most common

[1] Those interested in an official explanation should read John Dickinson's article in the *Atlantic Monthly* for August, 1933.

question is: "How can the President justify discharging government employes in Washington and making so many new appointments in connection with public works and other new programs?" Surely this seems inconsistent especially to the people who are being discharged and to their relatives. The simple fact is that this is a part of the revolution. The President feels that these old government employes have had their turn at the bat; and it is only fair that they should retire and give positions to others. Postmaster-General Farley is severely criticized for throwing out Republicans and installing Democrats, but he insists that a revolution in officeholding is only just and fair.

The President believes that the Democrats have not received a fair square deal or their share of appointments during the past twenty-five years and he is going to do what he can to rectify it. Furthermore, he will try to convince you that it is right and fair to "revolve" officeholders. Business men go to Washington and argue "economics." It is true that most business men never studied economics and know little about it. They have, however, an idea regarding "rugged individualism" and this is what they are arguing for when talking about "economics."

Business men go to Washington and talk about prices and profits, interest and dividends. They wonder why they do not make more of an impression. The difficulty is that they are thinking only of themselves and their group. They forget that less than ten per cent of the people in this country have ever seen a share of stock or a bond. The President and his associates will remind us that profits and even dividends consist of something besides money. In the last analysis profits must be expressed in terms of happiness, contentment and those spiritual qualities of all the people which cannot be measured by bank clearings, stock market prices or ordinary statistics. The new administration believes itself to be just as sane from an economic point of view as any of us. *They, however, take the position that we of the capitalistic group are narrow in our use of the word "profits" in confining it only to money.* Perhaps we are wrong!

Often when the business man has been to Washington before, it has been with the purpose of having the government help him collect debt—private debt, corporation debt, municipal debt, or foreign debt. Now when he goes to Washington he finds an ear deaf to such appeals. Why? The answer is simple. Washington is now primarily interested in the compromise or the reduction of indebtedness rather than in the collection of indebtedness. At first thought we say this is contrary to economic law, but the administration will soon convince us that such a question has nothing to do with economics. They even come back with the retort: "When you were last at church and repeated the Lord's Prayer, did you not say 'forgive us our debts as we forgive our debtors'?"

I received perhaps my greatest shock when going to Washington to secure a government appropriation for advertising to speed up the circulation of money. I had already been surprised in talking the matter over with leading magazine publishers to learn that they were skeptical of my being able to accomplish anything at Washington. However, I took the matter up with the administration. All I got was a blank stare until finally I learned that the real feeling is: *Nine-tenths of this advertising is bunk anyway. Instead of the government encouraging advertising it should wipe it out. One of the principal causes of both high prices and unnecessary debt is advertising. A great proportion of the advertising is to get people to buy things they have no business to buy and to pay prices they have no business to pay.*

Naturally I do not agree with this generalization. I feel that advertising played its important part in being responsible for the employment and prosperity of the American people from 1924 to 1929. On the other hand, I see both sides and the reason for the revolutionary attitude. The abuse of advertising has resulted in this feeling at Washington. They are much more interested in publicity that will help the buyer save his money, and not spend it for foolish things at high prices. They believe that it is too bad to have newspapers and radio used to encourage people to drink beer and attend cheap shows.

NEW SECURITIES ACT

Here is the real reason for the New Securities Act. The administration is not interested in interfering with bona-fide investments or speculation. But the administration has seen so many people ruthlessly lose their savings, through so-called investments, that they feel called by God to protect these innocent people, although they must admit that the investments were made to secure abnormal interest rates or perhaps to get something for nothing. The administration believes that the man in the street is much better off to put his money into a home or into education for his children or even into an automobile rather than into buying stocks. The administration believes the country is much better off to keep the money in Main Street rather than have it go to Wall Street. Hence, notwithstanding the justified complaints of the investment bankers, the President believes that more good than harm is being done by the New Securities Act. He believes that the legislation is in the interest of the underdog.

The same principle applies to the reasons for the Glass-Steagall Bill with its accompanying deposit insurance feature. Bankers go to Washington stating that the act is unfair to the bank stockholders, directors and officials. The administration freely admits it, but replies, "You bankers have had your day; now let the depositors have their day." Even the bankers must admit that the Glass-Steagall Bill is in the interest of the depositors, even though it is revolutionary. Heretofore when the Democrats have been in power, the Republicans have been out; and when the Republicans have been in power the Democrats have been out. *But in both cases the bankers have always been in and the small investor and the depositors have always been out!* Now the administration is attempting to revolutionize this condition. Bankers thought that when Franklin D. Roosevelt spoke about "the money changers in the temple" he was just giving some political talk. They could not imagine that he was in earnest. They realize it now.

THE NRA, THE AAA, THE CWA AND THE TVA

Leading Chambers of Commerce and the Republican National Committee criticize the NRA, the AAA and the TVA. They poke fun at the "Brain Trust" and "inexperienced children" who are operating the NRA and distributing the various aids to farm and home owners. Yet they must admit that the former vicious circle of cutting prices and sweating labor should not go on unrestrained. Industry needs to have some relief from the Anti-Trust Laws, so as to plan cooperatively; and if so, must be willing to submit to government supervision through codes and licensing.

The President's attitude toward organized labor is self-explanatory when one gets his point of view. He realizes the weakness and mistakes of organized labor. He has dealt with organized labor all his life. Were he a manufacturer he would perhaps endeavor to run an open shop. On the other hand, the President realizes that the goal of the labor unions is the same as his namely, to bring about a more equal division of the nation's income. Therefore, he works with union labor leaders believing that the end justifies the means. From this point of view you understand his interest in collective bargaining and other things which manufacturers know curtail their control of industry.

We complain about inheritance taxes and especially about income taxes. We say that the higher brackets are confiscatory. The administration will not deny this.

They even do not seem excited about it. Their reason is that these income taxes not only provide the government with funds, *but also help redistribute wealth. This means that the very thing which business men want to avoid is the real thing which the new administration wishes to accomplish.* This explains the issuing of such huge amounts of government bonds and even the mooted question of depreciating the currency. Therefore, instead of these revolutionary acts being inconsistent, they are very consistent with the goal of distributing more equally the national income, even although they retard building and enterprise, resulting in continued unemployment. *I especially have in mind sur-taxes on incomes.*

Even when I saw considerable of the President, during the World War, he was troubled with the fact that about 10 per cent of the people of this country own 90 per cent of the wealth, and that some 70 per cent have not enough money at their death to pay for probating their estates. This is a simple statement—one that has been repeated so often that its effectiveness is gone. However, anyone who seriously considers these figures must realize that a "new deal" is something to be considered, and should not be ignored. This is especially true when one considers that there are today enough idle factories, freight cars, labor, materials and capital, so that everyone in the country could enjoy a good home, warm clothing and plenty to eat, as well as normal comforts and pleasures. Only national planning is necessary to bring this about, yet the moneyed interests of our country consider such national planning as a revolutionary step!

WICKEDNESS OF WASTE

The President and his associates have also been inspired by the figures on waste which have been submitted by many of his friends. When the President considers that about one-half of the total national income is now being wasted, he cannot help becoming interested in national planning of some kind, which will give more of the good things of life to a greater percentage of the people. The waste, which I schedule below, is going on *in addition* to the waste that comes through the idle factories, idle freight cars, idle labor, idle materials and idle capital, to which I have referred above. Therefore, even the most conservative of us must realize that the revolution of 1933 is justified. Furthermore, that these revolutionists, of whom I am writing, are worthy of profound respect.

Let me add that it is not enough for us business men merely to stand on the side lines and criticize the honest attempt of President Roosevelt and his associates to solve this economic tragedy. We cannot afford to rest our case on the law of supply and demand and "let nature take its course." We are as backward economically today as were our forefathers when they looked upon cholera and smallpox as uncontrollable. If we are to avoid losing our liberty—to say nothing about losing our property—we must find some solution which will work. It is suicidal for us longer to remain inactive and let misled or ignorant radicals preach doctrines which never have worked and never will work. Therefore please note these figures:

Of our total annual income of $50,000,000,000, about

one-half is being thrown away, for which our people receive nothing in return. This one-half may be divided into three groups, as follows:

Group 1. Requiring only knowledge and common sense for saving.

(1) Foolish Investments and preventable business failures due to lack of facts and statistics $1,500,000,000
(2) Contagious sickness, largely amongst workers, due to uncleanliness, poor ventilation and faulty first-aid 1,500,000,000
(3) Preventable fire losses due to lack of fire alarms, sprinkler protection and police signals 1,500,000,000
(4) Automobile accidents and delays at street intersections, etc. 1,500,000,000
(5) Ignorant buying of adulterations, waste through dumping 1,500,000,000
(6) Losses through inexcusable advertising and management errors 1,000,000,000

TOTAL...... $8,500,000,000

Group 2. Requiring character and education for saving.

(1) Excess or harmful foods $4,000,000,000
(2) Excess drinking and excess smoking ... 1,000,000,000
(3) Unnecessary expenditures on criminals and insane due to failure to sterilize 1,000,000,000
(4) 25% of amount spent upon movies, cheap resorts, and joy rides 1,000,000,000
(5) Useless clothing 500,000,000
(6) Cosmetics and quackery 500,000,000
(7) Misdirected educational expenses 500,000,000

TOTAL...... $8,500,000,000

Group 3. Requiring planning and control, for saving.

(1) Needless overhead costs, due largely to
individual dishonesty and carelessness $3,000,000,000
    (Eliminating one-half of eight million
              workers)

(2) Failure to standardize on simple neces-
sities   1,500,000,000
(3) Unnecessary employment turnover losses   1,000,000,000
(4) Preventable miscellaneous accidents . . .   500,000,000
(5) Lack of elemental scientific management   500,000,000
(6) Obvious inefficient plant location   500,000,000
(7) Waste of coal, oil, gas and supplies
through 25,000,000 homes, stores and fac-
tories   500,000,000
(8) Miscellaneous   500,000,000

                TOTAL. $8,500,000,000

Of course, the first thought is that the elimination
of this waste would destroy present investments in
wretched homes and wasteful industries and throw out
of work those employed therein. It would destroy such
investments. Only thereby can the interest charge with
which the public is now burdened be reduced. *But the
labor would immediately become reemployed building
new houses and making useful goods.* All that is needed
would be the cooperation of parents, schools, churches
and newspapers. Next to present carelessness and ig-
norance in human breeding, those engaged in merchan-
dising and advertising may be most to blame for
present unjust economic conditions. These same people,
however, can be of greatest value in improving conditions by redirecting demand from useless and harmful

products to such as will make all healthy, prosperous and happy.

THE SOLUTION OF AMERICA'S ILLS

The above three groups make a total saving of $25,500,000,000 or about half the United States annual income. *This is without giving any consideration to what is spent for taxes, interest, fashions, recreations, education, literature, religion, art or even vice.* All of the above *means* as follows:

(a) That the cost of the present standard of living in the United States can be reduced about 50 per cent, or the present standard of living could be increased 100 per cent, by merely the elimination of waste. Furthermore, by the elimination of this waste the general health, comfort and happiness of all the people would be increased, while real estate taxes could be cut one-third.

(b) That with a reasonable amount of planning, the people now employed in the above useless industries could be put to work making goods and performing services which are truly useful, so that everyone could enjoy the necessities and comforts of life, with no abnormal unemployment.

(c) Also that hours of labor for executives and workers could be reduced so that there would be more time for spiritual, physical, intellectual and cultural development by all. Moreover, the nation's interest charge would likewise proportionately be reduced by the wiping out of these parasite industries.

(d) Or, by using the money saved through eliminating this waste, we could pay off in eight years all bond issues, all mortgages, and all corporation and personal loans, now aggregating $200,000,000,000.

No further inflation or other quack remedies are needed. The past century has been one of material progress; but the next century must be one of spiritual and managerial progress. The basic goal of the present revolution is that more people may enjoy a more equal distribution of the nation's income, due to better inheritance, more sensible training and more efficient planning. The Roosevelt administration believes all the above could be accomplished as follows: By a system of collecting penalties for waste and of using the funds to encourage the building of new homes, the manufacture of useful clothing, the distribution of healthful foods and the elimination of commercialism from amusements and recreation. Of course, those now guilty of this wicked waste naturally protest.

America has every natural resource to make everyone healthy, prosperous and happy. All America needs is to revive that religious creative spirit which causes men to have confidence in themselves, confidence in their brothers and confidence in their God. Yes, that spiritual creative power which causes men to want to pull the cart instead of riding in the cart—to work, think, promote and build instead of depending upon interest, bank accounts, pensions and government aid. From now on in the United States *activity* will be at a greater premium; while *passivity* will get a lesser reward. Men and women will be more anxious to own homes, farms and factories than to hold stocks, bonds or mortgages. Real estate and commodities will be worth more than money hoarded in bank vaults; while industry, initiative, courage and confidence will count for far more than securities, legal opinions, family trusts or even the Constitution of the United States.

CAMPAIGN PROMISES

I have already referred to the fact that the President is making a serious effort to carry out his campaign promises. Even this is a thing that troubles many business men today. They had seen so many political leaders make similar revolutionary promises before and never attempt to carry them out, that they are angry with Roosevelt for now carrying them out. Believing he never would do so, they were willing to let mud be thrown at President Hoover who was their real friend. They peacefully stood upon the side lines to "let nature take its course." Surely they then missed their chance to put in objections. Many of the business men who are complaining even voted for Franklin D. Roosevelt. However, at this late date is it fair for them to complain?

Business men of both political parties now realize that President Hoover was earnestly working to avoid this revolution. It could have been headed off if the conservative people had taken a greater interest in the less fortunate.

Still it may not be so bad. Roosevelt may now be making it easier for our children and grandchildren. In our sober moments we must admit that the *goal* of the President is right. It is far better for us to cooperate with him, even though it temporarily hurts, than to try to set back the hands of the clock. At least I have come to this conclusion. Now when I visit

Washington with this new goal sympathetically in mind, I feel at home and can talk the new language and get justice.

So far so good. Although the President would criticize us for thinking of "dividends" only in terms of money, yet we should impress upon the President and his advisers that there needs to be a redistribution of something besides property and income. *There needs to be a redistribution of energy, education, intelligence and judgment. There needs to be a redistribution of initiative, self-control, courage and a willingness to sacrifice. There needs to be a redistribution of those fundamental pioneering qualities developed by men and women enduring hardship*, working twelve hours a day and risking their lives to settle our great western farms and communities. In order that the new deal may be a success, the administration must devise some way to redeal these qualities, and not merely property and income.

It is true that some members of the administration have this point of view; but I fear that others still lack it. The fact that money is being so freely spent on bridges, highways and other things, not vitally necessary, while schools are being closed and school-teachers left unpaid, shows that the right point of view is lacking somewhere. I grant that these bridges and highways may be useful, but they could wait and be built a few years hence. This is not true in connection with the education of children who must be educated now or never. These children cannot wait four or five years before going again to school.

To help in this revolution the President has called

to Washington a group of able statisticians. Already many such men were to be found in the Bureau of Labor Statistics, in the Departments of Commerce and Agriculture, at the Federal Reserve, Interstate Commerce and other offices. But the President wanted a few trusties who had not only the figures but also the vision. He wanted some men who were seeking the same revolutionary goal that he is seeking. Here they are:

John Dickinson, Assistant Secretary of Commerce.

Oscar E. Kiessling, chief economist of the mineral statistics division, Bureau of Mines.

Mordecai Ezekiel, economic adviser to the Secretary of Agriculture.

Isador Lubin, commissioner of labor statistics.

E. A. Goldenweiser, director of research and statistics, Federal Reserve Board.

Alexander Sachs, chief of division of economic research and planning, National Recovery Administration.

E. Dana Durand, chief economist, Tariff Commission.

Corrington Gill, director of research and statistics, Federal Emergency Relief Administration.

Stuart A. Rice, assistant director, Bureau of the Census.

O. M. W. Sprague, financial executive assistant to the Secretary of the Treasury (W. R. Stark, chief of section of financial and economic research of the Treasury Department, alternate).

O. C. Stine, chief of division of statistical and historical research, Bureau of Agricultural Economics.

PLANNING THE REVOLUTION

I must not close this chapter without referring to another important factor of the administration's program —the bringing about this revolution by constitutional means. Italy, Germany and other countries are operating a system of planned economy designed to distribute the national income more equally and to give more people the good things of life. To do this, however, they are sacrificing one of the best things of life—*liberty*. Most people in the long run would rather have fewer material things but have the freedom to think and speak and vote as their consciences dictate.

It should be said that these revolutionists in Washington today are earnestly striving to bring about their desired changes constitutionally and without infringing the liberties of the people. They deserve the greatest credit for this attempt. If successful, this will be the great contribution of America to world political and economic progress. Furthermore, America should make this contribution because it was for this purpose that America was founded.[1]

It is important that business men and investors should recognize this point because there is gradually growing in this country a fascist movement centered in the industrial East among the leaders of the vested interests. When I go to New York, Philadelphia, Pittsburgh, and other large cities I hear bankers, captains

[1] See *Fountain Sources of American Political Theory*, by Florence A. Pooke. Published by Lewis Copeland Company, 119 West 57th Street, New York City.

of industry, and other ultra-conservatives talking in favor of fascism "which will put a stop to all this nonsense." At times when in the midst of wasteful struggles between capital and labor over collective bargaining, the open and closed shop, and so forth, I have felt myself that fascism, temporarily at least, is the answer to the problem.

When capital and labor get into conflict the public might ultimately get tired of the conflict and resignedly accept a dictatorship. Such a situation is a real and serious fear of the administration, because dictators are usually born and not elected. They secure their power through force of personal strength rather than through ballots. It can truly be said that the revolutionists about whom I am writing will hold fast to liberty as our most precious heritage. If we temporarily lose this heritage through a fascist government, this will be due either to the actions of capitalists or of labor leaders. The revolution in which President Roosevelt is interested is founded on liberty. If it cannot accomplish its purposes constitutionally, it will call a Constitutional Convention to amend the old document.

What distinguishes this administration from the last is not so much tempo, mood, atmosphere. That quickening always accompanies the transfer of power. It is the sense of *movement*. Everybody seems receptive, primed to go. "Let's try it," says the President, and there is ground-swell as if the nation had waited for the word. In the anteroom you realize that the movement is a movement of the national mind, which has at last reached the Capital, penetrated the White House. It is a manifestation that somehow moves you

as you wait here at the center, watching a new government taking shape. This is civilization, you say: a
people bent on change, yet disciplined and mature
enough to move toward new paths together, step by
step, patiently and with a tough and valorous humor.

The Executive desk is not quite so clear as it used
to be. There is a scattering of papers under the tall
bronze lamp. The schedule of appointments is not so
rigid. The President smashes through the order of the
day by sending for the people he wants whenever he
wants them—especially his revolutionary Cabinet
members. His secretaries find it hard to keep up with
him, but they are accustomed to his habits and have
survived a period of initiation not unlike the first few
months at the general headquarters of a revolution.[1] In

[1] The Act of Congress approved on January 19, 1886, provides the succession in the following order:

> Vice President
> 1. Secretary of State
> 2. Secretary of Treasury
> 3. Secretary of War
> 4. Attorney-General
> 5. Postmaster-General
> 6. Secretary of the Navy
> 7. Secretary of the Interior
> 8. Secretary of Agriculture
> 9. Secretary of Commerce
> 10. Secretary of Labor

The interpretation has been that should the man elected President die or become in any way ineligible, between the time of
the meeting of the electoral college and the following March
4, the Vice President-elect would become President. This interpretation has been made law by the Amendment of 1932 which

fact here is a newspaperman's thumb-nail description of these Cabinet members:

CORDELL HULL—He specializes in tariff and currency problems . . . he doesn't play cards . . . he doesn't attend the movies . . . he doesn't fish . . . he reads.

WILLIAM H. WOODIN—He composes symphonic music . . . he plays a guitar in bed . . . he collects coins . . . he builds locomotives . . . he fishes . . . he is quiet.

GEORGE HENRY DERN—A football captain in college . . . he was reelected Democratic Governor of Utah in 1928 despite national G.O.P. landslide . . . he is an expert organizer.

HOMER S. CUMMINGS—Liberal prosecuting attorney, who likes underdog . . . twice got votes at National Convention . . . former chairman National Committee . . . descendent of Robert Bruce's rival for crown of Scotland.

JAMES A. FARLEY—Five hours' sleep is enough for him . . . he writes thousands of letters . . . he shakes thousands of hands . . . he is six feet two . . . he smiles.

CLAUDE A. SWANSON—He collects mementos of the Confederacy . . . he speaks with the typical Virginia accent

---

was basically designed to reduce the period between election and administration.

In reading this old law, it will be observed that this succession shall, ". . . only be held to apply to such officers as shall have been appointed by the advice and consent of the Senate to the offices therein named . . ." This suggests a question. Since no Cabinet is actually appointed until after the inauguration of the President, this order of succession obviously cannot apply to the remote contingency of the removal of both President and Vice President-elect prior to their taking the oath of office and the subsequent approval by the Senate of the appointees. Who then would become President if both the President-elect and the Vice President-elect should die or become incapacitated?

. . . he wears pince-nez eyeglasses . . . he is a genuine Southerner.

HAROLD L. ICKES—A political reformer, he has been leading "lost" causes for 35 years as a Progressive Republican . . . firm-jawed, tight-lipped, he likes a fight . . . he has ideas.

HENRY A. WALLACE—He's a farm journalist of the third generation . . . son of a former Secretary of Agriculture . . . he advocates inflation . . . he's a Republican Independent . . . he writes.

DANIEL C. ROPER—His dish is numbers . . . even the filing of income tax papers is easy for him . . . he was clerk of the Interstate Commerce Committee of the Senate . . . he knows his commerce.

FRANCES PERKINS—She nearly always wears a black tricorne hat . . . she is an economist, sociologist, statistician . . . she insists on having the facts and figures.

Chapter II

THE REVOLUTIONISTS' HEADQUARTERS

FROM March 4, 1933, for the next few years at least, the White House will be the center of revolutionary power in Washington. Every department, bureau and official will give most careful consideration to summons, telephone calls or letters from the White House. A word from the White House has a tremendous effect toward getting things done. Bureau chiefs give great attention to requests from Cabinet members; Cabinet members give careful consideration to requests from key Senators and Representatives. But they all move fast when messages come from the White House. Those who have access to the White House have a distinct advantage. Therefore, it is well always to maintain a friendly relation and acquaintance with this center of authority in our national government. Furthermore, if one is honest and reasonable, such an acquaintance may readily be established and maintained.

Franklin Delano Roosevelt, as I have already indicated, has only about twelve to fourteen hours a day for work. A great portion of this twelve to fourteen hours he must take for study, conferences, dictation or other business routine. This means that his time for personal interviews, or for the reading of personal letters, is limited. Nevertheless, in fairness to President

Roosevelt, I will say that, even under these conditions, he takes time to meet more people and dictate more personal letters than the average business man of large affairs. The pressure on the President of the United States is almost beyond understanding. A conscientious citizen will do all he can to avoid asking for personal interviews or taking the President's personal time in any other way. Yet, there are other methods of accomplishing the desired "White House" contact.

With the exception of Cabinet days, which are Tuesdays and Fridays at two o'clock, it is usually possible to shake hands with the President at noon. It is customary for him to devote a half hour a day to shaking hands with people. This is purely a perfunctory affair and enables one only to say that he has "met the President." No time exists on these occasions to present any plans or to talk any business. People are necessarily rushed through the President's office like cattle through a dipping-vat, and this is only right and fair. Those desiring to bother the President in this way should get a letter of introduction from a Senator or Representative. Often a Congressman desires to accompany his constituent to the White House at that time, as it gives the Congressman himself an opportunity of keeping his face and name before the President. If one should be so fortunate as to have the President send for him, then one should by all means grasp the opportunity. If the President knows you, it might be wise to let him know of your presence when you are in Washington, but do not unnecessarily bother him.

THE OFFICIAL SECRETARIES

All of the above signifies that it is much more satisfactory to make your White House contacts through
one or more of the President's secretaries. Most Presidents have had only one secretary. President Coolidge
had two: Mr. Edward Saunders as official secretary
and Mr. Edward T. Clark as personal secretary. President Hoover had seven. President Roosevelt has three
secretaries—Colonel Louis McHenry Howe, Marvin
Hunter McIntyre and Stephen Tyree Early. In addition, Miss Marguerite LaHand, who has been his private secretary for twelve years, serves as his personal
appointment and file clerk. She lives on the third floor
of the White House and is called "Missy" by the
family. Miss Grace Tully is his stenographer. Another
stenographer is Henry Cannee. Any one of these persons may be useful as a means of contact and fortunate
are those who have the confidence of any of these
people.

The important ones, however, are Secretaries Howe,
McIntyre and Early, all of whom are old-time newspaper men. Right here let us say that a Washington
newspaper correspondent is always a good introduction
to the White House and this Washington representative
may be a better man to help you than even your Congressman. They all know the handsome, curly-headed
"Steve" Early. He is a descendant of Confederate General Jubal Early. He covered the Navy Department for
the Associated Press when Mr. Roosevelt was Assistant
Secretary of the Navy. He covered Roosevelt when

campaigning for Vice President in 1920 and has been a loyal worker for him ever since. I say, therefore, that when going to Washington on business it may be a good idea to get a letter of introduction from your local paper to its Washington correspondent and from this correspondent to "Steve" Early.

The above persons have all come to the White House since noon of March 4, 1933. There are two persons of real importance, however, who have been there through all recent administrations. They are Doorman Pat McKenna who is the first one you will meet when entering the Executive Offices on the west side of the White House, and Rudolph Forster who handles the mechanics of the White House business. When entering the Executive Offices, it is best first to inquire for Mr. McKenna and tell him that you wish to see Mr. Rudolph Forster. At the end of the long lobby, over which Mr. McKenna presides and where members of the press loiter, is a suite of three rooms. The first room at the right is occupied by Mr. Forster, a thin, worried, modest man wearing tortoiseshell glasses. He usually has a bouquet of roses on his desk. He is a friendly man, quiet, unselfish and exceedingly loyal to his chief. Moreover, he has excellent judgment and is "wise." He knows "who's who" and has an amazing memory for almost everyone who has been to the White House during the past twenty years.

The room adjoining his, looking out toward the Monument, is occupied by Secretary McIntyre. Directly adjoining his room, also looking out on the Monument, is President Roosevelt's private office. Beyond the President's office is another room called the

Cabinet Room. Between the President's private office and the above-mentioned lobby is where the press used to convene for conferences. When meeting the President, you will probably enter from Mr. McIntyre's room and pass out through the above-mentioned hall. Colonel Howe, with his bright red-haired secretary, Miss Durand, has an office over at the other end beyond the Cabinet Room, and Mr. Early is also out of sight.

WHITE HOUSE ARRANGEMENTS

Mr. Raymond Muir of Boston, a tall and lank individual, is now doorman of the White House proper (which of course no one will visit except on invitation or as a tourist to inspect). The public can come in on the lower floor and up the main staircase into the East Room every day except Sunday, from 10 to 2, and those who hold cards from their Congressmen and Senators may be shown the other formal entertainment rooms. There is a small dining room which is kept for the family, and the life of the family goes on upon the second and third floors. Mrs. Henry Nesbit, a former Hyde Park neighbor of the President's, is the White House housekeeper. Her husband, a lusty Irishman who used to sell whale oil, is superintendent of the Executive Offices.

Another interesting person is Miss Louise Hachmeister of New York City who takes charge of the White House telephone switchboard. She not only knows with whom the President cares to talk and with whom he does not care to talk, but also can distinguish the individual voices of these people so that the President or his secretaries cannot be tricked into talking with some stranger or anyone with whom they do not wish to talk. There also are numerous servants, some of whom have been at the White House for years and others have been brought by the President and his wife.

Mrs. Roosevelt is using the Lincoln Room as her workshop and office instead of the office occupied by other President's wives at the east end of the long corridor. Never has the oval room been so attractive as it is at present fitted up as the study of the President. The triple window looks down on the lawn and the fountain at the end of the grounds and the vista of the Monument. This is the airiest and most sunshiny room in the house. Here the President uses the desk-table for years in use in the President's study in the Monroe Room and in the Lincoln Study arranged by the Hoovers. This table-desk is made from the timbers of Her Majesty's Ship *Resolute* and was presented to the United States by Queen Victoria.

Since Mrs. Roosevelt does not use the raised alcove-like room at the end of the corridor for her office it has become an additional living room. The office of the secretary to Mrs. Roosevelt, Mrs. Malvina Thompson Scheiber, has been established in the wing of this corridor which runs out to the windows above the main entrance of the White House. This was formerly used as a second-floor playroom for the various White House children. The room used by Mrs. Hoover as a sitting room is now President Roosevelt's bedroom.

Markers have been placed telling of things which

happened in the various rooms. For instance, in one room you read on the mantelpiece an inscription:

"This room was used for Cabinet meetings from President Johnson's time until 1902. Here was signed the treaty of peace with Spain."

In another room:

"In this room Lincoln signed the Emancipation Proclamation freeing the slaves."

In another room:

"In this room Lincoln slept."

The President's bedroom, or lounging room, is on the second floor in the Oval Room where is the desk made from the timbers of the *Resolute*, with a copy of the inkstand used by George Washington at Mount Vernon. Before the fireplace is the President's favorite chair and the swivel desk and table reproduced for him in Mrs. Roosevelt's Val-Kill Shop, from one designed by Thomas Jefferson. There also hang some of his favorite pictures, including one of a destroyer over the mantelpiece, on one side a picture of the surrender of the German fleet and on the other the *Mayflower* being escorted into Queenstown.

Mrs. Roosevelt uses the suite which was occupied by Mrs. Hoover, but the bedroom was so large she has turned it into a study filled with photographs of places she has visited and people she knows. A smaller dressing room is used as a bedroom. Across the corridor from the President's room on the second floor is the one assigned to Louis Howe, the President's Secretary Number One. The Monroe Room nearby has been refurnished by Mrs. Roosevelt with green stuffed sofa and chairs brought from the Roosevelts' New York house. The old Monroe furniture has been removed to safer quarters in the broad corridor as the Monroe Room is now used as a sitting room for the younger members of the family. Over the mantelpiece is a picture of Mrs. Roosevelt's grandfather. In addition to her personal secretary, Mrs. Roosevelt has indirectly a number of women on her staff, such as Miss Nancy Cook, Miss Margaret Durand, and Miss Mary Ebing, the latter being of the State Democratic Committee.

One must be careful how one acts at the White House, even if it is the home of revolutionists! When waiting for an appointment, you are likely to be accosted by or innocently sat beside by a Secret Service man who may start a conversation. You naturally think that this is some other person like yourself awaiting an appointment. Before you know it, you have given him information which he takes in to Mr. Rudolph Forster. The Chief of the Secret Service is Mr. Richard Jervis.

There are a few men who have the run of the White House today as did Mr. Frank Stearns during the Coolidge administration. Among these may be mentioned Mr. William C. Bullitt, who has been dubbed the "Mystery Man" of the administration and Professor Raymond C. Moley. Professor Moley was Assistant Secretary of State, but has since left to found a magazine with Mr. Astor. For a time he occupied the same relation to the President on legislative matters as James Farley, the new Postmaster-General, occupies in connection with political appointments. In this connection, the following extract from an editorial which appeared in the Washington *Post* on a Wednesday in

March, 1933, is of interest, especially in view of Professor Moley's later retirement.

The prominent part that college professors played in the last campaign, particularly the group headed by Dr. Raymond C. Moley, professor at Columbia University, who has been closely associated with the President-elect ever since his nomination, has attracted much attention as a new element to be intimately connected with practical politics. At a meeting of Columbia graduates Dr. Moley spoke frankly of his experiences as economic adviser to the in-coming President. He believes that politicians and professors are being drawn together into closer relationship in solving governmental problems than ever before. In his new position as Assistant Secretary of State he will doubtless continue close relations with the President and be in a position to advance his own ideas of economic and international questions.

Dr. Moley disclosed that his recent experience outside the confines of academic walls had been an illuminating one. The professor explained that the so-called "brain trust" had worked directly with the Democratic candidate rather than with the campaign committee. However, he said, the professors like the politicians and the politicians like the professors, and he was frank to acknowledge that he had "learned more, not only of practice, but of theory, from Jim Farley and Louis Howe than from many of my books." By engaging in public service Dr. Moley found that the professor "came to sympathize with and appreciate fully the intelligence that the harassed public official exercises when meeting his problem; we have found that wisdom lives even when it does not wear the scholastic gowns of wisdom."

Another is Adolph A. Berle Jr., who was one of Mr. Roosevelt's technical advisers during the campaign and since has served on the President's "academic cabinet." He is 38 years old, is married, lives with his wife, the former Beatrice Bend Bishop, at 142 East Nineteenth Street and practices corporation law, with his brother Rudolph as partner, at 70 Pine Street, New York City.

Mr. Berle first attracted general attention more than a generation ago when he won the appellation "infant prodigy" by entering Harvard at the age of 13. He was graduated with his Bachelor's degree at 17, took his Master's degree the next year and, in 1916, at the age of 21, received the Bachelor of Laws degree from the Harvard Law School. He then entered the law office of Louis D. Brandeis, now a United States Supreme Court Justice, but left the following year to serve in the World War.

WHITE HOUSE CUSTOMS REVOLUTIONIZED

All agree that there is a pleasanter atmosphere in the White House today than has existed for many years. The White House of Wilson's day was clouded with his aloofness and illness; the White House of Harding's day was saturated with suspicion and unrest; the White House of Coolidge's day was filled with New England sternness; while the White House of Hoover's day was one of statistics. President Roosevelt, however, has brought to the White House that freshness and smile which were so effective during his campaign and the optimism and courage gained through years of suffering. When a person enters the Executive Offices today he feels he is entering a friendly atmosphere. No visitor is left in unhappy obscurity. If

· "Steve" Early or one of the other secretaries is too busy, some one else is ready to help visitors. Questions are quickly and honestly answered. The secretaries themselves freely enter the President's room at any time and the President calls them by their first names, "Louis," "Mac" and "Steve."

Another man who has access to the White House is Lewis W. Douglas, a young man from Arizona who is Director of the Budget. Others are of course the Cabinet members and the following: Vice President Garner; Speaker Rainey; Senators Robinson, of Arkansas, the majority leader; Norris, Nebraska; Wheeler, Montana; Pittman, Nevada; Harrison, Mississippi; and Representatives Byrns, of Tennessee, the house majority leader; McDuffie, Alabama, chairman of the special economy committee which reported the economy bill; Snell, New York, the house minority leader; Chairman Jones of the house agricultural committee; Chairman Buchanan of the house appropriations committee; Ragon, Arkansas; and Huston Thompson of the Federal Trade Commission. Also Professor Felix Frankfurter often comes from Boston, while Henry Morgenthau, Jr. and Prof. George F. Warren are constantly going in and out.

In nothing is the contrast between Mr. Hoover and Mr. Roosevelt more marked than in the President's conferences with the Washington correspondents. After President Harding's unfortunate contradiction of the State Department in an interview, all questions addressed to the President had to be written and he could answer them or not, as he wished. If this method had not been in vogue before Mr. Hoover took office he might have invented it, for never was there a man who so disliked answering direct questions as to his actions or policies. He seldom answered even written questions.

President Roosevelt abolished this rather clumsy way of keeping the public in touch with the Chief Executive and returned to direct conversation. Although it has obvious dangers, the method is, because of its unrestricted nature, a far better way to mold public opinion. Of course, the President cannot be quoted directly, except when he issues part of his interview in the form of a written statement, and much of what he says is confidential and for the information only of the men who are writing the news, material not to be used but to aid them in forming judgments as to public events.

FRIENDS OF THE REVOLUTIONISTS

In addition to the officials and clerks above mentioned, there are other distinctly private citizens who have entrance to the White House and the ear of the President at all times. Among these should be mentioned Colonel E. M. House, who is probably more responsible for President Roosevelt being in the White House than any other man, also Mr. Bernard M. Baruch, who was the most potent factor in raising the funds for the campaign, and of course former Governor Alfred E. Smith of New York. Although during the presidential pre-campaign Governor Smith temporarily forsook his old protégé, Franklin D. Roosevelt, yet there is no feeling of resentment on the part of the President. He still realizes what he owes to Governor

Smith and is always anxious to go more than halfway in meeting Governor Smith's wishes and personal requests. Another important Democrat who stands high is Mr. Owen D. Young, Chairman of the Board of the General Electric Company.

SOMETHING ABOUT MRS. ROOSEVELT

Mrs. Roosevelt is a remarkable woman, and unlike any previous President's wife who has presided over the White House. Some of these women, like Mrs. Taft and the first Mrs. Wilson, were invalids; Mrs. Coolidge was exceedingly gracious, but not in any way ambitious; Mrs. Hoover was a cultured woman who always did her part, but was naturally sensitive to the criticism cast upon her husband. None had the inexhaustible energy that Mrs. Roosevelt has. For years, in addition to being the wife of a busy man and the mother of five children, she taught school in New York City for three days a week and has operated a furniture factory (the furniture is exhibited by W. & J. Sloane & Company, 709 Twelfth Street, Washington) between Poughkeepsie and Hyde Park, N. Y., on the Val-Kill Lane, leading off Violet Avenue, which in turn leads off the state road.[1] The Roosevelts have their

[1] Motoring north from Poughkeepsie, if one bears to the right, instead of following the state road, one finds oneself on Violet Avenue. Years ago this was a pleasant dirt road flanked on both sides by miles of greenhouses in which were raised most of the violets for New York florists' trade. Nowadays, the air is no longer heavy with their fragrance, the greenhouses have disappeared, the dirt road has been transformed into a hard-

New York City home at 49 East Sixty-fifth Street, but
Mrs. Roosevelt has her own personal office at 331
Madison Avenue.

---

surfaced one and the origin of its name is remembered only by
the older inhabitants of Poughkeepsie and Hyde Park.

About five miles out on Violet Avenue swings a sign "Val-
Kill Lane," and if you are an adventurous, as well as a wise
person, you will turn right into this narrow road and follow it
to its end.

Between two fields it goes and presently finds itself following
the winding of a brook, or "kill" as they were called by the
early Dutch settlers of colonial times. Its banks are gay with
columbine, cardinal flowers, mallows, marsh marigolds, purple
loosestrife and goldenrod, that bring their riot of color with the
changing seasons. Over a little bridge and past a swimming
pool, the road swings around and up a gentle slope, to reach
its goal at the doorstep of a Dutch Colonial stone cottage surrounded by silver birches and tall cedars.

Four women are joint owners of this delightful place: Mrs.
Franklin D. Roosevelt, Miss Nancy Cook, Miss Marion Dicker-
man and Mrs. Daniel O'Day, and here they have started the
Val-Kill Industries, an enterprise that is of absorbing interest
to them.

They are manufacturing furniture. Not in the modern way,
but furniture fashioned with a craftsmanship such as was found
among the cabinetmakers of a hundred or more years ago.

The small staff of craftsmen work with loving care on their
products, and a piece of furniture must be perfect in order to
pass the scrutiny of the artist, Miss Cook, and be stamped with
the Val-Kill hallmark.

A flag walk leads from the cottage to the workshop, half
hidden by trees, and such a delightful workshop it is, airy, light,
with its many windows looking out upon a virgin forest, with
occasional glimpses of a rushing brook. The air is filled with the
pungent odor of the woods the men are working upon and it
is small wonder that the craftsmen here are a happy and con-
tented lot.

Mrs. Roosevelt often played with her cousin, Franklin, in the Hyde Park house and hence they have known each other from childhood, she having first visited

---

Over the workshop is a laboratory, where the various stains are made from previous formulæ by Miss Cook. Owners of antiques are eager to obtain Val-Kill reproductions as companion pieces of cherished heirlooms handed down by their forebears. Then, too, there are many modern rooms in which adaptations are needed to fit certain spaces, and these are so carefully designed that they have the beauty and color of the antique pieces and are perfectly in harmony with them.

It is a fascinating thing to follow the making of a piece of Val-Kill furniture. First, there is the selection of the wood from the racks of seasoned lumber that fill the bright, airy storeroom. Next come the careful measurements that must exactly follow those of the working drawing, then there is the making of the turnings, and the careful fitting of part to part with mortise and tenon joint pinned with wooden pegs. The common and usual way of putting furniture together in these hurried days is with dowels, none of which have any part in the construction of Val-Kill furniture.

When all of this has been completed, the unstained piece is taken to the finishing room. Huge glass jars filled with mysterious liquids are on the shelves that line the wall. Jars and bottles of gruesome-looking mixtures stand in corners and under workbenches. Indeed, the place might be mistaken for the workshop of an alchemist of old were it not for the collection of chairs and tables, chests of drawers, beds and benches piled high, awaiting their turn to be stained. This staining process seems almost a ritual, so carefully, almost reverently, it is done—a little color at first, carefully rubbed down, then a second and a third coat, but always preserving the beauty of the grain of the wood. The furniture gradually takes on the desired richness of tone. When this is finally satisfactory, the polishing begins. It is done entirely by hand, for hours and hours, until the wood becomes like velvet to the touch, and one is irresistibly

there when only two years old. She was Franklin's sixth cousin and they were married March 17, 1905. They have always been happy together. She has been a true helpmeet, both in connection with his official duties and also during his severe illness following the infantile paralysis stroke in 1921. The Roosevelt family now living consists of four generations, as follows, of which the President's wife is the grandmother of four.

Following is the entire family circle:

Mrs. Sara Delano Roosevelt.

The President and Mrs. Roosevelt.

---

reminded of the advertisement for a certain beautifying preparation much in the public eye.

Small wonder that the undertaking of these four women has proved a success, for into it they are putting their ideals of honesty, as well as of beauty, and the products of their workshop are finding their way to all parts of the country.

A memorial library has recently been furnished by the Val-Kill Shops as well as the children's room in the new Natural History Museum, in Buffalo.

Mirrors, fireside benches, and charming little gate-leg and butterfly tea tables are found to be in high favor as wedding gifts, and it is a lucky bride who finds herself the owner of three or four pieces of furniture bearing the Val-Kill mark. She has the nucleus of a collection to be handed down to future generations and prized as the old pieces of the seventeenth century are prized by their owners of today.

When you have inspected the workshop, examined some original pieces as well as those being copied from the seventeenth century and old provincial furniture, met the craftsmen, when you have been lured into a stroll through pines, birches and cedars, and perhaps seen a woodchuck or two, or a pheasant or covey of quail, and perhaps taken a plunge in the pool, you will, of course, want a cup of tea. (*Selected.*)

Their five children—Anna, James, Elliott, Franklin, Jr., and John.

Their daughters-in-law and son-in-law—Mrs. James Roosevelt, Mrs. Elliott Roosevelt and Curtis Dall.

And their four grandchildren—Anna Eleanor and Curtis Roosevelt Dall, Sara Delano Roosevelt Dall, Sara Delano Roosevelt, James' little girl, and William Donner Roosevelt, Elliott's baby son.

Mr. and Mrs. Dall live in the Roosevelt town house in East Sixty-fifth Street, New York.

James and his wife and baby daughter live in a little white house in Cambridge, Massachusetts. The Roosevelts' eldest son is engaged in the insurance business in Boston.

Elliott, who has since March 4 been divorced and married again, lives in California.

Franklin, Jr. and John are away at school most of each year. At present John is at Groton. Franklin, Jr., who graduated from Groton in June, entered Harvard.

Louis Howe has been a friend and political adviser of Roosevelt ever since the latter was in the New York legislature. He was with him as his assistant—a job created for him by Congress—when Mr. Roosevelt was for eight years Assistant Secretary of the Navy. And he has lived with the Roosevelts most of the time since the President was taken ill with infantile paralysis in 1921. Until now he has lived in the Roosevelt house in New York, spending week-ends at his own home in Fall River, Massachusetts.

Although they will not be living in the White House, the younger members of the Roosevelt family will be down there a good deal in the next four years. For, in spite of the fact that they have hosts of friends who are always about, they are an extraordinarily close-knit clan.

Some years ago, for instance, when Anna was a débutante, Mrs. Roosevelt made a rule that whenever the children were out in the evening they must stop in her room and bid her good night before they go to bed. If she was asleep, they were to waken her. The rule still stands for the younger boys. Mrs. Dall and James, when he is in town, frequently observe it voluntarily.

Both the President and his wife have been real pals with the children, entering into all sports. Mrs. Roosevelt has boundless energy and even now, with all her official duties, still finds time to ride horseback, fly back and forth to New York, and guide her furniture and private school interests.

Mrs. Roosevelt has been criticized for being away from Washington so much and leaving her husband alone. She replies by saying that she is "out on the road" securing information for him and getting converts for the New Deal. Perhaps so, but probably her following statement made to a reporter of the North American Newspaper Alliance on April 29, 1933, better explains the situation. Said she:

"The President's day is really spent in seeing one long succession of people. It begins sometimes even when he is still eating breakfast. But the variety of subjects discussed interests him so much and he has such a wide number of interests that it is often difficult to pry his visitors away from him, even when you know there are other people waiting to see him.

"When a visitor has stayed his allotted time, we go

in and say gently that some one else is waiting. But we are accustomed to have my husband turn, with a most delightful smile, and say 'Oh, just a few minutes more. Mr. So-and-so is so interested in ships or stamps,' or whatever the subject may be they are talking about.

"Here in the White House it is rare for us to have an evening alone. As a rule we dine together. The President and his wife do not dine out except once in the season, with the members of the Cabinet, but there are nearly always guests with us. Immediately after dinner, or at least by nine o'clock, people generally begin to come in to discuss again, often until late at night, questions which have not been sufficiently threshed out during the day.

"If, however, it happens that my husband is free for an evening, we are likely to have a movie which we can show on the second floor of the White House, a screen being let down from the ceiling for that purpose. Or my husband will sit quietly and happily a whole evening and busy himself with his stamp collection or go over book catalogues.

"When we are in the country and the boys are home for their holidays, we sometimes play cards, rummy and hearts being the favorite games, as more people are able to play these and the party, even when it is a family party, is usually large. Therefore, none of us is very good at bridge. There was a time when my husband and I used to play piquet, but now, if we are alone, he will often play solitaire, which seems to rest him more.

"The radio is turned on only when there is a special

thing my husband wishes to listen to, such as some speech, or music by the Secretary of the Treasury. You know, of course, that Secretary Woodin is a composer. These things appeal to my husband, but as a rule he prefers quiet.

"There are many evenings which he will spend looking over newly acquired books, sometimes books published many years ago, sometimes books that are just out. He has an uncanny faculty of apparently skimming through a book and yet knowing everything that is in it. Always after going to bed he will read, sometimes far into the night. That is a form of indulgence to which I also am addicted."

In the minds of many, Mrs. Franklin D. Roosevelt is more of a revolutionist than her distinguished husband. She has surely been more outspoken for collective bargaining, equal wages for women, old age pensions, and unemployment insurance than even her husband. She is a remarkable woman. Here are just a few things I have heard her say:

REMARKS AT BOSTON IN 1933

"I do a good many things, but I do them for my own education. It's no credit to me. I need the education. And I have learned so much in these recent years that I often wonder how I ever lived before with a feeling of carefreeness about the way other people lived and had to live.

"What we need is that we shall come to know each other, that we shall not remain in the small group in which we were brought up, knowing only our own conditions, only the lives we have happened to touch.

"We must know the life of our country as it is. We must make it the kind of country we talk about, that we believe in, that we think it is, but that we do not actually get at at all. Most of us really know nothing about it, as it really is.

"I hope that out of all these years of depression there are certain good things coming to us. I hope we are going to come to a day from which we have grown away in the rapidity of our material growth, in the changes brought by the machine age. We forgot that all business is founded upon the work of human beings. We have ignored what business did to the human beings in it. At the top we have had people who understood the economic end of the business but who could not imagine the problems of the human beings who underlie all business.

"No business can be called really successful which has at the bottom workers who are not able to live decently and happily." She gave as an example a mill in upper New York State whose owner, she said, an acquaintance of hers, had always been on intimate terms with the problems of every employe, and who knew them all by name. After years of freedom from labor troubles the mill was sold, she continued, and the sale was followed by a number of strikes. "The new people at the top," she said, "never visualized the condition of the people at the bottom."

She is democratic, has an inexhaustible supply of energy and is a mine of resources. She drives her own

roadster or else flies. Trains are too slow. They make
her nervous!

THE PRESIDENT HIMSELF

In closing, something should be said regarding President Roosevelt himself, although volumes have been
written about him. A brief summary of his life appears
herewith, but I wish to add a few details. Although only
a distant cousin of the great Theodore Roosevelt, yet
both the President and his wife come from old New
York stock and have a goodly share of the Roosevelt
blood. His father was James Roosevelt, a widower
with one son, James, Jr., the President's half brother,
by his first wife. James, Jr., after a minor diplomatic
career, died in 1927. James Roosevelt's home at Hyde
Park, New York, was known as "Krum Elbow" and
is now owned by his wife, the President's mother. It is
the legal home of both Mr. and Mrs. Franklin D.
Roosevelt. When James Roosevelt was fifty years of
age, he married Sara Delano, who was only twenty-six
years of age and who became the President's own
mother. Sara Delano was born in 1855 on the west
side of the Hudson River, near Newburgh, New York.
Her father was Warren Delano II, who was a wealthy
merchant importing tea from China. Her great-great-
great-great-grandfather landed at Plymouth, Mass., in
1621, aboard the *Fortune*. His name was Philip deLan-
noy. When President Roosevelt's mother was only eight
years old her parents took her and six brothers and
sisters around the Horn on the Clipper Ship *Surprise*
to Hongkong. The trip lasted a hundred and ten days.

There also were other trips to Paris and elsewhere, about which she has written.

James Roosevelt, the father of the President, was an aristocrat and a country squire. He died while his son, the President, was a freshman at Harvard. For a story of the President's boyhood see *My Boy Franklin*, by Mrs. James Roosevelt.[1] Thus, both sides have aristocratic blood. The President's uncle, Frederick Roosevelt, now owns his mother's birthplace at Newburgh and there lives his aunt, Mrs. Dora Delano Forbes. Another brother, Warren Delano, married the sister of the late Henry Walters, chief owner of the Atlantic Coast Line Railroad Company, which in turn owns the Louisville & Nashville. His son, Lyman Delano, is today Chairman of the Boards of Directors of these roads. Through him and Mr. Pelley, President of the New Haven, Mr. Curry of the Union Pacific and other relatives, the President has his railroad connections.

SUMMARY OF THE PRESIDENT'S LIFE

January 30, 1882—Born at Hyde Park, N. Y., son of Sara Delano and James Roosevelt.

1900   —Matriculated at Harvard.

March 17, 1905 —Married Anna Eleanor Roosevelt, a sixth cousin, President Roosevelt giving away the bride.

1907   —Admitted to bar and began practice in New York City.

[1] Published by Ray Long & Richard R. Smith as *My Boy Franklin* "as told by Mrs. James Roosevelt to Isabel Leighton and Gabrielle Forbush."

1910   —Elected to New York Senate.

1911   —Led fight of independents against Tammany choice of William F. Sheehan for United States Senate.

1912   —Delegate to Baltimore convention and worked for nomination of Woodrow Wilson; reelected to state senate.

1913   —Became Assistant Secretary of Navy.

1916   —Worked actively to bring navy into readiness for war.

1918   —Visited Europe on naval inspection trip which brought him into friendly association with British and French leaders.

1920   —Was vice presidential running mate with James M. Cox.

1921   —Stricken with infantile paralysis. Continued business and law interests with Louis M. Howe as his active agent.

1924   —Made first visit to Warm Springs, Ga., and became interested in its development as a health resort.

1924   —Placed Alfred E. Smith in nomination for Presidency at Madison Square Garden.

1928   —Placed Smith in nomination again at Houston.

1928   —At urgent request of Smith, ran for

governor of New York and was
elected.

1930   —Reelected governor.
1932   —Elected President.

HOW THE PRESIDENT WORKS

Some of the President's characteristics have been
well described by my friend Rodney Bean. They illus-
trate how the President tackles problems, handles so
many baffling ones and still retains his vigor and sunny
disposition.

He possesses, for instance, a keen sense of humor
and unbounded confidence that an objective can be
reached. It does not enter his head that a thing cannot
be done; he never quits, is never discouraged, and is
always ready to make a detour if that is necessary in
order to get ahead. If he finds a plan impracticable
after careful study, he drops it and tries another.

He has an insatiable curiosity and nothing which
affects the happiness and welfare of human beings is
without interest for him. Things that interest seldom
tire. The President refuses to take his trouble to bed
with him and if a final decision is not reached during
a discussion, he puts the whole matter off, to be considered again the next day. He never seeks to win a
decision while he lacks information, but always goes in
search of the essential data.

Once a decision is made he considers it final. With a
"Well, that's done," the subject is put aside and discussion turned into other channels. In his dealings with

business men, bankers, agriculturists, political leaders, he listens to arguments without entering into debate or immediately rejecting them, although in the end he may decide not to accept them.

All of the messages the President sent to Congress in the first few weeks of his administration were written or dictated by him at the White House before he went to the Executive Office. After he has breakfast of coffee, eggs, rolls and bacon, he goes over the mail selected for him by his secretaries and frequently consults with some of his advisers.

Decision in regard to the messages has usually been made on the night before their delivery, but sometimes final details are discussed and settled as the President is getting up. He talks things over with his advisers, either in his bedroom or in the Oval Room, a study on the second floor which Mr. Roosevelt uses also for night conferences. After calling in his stenographer he dictates a message, turns it over to his aides for minor changes and then it is ready for Congress.

A TYPICAL WORKDAY

A typical workday for the President thus starts before he begins to receive visitors in the Executive Office, to which he goes about 10:30 o'clock. Once there he faces almost continuous activity, receiving visitors on a fifteen-minute schedule, except when some question of unusual gravity is under consideration and a longer engagement is necessary. So far as possible the appointments are made for the discussion of some of the pending emergency questions, or in order that the President may hear the opinion of a visitor which has a bearing on the administration program.

To avoid loss of time, the President as a rule has his luncheon sent over from the White House and frequently calls for service for a caller, so that their discussion may not be interrupted. When possible he finishes up at the Executive Office not later than 5 o'clock, returning then to the White House for tea.

The President must meet groups, of course, as well as individuals. The Cabinet gathers on Tuesdays and Fridays at 2 P.M., and there are conferences between Mr. Roosevelt and his advisers in the Oval Room in the White House, morning or evening. Sometimes there are Congressional delegations to be received.

Cabinet and advisory sessions resemble meetings of a board of directors, with the members reporting to their chairman. There is usually a general debate in which the President takes an active part, drawing out the opinions of others. Unnecessary formality is dispensed with. The spirit of neighborliness also marks the dealings of the President with groups from Congress. Free exchange of opinion is invited.

I cannot close without saying a word about President Roosevelt's religious principles, which ultimately make or break any President and his administration. President Coolidge was a New England Puritan and President Hoover was a Quaker—both having been presented to the country in their campaigns as distinctly religious men. This was not done in the case of Franklin D. Roosevelt. His connections led many to believe that he did not wish to be classed religiously with his immediate predecessors. The fact that Roosevelt took such a decided stand for wide-open repeal of the Eighteenth Amendment cost him the confidence of many church people who stood almost a unit for prohibition. His relations with Tammany and the rank and file of Democratic politicians caused many to say "One cannot sleep with the dogs without getting fleas." Moreover, the fact that James Farley, his campaign manager, is a Catholic unjustifiably prejudiced many Protestants against Mr. Roosevelt. Incidentally, Mr. Farley is a sincere churchman and neither drinks nor smokes.

PRAYING FOR GUIDANCE

Let this author bear his testimony that President Roosevelt has a deeply religious spirit. This is emphasized not only by his professions and his life, but by his earnest interest in the "Forgotten Man." Instinctively, from the earliest days, Franklin D. Roosevelt has always been interested in Christian work. Of all Presidents, we know of none of whom we can more honestly say that he loves the Lord with all his heart and *his neighbor as himself*. Certainly he is the only President who, unostentatiously and most humbly, took time on that busy inauguration morning of March 4, 1933, to go to church and pray for guidance. He quietly drove to St. John's Episcopal Church at Sixteenth and H Streets.

Only a few knelt with him. There were the members of his family, members of his Cabinet and their wives, and a few personal friends, all of whom joined in the prayer that his régime would be blessed with prosperity for the people who have asked him to cleave for them the path to better times.

A solemn hush pervaded the little church as the Reverend Robert R. Johnston intoned a prayer for the then President-elect.

"Almighty and everlasting God, strengthen, we beseech Thee, Thy servant, Franklin, for whom we pray. Strengthen him, we beseech Thee, O Lord, with the Holy Ghost, the comforter, and daily increase in him Thy manifold gifts of grace, the spirit of wisdom and understanding, the spirit of counsel and ghostly strength, the spirit of knowledge and true godliness, and fill him, O Lord, with the spirit of Thy holy fear, now and forever. Amen.

"Almighty and most merciful God, grant, we beseech Thee, that by the indwelling of Thy Holy Spirit, Thy servant, Franklin, chosen to be our next President, grant that he and all his advisers may be enlightened and strengthened for Thy service, through Christ Our Lord. Amen.

"O Lord, our Heavenly Father, the high and mighty ruler of the universe, who dost from Thy throne behold all the dwellers upon earth; most heartily we beseech Thee, with Thy favor to behold and bless Thy servant, Franklin, chosen to be the President of the United States, and all others in authority; and so replenish them with the grace of Thy Holy Spirit, that they may always incline to Thy will, and walk in Thy way. Endow them plenteously with heavenly gifts; grant them in health and prosperity long to live; and finally, after this life, to attain everlasting joy and felicity; through Jesus Christ our Lord. Amen."

Then the clergyman lifted his hand in benediction over the small congregation. The strains of the recessional filled the church as the choir filed from the altar. As the last chords of the recessional died in the distance, the presidential party rose and walked through the church to waiting automobiles.

The Chief Executive was accompanied by his mother, Mrs. James Roosevelt, his wife and his eldest son, James, who rode to and from the church in an open touring car. Then came the other members of his immediate family and the members of his Cabinet and friends.

The service began at 10:30 o'clock and lasted only twenty minutes.

QUOTING THE BIBLE

Commenting on the President's religious training, Carl A. Glover wrote in the *Congregationalist*:

The inaugural address of Franklin D. Roosevelt reveals the speaker's acquaintance with the language of the Bible. Apart from indirect allusions, the inaugural contains seven distinct Biblical references. The phraseology of the Bible evidently fills the mind of the new President. Lifted from the lips of Jesus are some words in the sentence, "These dark days will be worth all they cost us if they teach us that our true destiny is not to be ministered unto but to minister." One recalls the scene in the Upper Room (John 13:3-16) where Jesus gathered the disciples for a farewell discourse. He girded himself with a towel, took the basin of water that he might wash the sand-soiled feet of his followers. Recorded in Matthew 20:28 is the statement by Jesus, "The Son of man came not to be ministered unto, but to minister."

Ancient Palestine was plagued by locusts, which stripped the fields of every vestige of vegetation, so that the inhabitants starved. Said Roosevelt, "Our distress comes from no failure of substance. We are stricken by no plague of locusts." I Kings 8:37 is one among many passages which refer to plagues of locusts. In the same paragraph that mentions locusts the inaugural address continues, "Nature still offers her bounty." It was Jesus who said that God maketh his sun to rise on the evil and on the good, and sendeth rain on the just and on the unjust (Matt. 5:45).

Jesus' encounter with the lawyer (Luke 10:25-37) whose question, Who is my neighbor? evoked the parable of the Good Samaritan, was the origin of the term "good neighbor" as used by Roosevelt. "In the field of world policy," said Roosevelt, "I would dedicate this nation as to the policy of the good neighbor . . . who resolutely respects himself and . . . the rights of others."

"When there is no vision, the people perish" is lifted verbatim from Proverbs 29:18 and incorporated by Roosevelt into the sentence, "They know only the rules of a generation of self-seekers. They have no vision, and when there is no vision the people perish."

A vivid reminder of the cleansing of the temple is found in Roosevelt's reference to the money changers in the temple (Matt. 21:12-17). Jesus overturned the tables of money changers and drove them from the sacred precincts, saying, It is written my house shall be called a house of prayer and ye have made it a den of thieves. Roosevelt said, "The money changers have fled from their high seats in the temple of our civilization. We may now restore that temple to the ancient truths. The measure of the restoration lies in the extent to which we apply social values more noble than mere monetary profit."

President Roosevelt's announcement that he will make Hyde Park the summer capital marks a deviation from the customs of the last few Chief Executives, who have not had estates of their own for such a purpose. While ex-President Hoover went regularly to the "Little White House," a camp on the Rapidan, other ex-Presidents—notably Coolidge and Wilson— spent summer holidays at rented places, and as a rule changed plans each season. The physical properties of Hyde Park, however, would seem to make it an ideal summer capital.

This homestead of the Roosevelt family is located a few miles above Poughkeepsie, in Dutchess County, New York. The estate forms a long, narrow parallelogram, with one end bordering the Hudson. Until recently it comprised 500 acres; the acquisition of two neighboring farms brought the total acreage to 1,000. The Albany Post Road pierces the eastern part of it.

A winding, tree-bordered drive runs from the highway to the huge rambling house, with its cluster of outbuildings, including stables, garages, laundry, greenhouses and servants' quarters. The entrance is on the east, with a broad open veranda facing the post road. On the west is another wide porch, from which a fine view of the Hudson may be obtained.

The house, built about a hundred years ago, is a clapboard frame, two stories high, with a roof of single

slant and a broad spread. The original floor plan con-
sisted of a central hall with two rooms at each side.
Some time before 1900 the straight staircase in the
central hall was removed and the stairs were built in
the northwest room, where other changes were made
and from which a service-wing was extended north-
ward.

The front veranda opens into the large central hall,
at one end of which is the "big room." This is a living
room, about 30 by 50 feet, with an eighteen-foot ceiling. Marble fireplaces are at each end, big enough for a
four-foot log. In a corner is President Roosevelt's
mahogany desk with a ship's clock that strikes bells
instead of hours. Walls and ceilings are white; the
woodwork is walnut. Bookcases almost cover the walls,
containing both classics and modern volumes, as well
as the bound volumes of a number of magazines. Ship
prints reflect the President's love of the sea.

Hyde Park's frontage on the river consists of un-
dulating terraces, rising gently from the Hudson. The
river is seen as it sweeps through the Long Reach—a
sailing course named in 1609 by Robert Juet in his
diary of the voyage of the *Half Moon*, and which was
later known to the Dutch as De Lange Rak. Inland is
a broad plain, which still bears the eighteenth-century
name of The Flatts.

The history of the Hyde Park estate properly begins
in 1697, when the Great Nine Partners Patent that
covered Springwood—the early name of the estate—
was taken out. In 1669 a small portion of the patented
area was divided into nine long strips of land border-

ing on the Hudson, which, because of their frontage on the river, became known as water-lots. Springwood was equivalent to the south half of the water-lot No. 6. It was purchased in 1867 by the father of the President, James Roosevelt, and there Franklin Delano Roosevelt was born in 1882.

A REVOLUTIONARY INAUGURAL

"I am certain that my fellow Americans expect that on my induction into the presidency I will address them with a candor and a decision which the present situation of our nation impels.

"This is preeminently the time to speak the truth, the whole truth, frankly and boldly. Nor need we shrink from honestly facing conditions in our country today. This great nation will endure as it has endured, will revive and will prosper. So first of all let me assert my firm belief that the only thing we have to fear is fear itself—nameless, unreasoning, unjustified terror which paralyzes needed efforts to convert retreat into advance.

"In every dark hour of our national life a leadership of frankness and vigor has met with understanding and support of the people themselves which is essential to victory. I am convinced that you will again give that support to leadership in these critical days.

"In such a spirit on my part and on yours we face our common difficulties. They concern, thank God, only material things. Values have shrunken to fantastic levels; taxes have risen; our ability to pay has fallen; government of all kinds is faced by serious curtailment of income; the means of exchange are frozen in the currents of trade; the withered leaves of industrial enterprise lie on every side; farmers find no markets for their produce; the savings of many years in thousands of families are gone.

"More important, a host of unemployed citizens face the grim problem of existence, and an equally great number toil with little return. Only a foolish optimist can deny the dark realities of the moment.

MANY BLESSINGS

"Yet our distress comes from no failure of substance. We are stricken by no plague of locusts. Compared with the perils which our forefathers conquered because they believed and were not afraid, we have still much to be thankful for. Nature still offers her bounty and human efforts have multiplied it. Plenty is at our doorstep, but a generous use of it languishes in the very sight of the supply.

"Primarily, this is because the rulers of the exchange of mankind's goods have failed through their own stubbornness and their own incompetence, have admitted their failure and abdicated. Practices of the unscrupulous money changers stand indicted in the court of public opinion, rejected by the hearts and minds of men.

"True, they have tried, but their efforts have been cast in the pattern of an outworn tradition. Faced by failure of credit they have proposed only the lending of more money. Stripped of the lure of profit by which to induce our people to follow their false leadership they have resorted to exhortations, pleading tearfully for restored confidence. They know only the rules of a generation of self-seekers. They have no vision, and where there is no vision the people perish.

"The money changers have fled from their high seats in the temple of our civilization. We may now restore that temple to the ancient truths. The measure of the restoration lies in the extent to which we apply social values more noble than mere monetary profit.

"Happiness lies not in the mere possession of money; it lies in the joy of achievement, in the thrill of creative effort. The joy and moral stimulation of work no longer must be forgotten in the mad chase of evanescent profits. These dark days will be worth all they cost us if they teach us that our true destiny is not to be ministered unto but to minister to ourselves and to our fellow men.

"Recognition of the falsity of material wealth as the standard of success goes hand in hand with the abandonment of the false belief that public office and high political position are to be valued only by the standards of pride of place and personal profit; and there must be an end to a conduct in banking and in business which too often has given to a sacred trust the likeness of callous and selfish wrongdoing. Small wonder that confidence languished, for it thrives only on honesty, on honor, on the sacredness of obligations, on faithful protection, on unselfish performance; without them it cannot live.

ACTION DEMANDED

"Restoration calls, however, not for changes in ethics alone. This nation asks for action, and action now.

"Our greatest primary task is to put people to work. This is no unsolvable problem if we face it wisely and courageously. It can be accomplished in part by direct recruiting by the government itself, treating the task as we would treat the emergency of a war, but at the same time through this employment accomplishing greatly needed projects to stimulate and reorganize the use of our natural resources.

"Hand in hand with this we must frankly recognize the overbalance of population in our industrial centers and, by engaging on a national scale in a redistribution, endeavor to provide a better use of the land for those best fitted for the land. The task can be helped by definite efforts to raise the values of agricultural products and with this the power to purchase the output of our cities. It can be helped by preventing realistically the tragedy of the growing loss through foreclosure, on our small homes and our farms. It can be helped by insistence that the federal, state and local governments act forthwith on the demand that their cost be drastically reduced. It can be helped by the unifying of relief activities which today are often scattered, uneconomical and unequal. It can be helped by national planning for and supervision of all forms of transportation and of communications and other utilities which have a definitely public character. There are many ways in which it can be helped, but it can never be helped merely by talking about it. We must act and act quickly.

SUPERVISION OF BANKING

"Finally, in our progress toward a resumption of work we require two safeguards against a return of the evils of the old order: there must be a strict supervision of all banking and credits and investments; there must be an end to speculation with other people's money, and there must be provision for an adequate but sound currency.

"These are the lines of attack. I shall presently urge upon a new Congress in special session detailed measures for their fulfillment, and I shall seek the immediate assistance of the several states.

"Through this program of action we address ourselves to putting our own national house in order and making income balance outgo. Our international trade relations, though vastly important, are in point of time and necessity secondary to the establishment of a sound national economy. I favor as a practical policy the putting of first things first. I shall spare no effort to restore world trade by international economic readjustment, but the emergency at home cannot wait on that accomplishment.

"The basic thought that guides these specific means of national recovery is not narrowly nationalistic. It is the insistence, as a first consideration, upon the interdependence of the various elements in and parts of the United States—a recognition of the old and permanently important manifestation of the American spirit of the pioneer. It is the way to recovery. It is the immediate way. It is the strongest assurance that the recovery will endure.

WORLD POLICY

"In the field of world policy I would dedicate this nation to the policy of the good neighbor—the neighbor who resolutely respects himself, and because he does so, respects the rights of others—the neighbor who respects his obligations, respects the sanctity of his agreements in and with a world of neighbors.

"If I read the temper of our people correctly we now realize as we have never realized before our interdependence on each other; that we cannot merely take but we must give as well, that if we are to go forward we must move as a trained and loyal army willing to sacrifice for the good of a common discipline, because without such discipline no progress is made, no leadership becomes effective. We are, I know, ready and willing to submit our lives and property to such discipline because it makes possible a leadership which aims at a larger good. This I propose to offer, pledging that the larger purposes will bind upon us all as a sacred obligation with a unity of duty hitherto evoked only in time of armed strife.

ASSUMES LEADERSHIP

"With this pledge taken, I assume unhesitatingly the leadership of this great army of our people dedicated to a disciplined attack upon our common problems.

"Action in this image and to this end is feasible under the form of government which we have inherited
from our ancestors. Our constitution is so simple and
practical that it is possible always to meet extraordinary needs by changes in emphasis and arrangement
without loss of essential form. That is why our constitutional system has proved itself the most superbly
enduring political mechanism the modern world has
produced. It has met every stress of vast expansion of
territory, of foreign wars, of bitter internal strife, of
world relations.

"It is to be hoped that the normal balance of executive and legislative authority may be wholly adequate
to meet the unprecedented task before us. But it may
be that an unprecedented demand and need for unde-
layed action may call for temporary departure from
that normal balance of public procedure.

ARDUOUS DAYS AHEAD

"We face the arduous days that lie before us in the
warm courage of national unity; with the clear consciousness of seeking old and previous moral values;
with the clean satisfaction that comes from the stern
performance of duty by old and young alike. We aim
at the assurance of a rounded and permanent national
life.

"We do not distrust the future of essential democracy. The people of the United States have not failed.
In their need they have registered a mandate that they
want direct vigorous action. They have asked for discipline and direction under leadership. They have made

the present instrument of their wishes. In the spirit of the gift I take it.

"In this dedication of a nation we humbly ask the blessing of God. May He protect each and every one of us. May He guide me in the days to come."

After such a revolutionary inaugural address, the writer of this book humbly added "Amen" to this fervent prayer.

The "Revolutionists' Headquarters" are at the White House, Pennsylvania Avenue, between Fifteenth and Seventeenth Streets, Washington, D. C.

Chapter III

THE MAN ON THE THRESHOLD

THERE is a single heartbeat between John Nance
Garner and the Presidency. If anything should
happen to President Roosevelt during the remainder
of his term—it is the prayer of the nation that nothing
will—Vice President Garner would be elevated to our
highest office in one of the most crucial periods of all
history. Even in normal times speculation is always rife
about the ability of the "second in command" in the
event he should become by force of circumstances the
Chief Executive. Naturally such speculation is inten-
sified in a period such as the present amid the extraordinary conditions that confront the nation and the
world.

Among conservative people certainly, and to some
extent perhaps throughout the rank and file, the attitude toward Mr. Garner is skeptical. Many who have
been in continuous contact with men of affairs in all
sections of the country feel that a consensus would be
that the Vice President is not "presidential timber."
Nevertheless, there is no warrant for a reaction so
adverse that it becomes indiscriminate hostility. Mr.
Garner is a man of parts. He has far greater ability
than the average member of Congress or—for that
matter—the average state or national executive official.

MR. GARNER'S BACKGROUND

Mr. Garner has the background, so essential for success, that can come only through years of experience. He has a distinctive personality that impresses those who know him, even though it is the rough-and-ready type. Over and above everything else, to use the parlance of politics, "he knows his way around." There are few men in public life today who are better informed on the workings of our national legislative body. He is rounding out twenty-nine years of continuous service in the halls of Congress. He has been through the mill. He is skilled in parliamentary procedure, versed in national affairs. There is hardly an issue of moment which he does not know forward and backward.

However—and here it is essential to perceive one of his shortcomings—he is said to be a stubborn partisan. He apparently can see no good in his opponents or in the principles for which they stand. He is apparently antagonistic to big business. Despite all his years of experience in the public service and his multitude of contacts, he remains very much the sectionalist. Uvalde, Texas, is still the center of his universe. He is a Southerner and proud of it. States below Mason and Dixon's line have first call at any and all times upon his attention. States to the north and west, he feels, are necessary adjuncts to the country but of secondary importance.

The foregoing picture is purposely painted broadly

to bring out the high lights. It is scarcely an exaggeration, however, of the impression gained of Mr. Garner by many who have had contact with him. During his first years in Congress, some of his early acquaintances in national life likened him to a bull in a china shop, a Texas steer breaking up Congressional crockery. But the chamber of the House mellowed him as it has so many others of similar temperament. His speech of today is not the rip-roaring type that it was in the years that have passed.

One characteristic of the man has survived the mollifying action of time. When his mind is set, there is no changing it. He is obdurate. For example, he projected the Public Buildings Bill in Congress despite protestations of leaders of his own party who felt that they had its best interests at heart. Thus he gave Hoover, then President, an opportunity of which he quickly availed himself, to brand the bill as an unexampled piece of pork-barrel legislation. Again, Mr. Garner flatly refused to cooperate with the Hoover administration at a time when the needs of the nation seemed to call for cooperation. His own party chieftains, Senators Robinson and Glass, among others, pleaded with him in vain.

PERSONAL CHARACTERISTICS

He has frequently fathered what would heretofore be regarded as radical legislation even in recent years. When he sponsors a bill, he works for it indefatigably, not only on the floor but off. He drives those subordinate to him into line. He makes them listen to him; it is said that he rarely will listen to them. A curious fact is that, in spite of the high offices to which he has attained, he seldom has participated in the national workings of his party. He is not a familiar figure on the public rostrum. Neither has he made the swings up and down the country at campaign time, as might be expected of a man who has been so honored.

Throughout his progress from an unknown member of Congress to the Vice President of the United States, Mr. Garner has clung to his original custom. Whether committee chairman, minority floor leader, or speaker of the House, he has quit Washington at the end of a session of Congress and hurried to hibernate in his beloved Lone Star State. There he has tarried until another session has called him forth. From his viewpoint, the wide-open spaces are preferable to the crowded cities. He obeys that impulse, uncontrolled by political or social obligations, formalities or any other behest than the dominant call of the wild.

By no stretch of the imagination can Mr. Garner be described as a "mixer," though he has notable facility for making friends of his own choosing. He has seldom appeared at the social functions which form so much of the life in the national capital. Whenever he has graced such gatherings, it was because he could not contrive to evade them. His preference is to close his office at five or six o'clock and disappear from sight until the work of the next day must begin.

The press, therefore, has had more trouble in making contacts with him after office hours than any other man of similar prominence in public life. The hotel at which he made his home is said to have had a standing order that under no circumstances could or should he be disturbed after six o'clock in the evening. According to recollections, the press associations were unable to reach him even on a certain historic night. That was the night in February, 1933, shortly before the inauguration, when the attempt was made at Miami, Florida, to assassinate the President-elect.

Despite his profound distaste for social life, Mr. Garner is a friendly soul when you get to know him. Newspaper men like him and call him a square-shooter. He has some intimate friends. They get together and enjoy the hours of relaxation in their own good way. It is noteworthy, too, that he does not draw a political line in making such friends. One of the closest associates he ever made throughout the last thirty years was the late Nicholas Longworth. Garner and Longworth were quite inseparable during periods of leisure.

Turning to the current situation, it is perhaps not stretching the point to say that Mr. Garner in one sense is more responsible than any other one individual for Mr. Roosevelt being in the White House today. Mr. Garner agreed to an arrangement by Mr. McAdoo, whereby the votes of Texas and California were switched to Roosevelt. Without this assent of Mr. Garner the Chicago Convention of 1932 might well have selected some one else as standard-bearer. Political analysts have conjectured that Garner's real purpose in seeking the presidential nomination was to put himself in a trading position for second place on the ticket.

ATTITUDE ON CURRENT PROBLEMS

Nevertheless, although Mr. Garner was a key man at that convention, he has played little part in the recovery program. The Vice President has been less in the picture than half the members of the Cabinet or scores of members of Congress. The Vice Presidency has swallowed him as it has many a man before him of greater prominence—Dawes and Marshall are recalled as examples. Mr. Garner has merely presided over the sessions of the Senate while the Congress was in session.

His inaction has caused comment and raised the question whether there has developed any lack of sympathy between the President and the Vice President. Has Garner been at odds with the New Deal? If so, the probabilities are that he leans toward greater radicalism in some directions and less idealism in others. If placed in the White House, presumably he could be expected to go farther than Mr. Roosevelt has gone to date. Mr. Garner's tendency might be to "shoot the works." He might tend to use any and all of the extraordinary powers that Congress transferred to the Executive. He is temperamentally anything but a watchdog of the Treasury.

As I have said, Garner is a man of real ability. No matter how much you may disagree with him, you must credit him with acting as he sees the light. He is a battler. He is fearless. He is skilled, trained and seasoned. For many months he has attracted little attention because the spotlight has been playing upon the other revolutionists of Washington. Nevertheless, if major calamity or even some minor turn of the wheel should project him into action, he is indeed capable of creating a revolution of revolutionists! Matched with some of the Brain Trust type, he would be a professional fighter among amateurs.

HISTORY AND ANCESTRY

Some idea of the Garner capabilities can be gained from an account of his career. He was born in 1869 in the hamlet of Blossom Prairie, which is near the village of Detroit in Red River County just south of the Oklahoma border of northeast Texas. For a man of his prominence he has one of the shortest biographies in the Official Directory. It reads simply: "John Nance Garner, Democrat, of Uvalde, was elected to the Fifty-eighth to Seventy-second Congresses; elected Speaker of the House, December 7, 1931; reelected to the Seventy-third Congress; but resigned having been elected Vice President of the United States, November 8, 1932."

The Garner line was of good American stock and the Nances trace back to English coat-of-arms families. John's father married the daughter of the local banker and, if the convention posters pictured facts, established his family in a log cabin—in the true tradition of families of presidential candidates. After some attendance at the public schools, John changed from work on the paternal farm to clerking in his uncle's general store. He played some "semi-pro" baseball, it is said. In his spare time he "read law" in the office of a county-seat attorney. He did this to such good purpose that at the age of twenty-one he was admitted to the bar.

While waiting for clients, he ran for city attorney and was defeated. Concerned about his health, he sought a more favorable climate four hundred miles south in the Rio Grande Valley, in Uvalde. From the start, he was successful in building up both health and wealth. He acquired farm lands, bank stocks, a local weekly newspaper—and an imperishable interest in politics. With the endorsement of party leaders, he was appointed to succeed the deceased county judge. He was elected to the same office for another term.

At about this time he met the future Mrs. Garner, a young lady of a nearby town who was then studying shorthand in San Antonio. She studied the art to such good effect that ever since her marriage she has been Mr. Garner's efficient secretary. He owes much to her help in his career, which was presently broadened by election to the Texas state legislature. There he was a member of the House of Representatives, 1898-1902. While in that body he conceived and executed a political strategy which placed him in the Congress of the United States and kept him there for three decades.

The old Seventh Congressional District was represented in Washington by a man of wealth and strength who was clearly too permanent a fixture to dislodge. In Garner's second year in the state legislature, however, it developed that Texas had become entitled to additional seats in Washington on the basis of the census of 1900. Garner managed to evoke and evolve a new Congressional district of his own, the present Fifteenth District. At the Congressional convention he was nominated and was elected, and took his seat in the United States House of Representatives in 1903. He has been returned every two years with the regularity of the calendar. Probably he has not delivered or even franked out an electioneering speech in the past twenty years. To do so would have been needless.

CONGRESSIONAL RECORD

Moreover, for about eight years after reaching Washington he apparently made no speeches. But he followed party leadership with fidelity and patience. He also was assigned to the Railways and Canals Committee. His first bill called for a coastwise canal in Texas. He also sought a federal building at Eagle Pass, Texas, and a federal courthouse at Del Rio. Especially he sought appointment to the Ways and Means Committee, and after a decade of faithful effort he reached this objective in 1913. The man is patient and tireless.

Although his philosophical views on the tariff conform to party principles, he has always been a Texan first, and a philosopher second. He cried for protection for the products of his district. In particular he demanded a duty on mohair, as befitted a representative of a goat-raising region. During the presidential campaign of 1932, a newspaper remarked of an outburst of Garner eloquence: "That sort of rude, rugged talk will certainly insure the cowboy-goat-herder-horse-wrangler vote for the Democratic ticket, but what it will do north of the mescal and pinto line is just horrible!"

Garner joined with Champ Clark in bucking the

Cannon dictatorship. In the Clark and Wilson friction of 1912, however, Garner played more the part of go-between than that of partisan. A few years later he gave forth the famous "ham-and-hog" dictum: "Now, we Democrats are in charge of House and I'll tell you right now every time one of these Yankees gets a ham I'm going to do my best to get a hog!" In quoting that alleged Garnerism, a hostile commentator is said to have added that John Garner has ever remained the smart county-seat politician, completely aloof from constructive legislation or experimental statecraft, with one hand always dipping into the barrel and the other hand scratching backs. That jibe, however, was uttered in the heat of the campaign. Further, in fairness, the same commentator was constrained to add that Garner has always been utterly frank in this attitude and has never assumed any pose to the contrary.

A quarter of a century of working while waiting put Mr. Garner in position to claim the rôle of minority leader in 1928. He won that post in a mêlée of attacks on Big Business and Wall Street. In that same year he was defeated as candidate for the speakership. In 1931 there was a scant Democratic majority, but it was enough to enable Mr. Garner to reach the goal. He was elected Speaker of the House of Representatives.

For a time everything went well. All was quiet—a quiet broken only by the shattering of gavels by the new Speaker registering the strength of the new leadership. In previous years, it was recalled, Mr. Garner himself had engineered a program of tax reduction. He now exemplified personal economy and talked of balancing the budget. Many of the plans of a Republican administration for combating the depression were ably furthered in the House.

As to the next chapter, the furious conflicts with the White House, this whole row is still too close at hand to be seen in perspective. It is too confused by the accompanying campaign complication to be appraised precisely. Both sides of the tangled controversies of that dark hour were publicized at length, and it must remain with the reader to decide.

REMARKABLE PATIENCE

Throughout Garner's career we find him the miracle man of patience. He can fight it out or he can wait it out. Only on the assumption of this characteristic can we explain the strange way in which the Vice Presidency has veiled him in obscurity. No later than August, 1932, an Associated Press dispatch quoted him as saying: "When my friends here in Texas and those in California decided I was fit timber to deal with Herbert Hoover, I assented to their wishes. I think now I may be big enough for that job, considering Hoover's weakness and vacillation. I now hold the most powerful position in this Government excepting that of the President of the United States."

At about that same period a view of Garner as others saw him is revealed in press comments such as this: "His proposals, his combats with President Hoover, and his dynamic personality, have completely overshadowed the colorless figure at the head of the ticket. The Democratic party has committed itself to Garner

and Garner policies, and will win or lose on them."
Another press dispatch in the summer of 1932: "No
nominee for Vice President on either ticket in many
years has called forth as much attention both from
friends and foes as has John Garner since he was nominated. Garner is going to be a real 'running mate.' He
is not going to trail behind the head of the ticket. He
will be in the middle of the picture."

The echo of such words as the foregoing had hardly
died away before Garner began to retreat from the
headlines. History, however, shows that while Garner
may retreat he never surrenders. He may retire but he
never reforms. We can be assured that within the sanc-
tuary of the second highest executive office in the nation he is still further solidifying his ideas. It is morally
certain that he is ready at any moment to emerge from
obscurity, with freshened firmness, just as he returns
from the fastnesses of his beloved Rio Grande Valley.

Because of this fixity of character it becomes doubly
significant to inquire into his complexion as a revolutionist. Probably no man in Washington or elsewhere
has been less transformed by the policies of the New
Deal than the Vice President of the United States. He
is at the opposite pole from the experimentalist. From
Garner's unchanging viewpoint, why experiment when
hundreds of years of politics have already shown what
will work? If the dice-box of destiny ever tumbles John
Garner again into an area of activity, what we may
apprehend is not a revolution in the current significance of that word but rather a revolution within a
revolution.

Such a counter-revolution might stop short of moving the national capital from Washington to Uvalde. It would, however, continue a policy of "bawling out" the big bankers and with even more resounding epithets—you may be sure that Garner would never call the bankers anything so polite as "money changers." The *national* viewpoint, which for a time at least has been in ascendency in Washington, would almost surely become tempered with "sectionalism," geographic, industrial and political. Conceivably, Washington might be revolutionized into an even better Washington. Surely Garner would stand no nonsense from communists.

Understand, of course, that any such foreboding has never assailed Mr. Garner's personal integrity, which is irreproachable. In fact, it is one of the paradoxes of politics that a man into whose keeping you could entrust your private estate with complete assurance should apparently view as so much spoils the economic estate of the nation. This is why many conservatives will continue with fervor their prayers for the safety of President Roosevelt. They will not be disarmed merely because Mr. Garner is "under wraps." They will not reckon him indulgently among the other Washington revolutionists. They insist on classifying him as what they fear him to be—the counter-revolutionist, patient and imperturbable, undedicated to the aims of the New Deal because unalterably cast in the die of the old deals.

The Vice Presidency imposes upon the incumbent three chief duties: (a) To preside over the Senate; (b) to advise with the Cabinet, and (c), in event of necessity, to succeed the President. The last-named potential function is of great importance. As to what Mr. Garner would do under such circumstances, I frankly do not know. My friends tell me he would raise havoc, but I have a hunch he might give us an old-fashioned common-sense administration.

"The Man on Threshold" lives at Washington Hotel, Washington, D. C.

Chapter IV

"THAT WOMAN!"

THE chief revolutionist is Mrs. Paul C. Wilson who in Washington is known as "Miss Frances Perkins." She is an intelligent and conscientious woman, with an ardent interest in the underdog. I have heard Congressmen say that they would hate to have "that woman" for a wife, but they all respect her earnestness. Some insist that she is the ablest member of the Cabinet, certainly the one who "best knows her unions." However this may be, she is held in great respect by both President Roosevelt and his wife. She is a credit to womanhood and lucky are those who have her friendship and confidence.

IMPORTANCE OF WOMEN

The advent of "Miss Perkins" into the President's Cabinet was a part of the revolutionary program. So long as women have the vote, there is no reason why they should not be given office. Certainly there is no position in the Cabinet for which women are better fitted than to serve as Secretary of Labor. This does not mean that the Secretary of Labor should always be a woman, but it does mean that the position should be held by a woman at least a third of the time. Not only has the Department of Labor two or three divisions which deal almost exclusively with women and children, but women are constantly becoming a greater factor in industry, finance and commerce. Every census shows a greater proportion of the employed to be women; every new stockholders' list published shows a larger percentage of women stockholders; while the percentage of women in trade is constantly increasing. For some time women have had the majority of savings bank accounts in many cities and are fast becoming the greatest income tax payers. Therefore, President Roosevelt showed wisdom in selecting a woman as Secretary of Labor.

If a woman was to be selected for this position, it was natural that the President should select Frances Perkins. He had worked with her for some time. He knew her to be honest, intelligent and courageous. He knew that she had the respect of labor experts and had won her fame through painstaking work. Whenever Franklin D. Roosevelt, as Governor of New York, consulted Frances Perkins he got a definite and intelligent answer. At times when employers or labor leaders or even the Department of Labor in Washington disagreed with Miss Perkins, it usually developed that Miss Perkins was right and the others were wrong. Moreover, when Governor Alfred E. Smith turned the administration of the state of New York over to Governor Roosevelt, Governor Smith gave this same testimony as to Frances Perkins: "She's an able and conscientious woman. You better hold on to her." Governor Roosevelt took this advice, and because he did, Frances Perkins became the first woman to enter the

President's Cabinet. Without doubt, she feels grateful to Alfred E. Smith for his part in this connection.

Because Miss Perkins is a woman, do not think for one moment that she is easy to handle. Both employers and wage workers have already found her the most difficult Secretary of Labor to influence of all that have ever held the office. I have been personally acquainted with them all. Secretary William B. Wilson was a kind-hearted and fair-minded man, but he was appointed by organized labor and always remembered it. He is still alive, doing odd jobs for the labor interests as occasion offers. No finer character ever sat in the President's Cabinet. He was followed by James J. Davis, who is now Senator from Pennsylvania. Mr. Davis was distinctly of the "glad hand" and pacifying class. He was a friend to all groups and earnestly tried to "sell" labor to the people of the United States. He, however, knew little about the technique of the labor movement and, although he carried a labor union card in his pocket, having once been a steel worker, he was not a labor man at heart. The last Secretary of Labor, W. N. Doak, was a personal friend of President Hoover. Although technically a labor man and fully acquainted with the technique of labor organization, he was not under the control of the American Federation of Labor. It is generally believed, however, that he took orders from President Hoover rather than that he gave advice to President Hoover.

Those who are now visiting Washington on business or legislative matters should realize that the situation has entirely changed. Whether for good or for evil, there certainly has been a revolution in the Department of Labor. There is a different atmosphere in labor circles than has existed for many, many years. President Roosevelt is determined to give the country a new revolution, based upon untried economics. He has selected Frances Perkins to handle the labor end of this revolution. He will depend upon her for advice and will back her in her policies.

MISS PERKINS' TRAINING

Now as to Frances Perkins: Frances Perkins was born in Boston, Massachusetts, April 10, 1882. Her mother was Susan Wright and her father was Frederick W. Perkins. Both were of good stock and in moderate circumstances. Owing partly to her environment and partly to inheritance, she was always an "offish" child. She was both serious and set in her ideas. Those who knew her in those young days remember that she was a thoughtful child. As they now review her early life they are not surprised that she has been a leader in this worth-while movement for a more equal distribution of the nation's income. The point I wish to make is that her interest in the welfare of others has come about through neither personal privation nor sudden conversion, but through constant study and experience.

Most of us when young tend to accept family political loyalties as we do our religion. Not so Frances. She was still in high school when she dropped a mild bombshell into her staunchly Republican family circle by announcing that she was a Democrat. She had worked out to her own satisfaction the idea that the

Democratic party stood for the welfare of the masses more than did the Republican party—a viewpoint which she has never changed, despite the disillusionments which close contact with practical politics and politicians have brought to her. From adolescence onward Frances was an idealist and she translated her idealism in terms of social service. She was actively interested in church and Sunday school work when in high school and during the year following her graduation from college. The family had left Boston when Frances was a baby and in Worcester her father founded the firm of Perkins & Butler, twine manufacturers, which is still in existence.

Entering Mount Holyoke College at South Hadley, Massachusetts, in the fall of 1898, "Fanny", (she was designated in the college year books of her day as Fanny Cora Perkins) showed herself a good but by no means scholastically brillant student. She was extremely likeable and by the time she had reached her junior year she had been elected vice-president of her class, an honor which was further improved upon the following year when she became president of the class of 1902. According to several of her classmates who recall her vivid, warm qualities of leadership, she possessed a high degree of executive ability. She was so efficient as a class officer in delegating work and shrewdly devising sources of class revenue that she brought sufficient funds into the exchequer to more than balance the class budget, an extraordinary feat in those days. In addition she was tremendously active in extra-curricular affairs, being chairman of the Y.W.C.A. committee, member of the Athletic Association, member of an ambitious literary society which sported the title "The Sophocles Authors Club." She also showed some slight histrionic talent as Brutus in a farce entitled *"The Lamentable Tragedy of Julius Caesar"*.

Miss Perkins has recently paid high tribute to the influence which the impact with certain members of the faculty made on her during these college years. I feel she is a bit too severe on herself in the following statement, but she undoubtedly reflects the unchanneled confusion of the average student in those formative years of college. Emotionally interested in the humanities, she found herself a rather bewildered freshman in the required chemistry course given by Dr. Nellie Esther Goldthwaite.

"It was Dr. Goldthwaite's hounding personality, the pounding impact of her intelligence, which first aroused in me the consciousness of intellectual life," said Miss Perkins. "I discovered for the first time, under the stimulus of that course and of that teacher, that I had a mind. My intellectual pride was aroused and the grim determination awakened in me to get the most I could out of college.

"Again, I made new discoveries in another field. Miss Esther Van Dieman, a curiously emotional personality of fine intellectual type, was my instructor in freshman Latin. Up to that time, I had bluffed successfully through my years of schooling. Miss Van Dieman aroused in me an emotional state; she made me ashamed of my attitude, reduced me, a naturally light-hearted person, even to tears on one occasion, made me see that Latin prose was something that I had to master whether I liked it or not. For the first time, I became conscious of character.

"These two persons literally forced me into the election, not of the easiest, but of the hardest course. Chemistry was my major subject, physics and biology my minor. I was almost the only student who took advanced physics under Professor Laird, and I also took the supporting mathematical work. All this, though, as I said, I was emotionally interested in the humanities."

Such Spartan intellectual discipline was excellent ground work for a girl who was soon to plunge headlong into the "humanities" and who has never since left them. For a few months after graduating from college she remained at home, serving as an instructor at Leicester Academy. But a restlessness for larger fields of activity was upon her. This discipline was added to her New England ancestry. In addition to being born in Boston, her parents were New England people; in fact they were married in New Castle, Maine. From Boston she moved when a young girl to Worcester, living at 4 Linden Street and later at 16 Cottage Street. Both her father and mother are now dead but she has a sister living—a most estimable woman—Mrs. Frederick H. Harrington of Holden, Mass. Frances joined the Plymouth Congregational Church of Worcester and attended high school there.

FRANCES' SCHOOL RECORD

She graduated from the Worcester Classical High in June 20, 1898. She was not on the Honor List and took no part in the program. She was an "A" student in physiology, English and elocution, but did only moderately well in most other subjects. In general, she was a good student but not an outstanding one. While at the High School she was a member of the Aletheiai Debating Society and always was a good talker, extremely ambitious but very loyal to her friends.

Miss Perkins went to the Oxford Street Grammar School in Worcester before entering the Classical High School. During the latter part of her high school days and after she came back from Mount Holyoke, she taught Sunday school in the Plymouth Congregational Church at Worcester which her family attended. She was always an original girl, quite creative and very resourceful. She particularly shone in her diversion and her play rather than in the classroom. Where others were satisfied to follow, she always led. An incident of her resourcefulness was shown when she was only seven years old. A playmate of hers was gashed badly on the leg when climbing a picket fence. Miss Perkins used such bandages as could be made on the ground and dressed the leg and gave first aid before the girl was taken to a doctor.

After leaving college and while teaching at Leicester Academy, she became interested in social welfare and settlement work. She left Worcester then and went to Lake Forest, Illinois, to teach in an exclusive boarding school for three years. From there she went to Hull House to do settlement work. After a few months she returned to Worcester. She hired herself out for domestic positions to investigate employment conditions under the auspices of the Employment Research Bureau of Philadelphia. From there she went to New York, observing working conditions.

FRANCES PERKINS AT MOUNT HOLYOKE

Members of her class still remember her energetic and vivid personality. They relate that it was she who organized "junior Lunch", the mid-morning sale of sandwiches in aid of junior class funds, still a feature of college life today. According to one of her classmates, Miss Alice Little, owner-manager of the College Inn at South Hadley, who knows executive ability when she sees it, Fanny was a good executive, efficient at delegating work and seeing that it was carried out, keeping everybody in good humor meantime. Miss Little describes the present Secretary of Labor as she remembers her from association with her both in her undergraduate years and in many more recent encounters. In spite of growing responsibility and fame, Miss Perkins has continued in most cordial relation with her classmates and, as a loyal alumna of Mount Holyoke, has been present at many class reunions at the college. She was one of the members of the class of 1902 to return for the alumnae fete in June 1930.

"Very popular with her classmates, very pleasant to everybody, extremely goodnatured, given to practical joking (as we all were), a splendid organizer and extremely efficient as an executive." Not always so very popular with all the faculty members, perhaps. She had not exactly "the student mind" according to Miss Little.

AN ARDENT MODERNIST

During her early post-graduate years she returned from the big city atmosphere of Chicago and New York to the New England campus for her fifth and tenth reunions and astonished, even shocked, some of her contemporaries with her endorsement of modern ideas, fads and fancies. She was regarded by her classmates as "very advanced" and not all approved of her "modern notions". Some there were who openly disapproved of her modern idea of retaining her maiden name after her marriage and after the birth of her daughter. She went ahead and turned her modern ideas into achievement and put the abounding vitality which had characterized her undergraduate years at the service of the State.

Many who had formerly criticized her or held aloof from her came to recognize that behind the modern ideas was a definite purpose and real constructive ability. The Fanny who would give up a course she had flunked at college rather than repeat a part of it, once having found her bent, had amazing energy, directness and power to put through her constructive ideas. They also found in the now famous classmate, the successful executive, the same amiable and cordial person of undergraduate days. The present Secretary of Labor showed no evidence of swell-headedness, no standoffishness or evasion of her former college associates. No remembrance of former disapproval or criticism lingered in her mind.

GETS INTRODUCTION TO SOCIAL WORK

Thirty years ago there was no course in sociology or economics at Mount Holyoke. The nearest approach to such a course was given by Miss Annah May Soule, Professor of American Colonial History, who gave a course scaled on the plane of economic and social history, employing perfectly sound research methods. It was Miss Soule who introduced the future expert to the field of social service and to whose teaching she owed the fact that she was not entirely unoriented in the sphere of labor she was soon to enter.

As a member of Miss Soule's course she had undertaken a survey of factory conditions in the neighborhood of the college and, during the year which followed her graduation, she occupied her leisure time with church settlement work in connection with a girls' club, many of whose members were employed in big factories under extremely bad working conditions. Here she gained an insight into the inequalities of life and discovered the crying need for legislation for the young women workers who were at that time entirely without legal protection. She began to dig for information, to forage among the books her Mount Holyoke instructor had recommended to her class.

Her family, opposed to further study, hoped she would marry and had even a choice of suitors for her ready at hand, but instead she took a little money of her own and set out for Chicago where she became interested in the work of two well known settlement houses, Hull House and Chicago Commons. It was there that she definitely decided to enter the field of social service. Her first job was with a Philadelphia social agency and paid $40 a month. Further study under Dr. Simon Patten of the Department of Economics at the University of Pennsylvania and later at Columbia University furnished her with a yet stronger incentive for achievement. This incentive has spurred her on throughout her career.

She has degrees in sociology and economics at the University of Chicago, University of Pennsylvania, Columbia University, and an honorary Master of Arts from Mount Holyoke. She has written treatises on Life Hazards from Fires in New York Factories, in 1913; Problems of Mercantile Fire Hazards, in 1914; a Plan for Maternity Care, in 1918; Women as Employers, 1919; Social Experiment under Workmen's Compensation Jurisdiction, 1921.

Both while in college and during teaching, Frances Perkins was stimulated by the writings of Jacob Riis (*How the Other Half Lives*) and Lincoln Steffens (*The Shame of the Cities*) and other social pioneers. She developed an enthusiasm—not for labor *per se* —but rather for the unfortunate. This was what led her to Chicago, to enter Hull House and work there for some months with Miss Jane Addams. This was really her first actual experience of living and working with the poor. It awoke her sympathies to even a greater degree and she determined to give her life to helping others. She felt that the first step was to learn what she could of sociology and economics, and hence took certain postgraduate work at the University of Chicago, the University of Pennsylvania and Columbia

University. Hence, she spent these few years in teaching and studying and social settlement work. As her family was in fair circumstances financially, she was not called upon to support others and was free to study, experiment, travel and observe. From 1907 to 1909 she was secretary of the Philadelphia Research and Protective Association.

ACTIVE IN CONSUMERS' LEAGUE

After working with various groups, from conservative organized labor to radical syndicalists, the efforts of the Consumers' League seemed to be the sanest and most effectual. The league was operated by cultured people with whom she liked to associate, and yet was truly helping the poor in a practical way. For a long time she has been a member of the league and regularly attended its meetings. She gave considerable personal time to the work without any recompense. Finally, in 1910, she was elected executive secretary of the Consumers' League in New York City. In this position, which she held two years, Miss Perkins made and directed investigations of mills, factories, mercantile establishments and tenement houses. She especially studied and personally investigated sweatshop work, bakeries, laundries, etc. The more she investigated the more she was convinced of the great need of industrial protection for the poor and unfortunate. Although moved by her heart, she kept her feet on the ground. She was not a talker, but a great worker. Let me here say that the revolutionary minimum wage feature of the National Recovery Act was largely due to Miss

Perkins' influence. In fact, the entire N.R.A. movement is largely a glorified consumers' league.

The story is told that one afternoon in 1911 Miss Perkins was having tea with friends in New York City in the vicinity of Washington Square. Washington Square is near Greenwich Village, which is now the haunt of the "pinks" of New York City. It is a section where industry, boarding houses and restaurants converge. The story is that while Miss Perkins was sipping her tea, in this comfortable home and discussing theoretical social questions, a fire broke out nearby which burned nearly one hundred fifty factory girls before her very eyes. This was the famous "Triangle Shirt Waist" fire. Miss Perkins sipped no more tea and no longer discussed theoretical problems with "pinks" and college professors. She accepted the position of executive secretary of the New York Committee on Safety in 1912, which position she held through 1917. She then became executive director of the New York Council of Organization for War Service, which she held through 1919, when she went to Albany. She has been on the trail ever since, but she looks for results rather than for arguments or glory.

HER PUBLIC CAREER

She first went to Albany as a representative of the Consumers' League and in charge of their legislation. While there she conducted a successful campaign for the passage of what is commonly known as the 54-hour Bill. This is the law which limits the hours of labor of women in mercantile establishments to 54 hours a

week, or 9 hours a day. The bill became a law for
New York State in the spring of 1912 and has since
been adopted by many other states. During these years
when she was lobbying—not for organized labor, but
for unorganized women and children—in Albany, she
met three men who were then winning their spurs.
These men were Al Smith, Franklin Roosevelt and Bob
Wagner. They have been her friends ever since, convinced of her intelligence, fairness, industry and courage. During this period Miss Perkins successfully urged
amendments to other labor laws in regard to the protection of women and minors and the regulation of
tenement homework manufacture. Hence she has always been looked upon by irresponsible landlords and
manufacturers as a revolutionist.

It was while Miss Perkins was leading the fight in
behalf of the fifty-four-hour bill that an incident occurred which shows that she already knew her way
around in the field of practical politics. When the final
vote on the bill came up in the Senate it was found
that with several members absent the measure lacked
two votes of passing. President Roosevelt, then a member of the upper branch at Albany, led the filibuster
on the bill which delayed the vote sufficiently so that
Miss Perkins had time to use the telephone frantically
and to good effect. She headed off two New York City
members of the Senate who were on their way to take
the night boat from Albany back to the city and got
them back into the Senate Chamber and saved the day
with their votes.

In 1911 Miss Perkins conducted an investigation into
the cellar bakeries of New York City in cooperation

with the Commissioner of Accounts and published jointly with him the results thereof. This led to a thoroughgoing regulation of the sanitary conditions in cellar bakeries in New York City. Incidentally, this campaign should have taught her a lesson, although whether or not it did I do not know. Her exposure resulted in giving the people of New York bread produced under far more sanitary conditions and eliminated the "sweatshop" conditions in the bread industry; *but it resulted in throwing the manufacture of bread into the hands of a few large corporations.* The General Baking Company, the Continental Baking Company and other members of the so-called "Baking Trust" give Miss Perkins the credit of securing for them a grip on the baking industry of New York City. This seems to be universally the case. The breaking up of sweatshop work and the regulation of industry lead invariably to large corporate organization control. The next question to answer is whether or not large corporate control is to lead to government ownership with its inefficiency and bureaucracy or merely to government control with dictatorship as its goal.

INTERESTED IN FIRE PROTECTION

As a result of the Triangle Fire, an organization of private citizens was formed in New York in 1912 to promote measures designed to prevent a repetition of such a catastrophe. This organization was known as the Committee on Safety and Miss Perkins was chosen to become its secretary. In this capacity she operated investigations into mill, factory and store fire hazards throughout the state of New York. With the help of an advisory committee of experts on various phases of fire protection, this Committee on Safety built up a co-operative lobby in Albany and other state capitals. With the assistance of professional interests and scientific societies, having interest or knowledge of this field, she became recognized as the leading authority and the most potent factor therein. She not only had the backing of labor, charitable and social organizations, but also the help of architects and corporations such as the Gamewell Company, Rockwood Sprinkler Company and others engaged in fire protection. Combined with this work, Miss Perkins acted as director of the State Factory Investigation Commission, appearing before them with testimony as to the results and conclusions of her investigations.

From 1913 to 1917 Miss Perkins was an exceedingly busy woman, traveling throughout the state of New York to collect evidence, to direct investigations and to secure legislation at Albany. This gave her a wonderful opportunity to understand legislative bodies and to handle legislative committees. In consequence our Senators and Representatives in Washington are having their eyes opened as she appears before them on various legislative matters. During these years she represented not only the Committee on Safety and co-operated with the State Factory Investigation Commission, but she helped every good cause that appealed to her. She boosted all sane new provisions of the labor law, relating to safety, working conditions, hours of work and wages. She acted as secretary of the Committee on Safety until January, 1918. During this time she continually cooperated with city, state and federal departments in the establishment and enforcement of standards for fire, accident and sickness prevention. She holds the entire confidence of the above-mentioned organizations and also the National Safety Council, the Committee on Safety of the National Fire Protection and other organizations.

MARRIED IN 1913

During the above period, that is, in 1913, Miss Perkins was married to Paul C. Wilson, who at the time was secretary to John Purroy Mitchel, New York City's reform mayor. Since that time, Mr. Wilson has held various positions and is now doing research work for banking interests in New York City. He naturally is interested in her success but he never appears with her professionally in connection with her work. They have a daughter named Susanna Winslow Perkins Wilson, born in 1917 who is now at a private school near her, with Balto, her reddish-brown, stubby-tailed Irish terrier. It is said that Mrs. Wilson kept her maiden name "Miss Perkins" so as not to embarrass her husband with her political activities.

Although Miss Perkins is listed by many with Jane Addams and her other friends as a "pink," she has no Lucy Stone ideas that women after being married should continue to use their maiden names. Frankly, she sees no reason why they should not do so if they desire; but if she had not been in public work would doubtless insist that she be called Mrs. Paul C. Wilson. In this same connection it should be mentioned that olive-skinned Miss Perkins always wears black dresses and usually a tricorne hat almost as distinctive as the brown derby worn by ex-Governor Smith of New York.

When her child was two years old, so that she could be left to the care of others, Miss Perkins decided to return to active social work. She found it advisable, however, to give up some of her traveling and personal investigating work, and rather confine her activities to the office. Therefore, she was naturally pleased when Governor Alfred E. Smith sent for her after his election in 1918 and asked her if she would like to be commissioner of the State Industrial Commission for New York. She graciously accepted and received the appointment on February 18, 1919, and served in this capacity until April 15, 1921. From April 15, 1921 on, she was useful in various capacities. In January, 1923, she was appointed a member of the New York State Industrial Board by Governor Smith. She served in this capacity until January 19, 1926, when she was appointed by Governor Smith as chairman of the Industrial Board. On January 9, 1929, Miss Perkins was appointed Industrial Commissioner by Governor Franklin D. Roosevelt.

As Industrial Commissioner of the State of New York, Miss Perkins thought she had reached the top round of the ladder. She was then directing head of the Department of Labor of the leading industrial state of the United States. During these three years (1929-33) she continued her legislative work, writing and public speaking, giving special attention to the problem of unemployment. She has been largely responsible for the monthly statement on employment trends in 1,800

New York factories, which statement is accepted as an authoritative index of employment conditions in New York State. This report is also used as a barometer of employment conditions throughout the country. It is not only issued in advance of the Federal Index of the Bureau of Labor Statistics of the Department of Labor, but it is generally accepted as more reliable. During the Hoover administration there was a tendency for the federal Department of Labor to edit its statistics to back up the statements of President Hoover.

ACQUAINTANCE WITH ROOSEVELT

Both as Industrial Commissioner of the State of New York and ex-officio member of Governor Roosevelt's Commission on Unemployment Problems she has assisted in devising and inaugurating plans designed for industrial stability. She has continually stressed the importance to the general economic welfare of maintaining the wage earners' purchasing power. During her administration as Industrial Commissioner, she succeeded in getting her original 54-hour Law changed to a 48-hour Law, which now limits the hours of labor for women and children in mercantile establishments to 8 hours a day, or 48 hours a week. This law became effective in New York State, July 1, 1931. She has appeared as speaker before many large organizations including the National League of Women Voters, National Democratic Club, American Academy of Political and Social Science, National Consumers' League, National Safety Congress. Articles of her writing, discussing various phases of social and industrial problems, have been published in *Harper's Magazine*, *New Republic*, *Annals* of the American Academy of Political and Social Science, *Survey* and others.

Although many of Miss Perkins' ideas seem revolutionary to most employers, yet all recognize that she is honest, intelligent and courageous. Unlike most revolutionary leaders, she never goes off "half-cocked." She always bases her conclusions on thorough studies and investigations. When she makes a statement or takes a position, you can always be sure that she has the evidence to back it up. No one has ever questioned her integrity or her intelligence. She is probably the best-trained social worker in public office today. Moreover, she cannot be coaxed, frightened, bribed or bulldozed. If she has any one outstanding trait, it is her stubbornness and determination. When dealing with Miss Perkins, the only way to get results is to present definite evidence to support your case. The old methods which were used with other Secretaries of Labor and their assistants are of no avail when dealing with Miss Perkins. You might as well make up your mind to this first as last.

Miss Perkins may or may not be right in all her conclusions. People may be honest and intelligent and courageous and still make mistakes. Many who respect Miss Perkins' ability believe she is wrong in some of her theories. This applies both to leaders of organized labor, such as William Green as president of the American Federation of Labor, and to leaders of the employers' group, such as Henry I. Harriman, president of the

United States Chamber of Commerce, Secretary Quinn of the National Manufacturers' Association and Mark Daly of Associated Industries. Both the American Federation of Labor and the National Manufacturers' Association fought her appointment as Secretary of Labor. Mr. Green's official explanation for his opposition was that she was not a definite representative of labor—meaning, probably, that she never held a labor card or union office. His real reason, however, probably was because he knew that he could not control Miss Perkins. Certainly, he could not claim her to be too conservative!

The new Secretary of Labor says her first aim is to aid in providing effective relief for unemployment. She promises to give "prompt, regular, candid and uncolored" reports on conditions, and adds "there will be no manipulation of statistics." She is also trying to coordinate and harmonize the unemployment relief measures of the federal government and the forty-eight states. Her first step in this direction was the calling of a conference in Washington on March 31, 1933, to consider shorter working hours, unemployment insurance and other subjects in which she is especially interested. The agenda of said conference were as follows:

PART I OF LABOR PROGRAM

EMERGENCY ITEMS

1. Unemployment relief measures.
2. A program of public works.
3. Short hours as a means of further employment.
   (a) One day of rest in seven.

(b) Short hours or short week or both.

(c) Best methods of achievement—Federal legislation? State legislation? Contracts? Compacts between the States?

(d) Voluntary joint agreements between employers and between employers and employes.

4. Increase of purchasing power of the wage earners and its effect on stimulation of employment.

(a) How can this be brought about? Minimum legislation? By States? By Federal Government? Joint action between employers and employes? Through government machinery for the regulation of wages by boards composed of representatives of the workers, employers and the government? Fixing of minimum standards of wages in government purchase contracts?

5. Unemployment insurance or unemployment reserves as a method of achieving security of employment.

6. Home mortgage problems of wage earners and unemployed workers.

7. Canvass of possibilities of re-absorbing labor into its normal employments.

PART II OF LABOR PROGRAM

PROGRAM OF PERMANENT IMPROVEMENT OF LABOR AND INDUSTRIAL STANDARDS

This should be considered as possible guides to legislation and to standard practice.

1. Formulation of industrial standards to assure wage earners who are still employed a constructive standard of living and working conditions, to arrest the progressive breakdown of industrial standards which has been going on and to

assure a progressive rise in standards when industrial revival begins to take place.

There is grave danger lest the depression and unemployment may have caused a lowering of industrial standards which will be felt for years to come.

The fields to be considered include:

    (a) Industrial safety and accident prevention.
    (b) Workmen's compensation laws.
    (c) Prevention of industrial diseases.
    (d) Industrial sanitation.
    (e) Wages and hours so far as these may not be covered in the emergency program.
    (f) Industrial relations practice.
    (g) Machinery for joint relations.
    (h) Methods of representation; settlement of disputes.
    (i) Constructive industrial relations.

2. Labor's relation to industrial reconstruction such as railroad organization; extent of shrinkage of capitalization in basic industries; provision for old age and prevention of child labor; employment exchanges. Relations between the States and Federal Government. Desirable legislation for the achievement of these ends.

At the close of this conference Miss Perkins made the following announcement:

"The program advanced by the labor leaders voiced demands for the immediate appropriation of at least $1,000,000,000 for relief, a bond issue to provide a 'generous' part of the cost of $3,000,000,000 public works program, labor representation on all relief boards and in the enrolment of the conservation corps provided for in President Roosevelt's reforestation bill, and ratification of the pending child labor amendment or enactment of drastic child labor laws in view of the widespread unemployment of adults throughout the country."

Miss Perkins pointed out that there was agreement on many major questions of policy, with specific questions as to wage standards and methods of maintaining them postponed for further consideration.

Regarding a public works program, Miss Perkins said, there was complete agreement that the nature of the work to be undertaken first should be that of a nature calculated to raise the standard of living, such as low cost housing and slum clearance, waterworks, sewerage systems and sewage disposal plants and flood control, and that the money for financing it should be raised by the issue of "baby" bonds that could be bought by the "man in the street."

She stipulated that great care should be taken in the distribution of relief funds so that encouragement would not be given to those who are "sweating" labor and that relief funds should not be used to supplement wages and so enable employers further to depress labor conditions.

The delegates were emphatic in demanding a shorter week and in protesting against "the spirit of opposition on the part of employers to the organization of workers," the miners leading in this phase of the discussions

A plan to fix and adjust wages and to plan against depression by means of labor boards, on which would be representatives of labor, or industry and of the public, was suggested by Sidney Hillman of New York, president of the Amalgamated Clothing Workers. It was at this conference that the NRA movement started.

REVOLUTIONIZES HER DEPARTMENT

Miss Perkins is overhauling the Department of Labor. She feels that the Employment Service deserved a reorganization, especially in view of the Wagner Bill. She has worked closely with Stuart Rice, president of the American Statistical Association in connection with the Bureau of Labor Statistics, so as to make its work more adequate and practical. She especially differs from preceding Secretaries in relation to immigration. When James J. Davis was Secretary of Labor he talked a great deal about the "criminals and communists who were coming into this country to undermine Americanism" and this same fear developed into a complex during the administration of Secretary Doak. Secretary Perkins desires to comply with and enforce the immigration laws, but not to make these laws a fetish as has been desired by the capitalistic friends of the Department of Labor. Honest foreigners in this country—even if not technical citizens—will receive fair treatment under Secretary Perkins. They will not be considered criminals merely because they are working for revolutionary changes.

Miss Perkins seems to be well satisfied with the work of the Children's Bureau under Miss Grace Abbott and the work of the Women's Bureau under Miss Mary Anderson. Both of these are pet projects of Miss Perkins' and will probably not be cut down as will be the Immigration Service, which she feels has been abused by the ultra-conservatives, among both employers and union labor. The position of these conservatives is well expressed by the following editorial in the Washington *Post*:

A rigid immigration policy has been followed since the depression began. President Hoover decided that one of the most positive contributions the Government could make toward relief of the unemployed would be to cut off the competition of foreign laborers who are accustomed to working for a pittance. That clause in the law forbidding the admittance of aliens likely to become public charges was invoked and the flow of immigrants was almost cut off. It is doubtless true that some hardships have been created by these regulations, but they are insignificant in comparison with the hardships that would have been imposed upon American labor if the regulations had not been set up.

Along with this policy went the movement to rid the country of criminal aliens and other foreigners illegally living in the United States. Congress and the Department of Labor have recognized that this is expensive work, but it is the only way in which the law may be enforced in the absence of a bill requiring the registration of aliens. Administration of the immigration laws can never be entirely satisfactory until Congress acquires sufficient courage to establish a roll for all individuals living in the United States who are not citizens.

The policy of rigid control over immigration and deportation of undesirable aliens has the unqualified approval of the public. The workingmen of America will not approve a weakening of the immigration service, not even on the grounds of economy. There could be no real economy in thus exposing unemployed Americans to competition with alien paupers. If Secretary Perkins intends to maintain the policy of rigid control over immigration, she would do well to make her plans known along with her reorganization program.

Miss Perkins has made changes in the personnel of her department. The one which interests me most is her appointment of Edward F. McGrady of the American Federation of Labor as her No. 1 Assistant. The rumor is that Secretary Farley brought this about.

Miss Perkins' whole career has been in training for her present position. The President may have the honors of the national recovery movement and other revolutionary and forward steps; General Johnson and his associates may have the publicity of putting into effect the codes and agreements. But the program was largely conceived and formulated by "that woman"— Miss Perkins. Furthermore, she was the only government official who had the courage to combat the steel operators, the coal operators and truly big business. Without her, the entire NRA program might well have failed at the outset.

Miss Perkins' goal is briefly this:

More pay, more comfort, more security, more peace of mind for the ordinary worker. What is a fair wage? "Enough to permit a worker to call a doctor when his baby is sick without going on half rations for a month after." Unemployment insurance? "Many corporations dipped into their surpluses and reserves during the last few years to meet their dividend payments. Would it not be equally wise and just to make some of these reserves available for meeting payments in lieu of wages for employes who must be laid off from time to time?" Consuming power? "If we see the wage which goes to the investor is less because the wage which goes to the worker has got to be greater I think you'll hear all over this country 'aye' from people who will be glad to make the sacrifice." Miss Perkins sums up her philosophy thus: "It's time to treat ourselves to some civilization even if it requires revolution."

REPORTERS' COMMENTS

Newspaper men believe that President Roosevelt's Reforestation Scheme was devised by Miss Perkins. She surely personally took the responsibility for fighting for it before the Legislative Committee in March, 1933. She fought industrialists in insisting that work should be given in the form of federal aid; but she also fought the American Federation of Labor in insisting that the work should be paid for at not exceeding a dollar a day. The bill was finally amended by not mentioning any rate of pay, but those who know Miss Perkins believe she had her way in the end. She answered Mr. Green by saying that the dollar-a-day workers will not take the place of laborers now getting regular wages, as they would be engaged on projects that otherwise would not be undertaken. She opposed Chairman Connery of the House Committee on Labor just as violently as she opposed bankers who objected to the government wasting federal funds by such an experiment.

Readers may be interested in an interview which she gave in her office in New York City, which was reported in the press at that time. Referring to one of her major interests, Miss Perkins said that there was an acute need for revamping the federal employment system in order to take full advantage of the Congressional appropriations in this field. She pointed out that in some states the Department of Labor's federal employment organization had put into the field employment bureaus in competition with state employment bureaus. This was "not economical in these times."

Miss Perkins did not say what could be done in Washington to further the movement for unemployment insurance but recalled that she had recommended legislation in New York. On the occasion of her valedictory before the legislature she had again referred to the need for unemployment reserves in industry. Regarding a national policy on labor and industrial standards, she said that such a policy could only be arrived at in cooperation with the states "and not by the domination of the Federal Government." "I shall certainly not try to be a schoolmistress to Congress," she replied with just a shade of annoyance in her voice in reply to persistent questions as to her recommendations along labor lines. In reply to a question as to her policy for the Children's Bureau whose budget some legislators have sought to curtail, Miss Perkins shot back quickly with the statement that she would "maintain it in strength and health."

Asked whether she had any special plans to relieve unemployment, Miss Perkins said she had always favored proper utilization of a public works program as one method of helping unemployment, although not as a panacea "because there is no one panacea that can relieve all forms of unemployment." Any stabilization program, she said, would have to include a definite improvement in standards of work and health, in the prevention of accidents, in the establishment of a basic minimum wage that would represent "the fair value of services" and in the rule of one day of rest in seven. All this she sought so that through mass consumption more money might flow into wage earners' pockets to permit them to buy something more than the mere necessities. Miss Perkins praised Governor Lehman for having introduced minimum wage bills for women and children. The one she favors most is the bill that provides for application of a penalty if the employer refuses to abide by the recommendation of the minimum wage board. She also favors extending the minimum wage law to cover women in other than factory occupations. All these measures she later made a part of the National Recovery Program.

"What will be your immigration policy?" was another question.

"On that, the Bible I have to go by is the Wickersham Committee report, which recommended that a board be formed which would exercise its discretion under proper safeguards to see that the immigration law was carried out with humane consideration for those involved."

MISS PERKINS' DISLIKES

"Will you engage in social life in Washington?" she was asked.

"I enjoy my friends—if you mean just superficial social life; in times like these such a social life for a Secretary of Labor would not be very extensive."

As for her hobbies and hates, Miss Perkins said she was "semi-illiterate" in the technique of music, gave up tennis ten years ago, plays a little golf but would not go a long distance for it and is interested in painting, particularly modern art.

"I hate telephones, automobiles, airplanes and everything that makes noise," she said as her interviewers rose to leave. "That includes the radio. No, I do not possess one."

When I was in Washington in April she was much interested in the hundreds of "slump panaceas" which were coming to her office. These she classified into six groups as follows:

1. Those advocating that the government take over all industry and operate it for the benefit of the people.
2. Those favoring some form of subsidy to private industry to aid reemployment, fixed wages, etc.
3. Those urging that industrial boards similar to the War Labor Board be set up to act as industrial arbiters, setting quotas of production.
4. Those based on a conception of a permanent future for America combining agriculture and industry, placing the unemployed on thinly-settled spots near industry where farm eating could be combined with some wages.
5. Those contemplating an enormous program of a great variety of public works.
6. Those establishing barter plans "in a big way."

Miss Perkins is truly interested in improving the statistical bureau of the Department of Labor, revising both the Commodity Price Index and the Cost-of-Living Index. To aid her in these studies she has appointed the following committee:

Bryce M. Stewart, president of the American Statistical Association, Morris A. Copeland of the Economics Department of the University of Michigan, J. Frederic Dewhurst of the American Wire & Steel Institute of New York, Meredith Givens of the Social Science Research Committee, Ralph G. Hurlin of the Russell Sage Foundation, Miss Aryness Joy of the research and statistical division of the Federal Reserve Board, Howard B. Myers of Chicago University and Sidney W. Wilcox of the New York State Department of Labor.

FIRST LABOR DAY ADDRESS

Perhaps I can best close this chapter on this remarkable woman whom nobody really knows, everyone respects and many fear, by quoting from her first Labor Day address as Secretary of Labor. This address was given in her natal city of Boston on Monday, September 4, 1933. Said she:

"Wage earners today occupy a more important and more strategic and significant place in society than ever before. Realizing this, the Department of Labor stands ready to accept and fulfill its responsibilities in making it possible for labor to enjoy its just share of national well-being. It has a large share of responsibility in informing the nation of the needs of our 40,-000,000 wage earners. Not only must it make employers aware of the necessity of providing fully and equitably for wage earners, but it must make labor itself aware of the problems it has to solve and aid in their solution.

"For this purpose I plan on establishing in the Labor

Department a division of labor service and labor standards. Its function will be to study the problems of
industrial health and safety, of labor insecurity, wages,
working hours, housing, adult education, and other
factors which bear on a worker's life. But we shall not
stop at merely studying these problems. We shall keep
both labor and industry acquainted with the results
of our investigations, and have available for the wage-
earning population an information service to which the
country's workers may turn for aid and advice in dealing with the issues which confront them in their daily
relations to their jobs.

PART OF MODERN STATE

"This is more than ever needed, for the National Recovery Act has made labor an integral part of our modern state. The act includes among its basic ideas the
idea that employers are not the sole arbiters of their
industries. Labor is to be recognized as a factor in
formulating the policies of industry and is to be permitted and in fact expected to play its part in deter-
mining the course to be followed by our industry.
Behind the NRA is the philosophy that we can no
longer hope to build up the economic life of the nation
without first building up the life of our working population. To create prosperity we must develop opportunities for work; we must stabilize the incomes of wage
earners; we must create opportunities for leisure.
Without these we cannot have the purchasing power
necessary for sound industrial activity. Upon these are
dependent a steady flow of consumption demand, with-

out which, in the last analysis, the wheels of industry cannot keep turning.

"Accompanying this philosophy is the recognition by the National Recovery Act that our country is becoming a unified nation. It recognizes that the prosperity of every section of this broad land is dependent upon the prosperity of every other section. With this idea underlying it, the NRA has undertaken to bring a measure of uniformity into the labor conditions of the nation as a whole. It has provided the machinery whereby it has become possible to make national labor legislation and regulation a reality.

NEW RESPONSIBILITY

"Industry has now had thrust upon it a new social and public responsibility. It is coming to realize that it holds its plant and equipment as trustee for the nation as a whole. By the bitter lesson of the depression it has come to realize it must use its factories, its mines and its warehouses for the public good. No longer will any single business man be permitted to profit at the public expense by paying wages which depress the nation's standard of living or by working his employes for inhuman hours at the expense of the nation's health.

"American industry has nobly risen to these new responsibilities. It has accepted its trusteeship in an unselfish manner. It has undertaken its new functions with commendable vigor. It is in keeping with the observance of Labor Day that we should look forward to inaugurating a program for the prevention of unemployment in the future. We already have under NRA shorter work hours aimed to employ all the people willing and able to work. Then, too, they are being paid wages designed to increase the purchasing power of the worker—consumer. We have also made long strides toward the abolishment of child labor."

ADDITIONAL PLANS

We should keep these gains and Miss Perkins suggested that these additional points be added to a forward-looking program:

Social and industrial provision for old age.

Reserves for payment of supplemental compensation during involuntary unemployment.

Public works or government expenditure for stimulating employment and business in time of early slack in employment.

Free public employment exchanges on a national scale.

Development by industry of programs of stabilization of employment within itself.

An agricultural program integrated with the industrial program.

She then continued:

"Let us take the question of provision for old age. Elderly people who are past the years when they are expected to work hard should have some sort of security. They should not be competing with young workers and those of middle years in a market for the relatively few jobs. Certainly every state should have legislation providing for persons who are no longer

able on account of advanced age to earn for themselves
and on account of meager pay and heavy responsibilities in the past have been unable to save for the future.

HARDSHIP AND INJUSTICE

"This question of the older worker brings up another aspect that has been to the fore in the past five
years. The age at which men and women have been
considered undesirable for many types of work has
been creeping lower and lower. This trend has been
working considerable hardship and injustice. With the
increase in labor-saving devices cutting down the number of workers required in many plants and with the
running of automatic machines tending to lessen the
need for the skill and the experience of old workers in
a number of lines, it is imperative to formulate a program to safeguard their interests.

"With proper functioning of adequate government
employment agencies greater effort can be made to adjust and retain many of the so-called older workers
who are still capable and for whom there should be
a foothold in the occupational scheme of things with
proper value upon their experience and mature judgment. And now let us take up another innovation, the
matter of establishing unemployment reserves. I believe
that some form of compulsory reserves against unemployment should be built up by employers when business is good again. They build up surplus funds for
payments of dividends in an industry over lean years,
and it is expected that they will provide for supple-

mental compensation to be paid people out of work through no fault of their own in the future.

"Some kind of fund—unemployment insurance or whatever it might be called—that would compel employers to sharpen their wits and prevent these valleys and peaks of activity is highly desirable. We Americans are an ingenious people, as proof of which witness our mechanical inventions and system of mass production. Surely a people that can point to such achievement could evolve satisfactory schemes to take care of the other side of the problem—the human equation—to guarantee steady employment and an adequate system of mass consumption through a maintained purchasing power."

"That Woman" lives at 1344 Thirtieth Street, Washington, D. C.

Chapter V

"HONEST ICKES"

THE second most active revolutionist is Harold L. Ickes, Secretary of the Interior. Secretary Ickes'[1] first revolutionary act was to drag his desk from its private cloister and set up headquarters in the open. He revolutionized the ideas of any of the public who may have thought that a Secretary is a hard man to see. Equally he revolutionized the ideas of any who may have thought that the Secretary is an easy man to engage in prolonged and personal chatter. Ickes does not shrink from a long line of callers—but how he keeps that line moving. Cæsar was supposed to have set an immortal standard of terseness when he reported, "I came, I saw, I conquered." The caller who comes to the Department of the Interior to see the Secretary, however, can summarize the experience even more briefly: "I came, I saw."

In the Department of the Interior is a regular revolutionist. It requires no particular angle or special light to bring out Ickes' revolutionism. It is glaringly apparent in any light and from all angles. Whenever it has appeared to him that it was a case of "People vs. Privilege," lawyer Ickes has been ever ready to make a pass at the high and mighty. Years ago when Samuel Insull, of Chicago and Athens, was after a perpetual

[1] Pronounced e-keys.

street railway franchise which looked iniquitous, Ickes, in the rôle of president of the Peoples' Traction League, joined battle valiantly. Such action at that time was equivalent to declaration of war on some of the holiest political and social circles of Illinois.

Ickes opposed William Hale Thompson zealously, indefatigably. Ickes was in that little group of willful men who, after the nomination of Senator Harding, loudly voted "No" on the motion to make the nomination unanimous. It was his view that Harding had broken every idol of Progressivism and cast a slur on Theodore Roosevelt. Thereupon, though a delegate-at-large from Illinois to the Republican Convention, Ickes wrote a statement supporting the Democratic candidates, Cox and Roosevelt. Yes, he is a revolutionist and you usually can forecast when and how he will react.

One thing, however, is always predictable: The Secretary of the Interior will be found fighting on the side of that symbolic figurehead of the New Deal, "the forgotten man." Ickes has championed that cause for a generation. He has continued to stay in the conflict —repeatedly proving that he can take it and that he can fight back. In fact, it seems a good guess that if he had chosen to align himself on the side with the politicians, he could have been as big a regular as he has been a revolutionist.

In other words, though he instinctively has the public welfare at heart, the Secretary of the Interior is a politician in the sense of knowing the game from start to finish. He has been called, without shade of aspersion, the most accomplished politician in the Cabinet. Observers admit that had he not been working for others, he might have gone far. Ickes himself, however, has never become embittered or cynical over his collection of lost causes and defeated candidates. He summarizes with judicial calmness and absence of rancor: "The trouble has been that not enough people have cared enough to work for their own best interests."

Not all his drives have gone for naught. He has administered some resounding defeats to political opponents. Moreover, it normally happens that while a battle-front as a whole may be lost, the particular sector under command of Ickes has been decisively won. He has long been at his crusading. He was still in the senior class of the University of Chicago when he participated in his first political campaign. That battle of the century centered around a franchise grant desired by Charles T. Yerkes. John Maynard Harlan was the son of the late Mr. Justice John Marshall Harlan, at that time member of the City Council. The younger Harlan decided to run as an independent Republican for mayor against the machines. At the call for volunteers, Ickes shed cap and gown and plunged into the fray for the remainder of the campaign. He again supported Harlan in several later campaigns.

It was Ickes who proposed to Professor Charles E. Merriam that Merriam go after the Republican nomination for mayor. Professor Merriam replied that he would run if Ickes would run the campaign. The result was one of the most spectacular affrays ever witnessed in Chicago—which is high praise—and Merriam got the nomination. At the polls he was defeated, but only because bankers and investors lined up with the gangsters and grafters. This made Ickes more determined than ever to fight.

That fight was not wholly wasted, for it created a volunteer organization under Ickes as manager of the Merriam campaign, which continued to function. Within a year it was called upon to take part in the famous Progressive movement of 1912. In that campaign, Ickes was chairman of the Cook County campaign forces. Theodore Roosevelt's national manager was Joseph M. Dixon, then Senator from Montana. More than a score of years later when Secretary Ickes assumed office in Washington, he met Dixon as First Assistant Secretary of the Interior. In that 1912 campaign, Theodore Roosevelt carried Cook County by a majority of 27,000, though failing to win Illinois.

AN ARDENT PROGRESSIVE

Ickes liked the atmosphere of the Progressive camp and he continued his activities. These included: State Chairman, National Committeeman, member of the National Executive Committee, delegate-at-large to the Progressive National Convention. Ickes labored to persuade the Progressive party to fight things out on a long-pull basis. He argued that Rome was not built in a day and that by continuing the battle through one lost election after another the party would eventually establish itself. If that policy were adopted, Ickes foresaw that the day of victory would finally arrive.

Disappointed at Theodore Roosevelt's refusal to run as the Progressive party's candidate in 1916, Ickes turned to the support of Charles E. Hughes. The Hughes campaign was not run in regular form by the Republican National Committee, but with the instrumentality of a campaign committee of nine regular Republicans and six Progressives; Mr. Ickes was one of these half-dozen placed by Mr. Hughes on this committee. Ickes was active in western headquarters at Chicago, with the particular assignment of working with former Progressives. These, however, could not be successfully herded into line in the face of the attitude of regular Republicans. Weeks before the election, a private state-by-state analysis constructed by Ickes pointed to Hughes as the probable loser, with the onus of defeat placed on the party regulars.

In 1920, Mr. Ickes supported Frank O. Lowden until the final ballot and then voted for Hiram W. Johnson. It is significant that prior to the Democratic Convention of that year, Ickes had urged upon Democratic leaders as the best man who could be named for Vice President on their ticket, Franklin D. Roosevelt of New York; and in the convention the Illinois leader did support Roosevelt for that office. Here is when his acquaintance with the President began. It has continued ever since.

In Illinois, Hiram W. Johnson's 1924 candidacy for the Republican nomination was under the direction of Ickes. The Johnson vote in that state was surprisingly large, especially in view of the limited funds available, the small organization, and the fact that the Senator was running against Calvin Coolidge, then President.

At a later date, the campaign of Hugh S. Magill, as an Independent candidate for the United States Senate, was managed by Ickes. He did not participate in the 1928 presidential campaign but he voted for Alfred E. Smith. This further cemented him to the Roosevelt bandwagon as Roosevelt nominated Smith.

The foregoing details have been narrated to paint in a broad way the political complexion of our Secretary of the Interior. It is clearly of revolutionary cast. Whether struggling vainly for the permanent establishment of a Progressive party or blocking successfully the attempt to give Illinois a reactionary state constitution, Ickes is discovered in the ranks of the revolutionists. He never appears, however, either the parlor type or the soap-box ranter, but an effectual and practical politician. Sometimes he has won, sometimes he has lost; but win, lose or draw, his opponents have always known they have been in a fight. Ickes has emerged from conflict, never crestfallen or embittered, but apparently aroused to fight all the harder.

ICKES FAMILY HISTORY

Ancestrally he comes of Pennsylvania stock. On both mother's and father's side, the family tree has flourished for nearly three centuries. Its founder sailed to this country on one of the voyages of William Penn. That Ickes settled in the Philadelphia region. Our Secretary's great-grandfather, Nicholas, fought in the Revolutionary War at the age of sixteen, and later settled in Perry County, Pennsylvania. In that county, on the site of that original farm, is the town of Ickesburg;

and in the local cemetery are buried Nicholas Ickes and his wife. We may squirm at some of the Secretary's proclivities, but we can hardly pass them off in the convenient category of foreign propaganda. Friend or foe, we must grant he is an American revolutionist.

The Secretary's grandfather migrated west to Blair County and settled in Altoona. The Secretary's father, Jesse Ickes, was Comptroller of Altoona at the time of his death about ten years ago. The mother of Harold L. Ickes was Martha Ann McCune. That name was originally spelled "McEwen" and both sides of her family were Scotch Presbyterians. They had settled in the Alleghany foothills before the Revolution, among the oldest families of the region. For thirty-six years the Secretary's great-grandfather, Joseph McCune, served as Judge for Huntington County from which Blair County was carved. We will admit respectfully that Harold L. Ickes, whatever may be the novelty of his views, cannot be classified as upstart or newcomer in this country of ours.

Date of his birth: March 15, 1874. Place: Frankstown Township, near Hollidaysburg, in Blair County. At his mother's death, when he was sixteen years old, he was sent to Chicago to live with an aunt. In three years he finished the four-year requirements of the Englewood High School. Then he worked his way through the University of Chicago by teaching in the public night schools. He struck into life as a reporter on the old Chicago *Record*, Victor Lawson's morning paper. Somewhat surprisingly, the annals disclose him later as assistant sporting editor of the paper! Not at all surprisingly, the next view shows him in the political department, in which he had asked to be placed. He had arrived at destination.

Until lately, the secretary of the Board of Indian Commissioners in the Department of the Interior was Malcom McDowell. This man was Ickes' superior in the old days in the political department of the Chicago *Record*. Curiously enough he has crisscrossed with Ickes by recently returning to the newspaper industry. Another former associate of cub-reporter Ickes was Frederick William Wile, famed news broadcaster from Washington. Ickes also worked on the Chicago *Tribune and Chronicle*. While on the Chicago *Record* he helped to report the Republican National Convention and a Democratic National Convention.

It is not altogether clear why a potential revolutionist should be attracted to the law, unless as a field in particularly urgent need of reform. For some reason, Ickes had long wanted to become a lawyer; and after a period of reporting and reforming, he returned to the University of Chicago and entered the Law School. With his usual persistence in reaching a goal he was duly admitted to the bar.

A GOOD WAR RECORD

That in fragmentary account is the Secretary's background. Two more passages remain to be related. They are especially interesting because they help to show this man in a light somewhat different from the almost monotonous turmoil of progressive politics. Harold Ickes drove into the World War with admirable energy and devotion. He proved himself ready to fight for the right as he saw it, whether the decision was by bullet or by ballot. Such has not always been an outstanding characteristic of all revolutionists. He was not content with service as director of patriotic propaganda for the Illinois State Council of National Defense. He sheered away from an army commission with assignment to the War Department at Washington. What did appeal to him was the opportunity offered by the Y.M.C.A. to go to France.

In France he was attached to the 35th Division. With that division he served in Alsace-Lorraine and in the final drive in the Argonne. Former Senator Henry J. Allen was at the head of the Y.M.C.A. unit, and during his long illness full charge devolved upon Ickes as next in line of command. Ickes was then over age and a married man with a family. Nevertheless, he succeeded in obtaining from the General in command of the 35th Division a recommendation that he be given a commission as captain in the Commissary Department and sent into active service. Ickes was in Paris on his way to General Headquarters, when the Armistice was declared.

The second of the two passages which give us a glimpse of the man within the revolutionist is of lighter tone. Secretary Ickes is a dahlia fan! For years his hobby has been gardening and his specialty has been the petaled curls of dahlias, with their richness of red, or pink, or salmon, or lavender or white. Various varieties have been originated by him. One variety he has named for his wife, the "Anna W. Ickes" dahlia. This he has patented under some rather revolutionary patent legislation which he also originated. Still you can always trust a man who loves flowers and birds.

Anna W. Ickes, I may remark, is more than the name of a flower and more than the name of the wife of a famous man. Mrs. Ickes is a public person in her own right. For several years she has represented her district in the Illinois legislature as a regular Republican. They have three sons and a daughter. The family home is at Winnetka, Illinois, where everyone knows them. Mrs. Ickes has backed her husband both sympathetically and financially in all his endeavors.

Among the memberships with which the Secretary is listed: National Roosevelt Memorial Association, in which he was president of the Greater Chicago branch; Chicago Forum Council, of which he was former president; American Bar Association; Phi Delta Theta and Phi Delta Phi fraternities; University Club of Chicago; Congressional Country Club; Indian Hill Club; Shawnee Country Club. Moreover, he has helped every good cause and has been a friend to many.

Under the New Deal, the fundamental viewpoints of the Department of the Interior may be somewhat revolutionized. As defined of old:

"The United States Department of the Interior, established by the act of March 3, 1849, is the land, home and education department of the Government. Its work is a permanent contribution to the educational, scientific, historical and conservation functions of the Government. It is a fact-finding department.

"Its mission is largely educational and many of its activities are devoted to the discovery and dissemination of knowledge. It contributes to education through its Office of Education. It operates directly 205 schools for the American Indians and 86 for the native Alaskans. It maintains Howard University, training schools for nurses at Freedman's and St. Elizabeth's Hospitals, with a graduate school for psychiatrists at the latter, and Columbia Institution for the Deaf. Its work in the General Land Office Geological Survey, and the Bureau of Reclamation touches the scientific field; through the National Park Service it handles the national playgrounds of the people."

PUBLIC WORKS PROGRAM

True, the activities such as described above will continue. But the New Deal has put upon the Secretary new duties. It has charged him with the administration of a program of public works calling for the expenditure of $3,000,000,000. Now this is more than "education"—it is disbursement! Heretofore the Department of the Interior has conceived of itself as keeping an eye on economic resources; oil, for example. Under the dictates of the New Deal it looks as if the department is going to do more than keep an eye on the battles of the petroleum industry; the department is going to take a hand in them if necessary.

Even under the old deal, however, the department had quite a sizable job of procurement. Departmental activities requiring materials purchased include normally: Office of Indian Affairs, Geological Survey, Bureau of Reclamation, General Land Office, Office of Education, National Park Service, Alaska Railroad, hospitals and institutions. The department buys things ranging in size from a paper of pins to Boulder Dam. One office alone, the Office of Indian Affairs, does buying for groups equivalent to a city of 350,000 population. One hospital, St. Elizabeth's, expends about $1,500,000 annually. So it was only natural that the President gave the $3,000,000,000 Public Works appropriation to Secretary Ickes to spend.

Purchasing conditions can be outlined in part as follows. Indian Service: Buys all supplies under supervision of Purchasing Officer, visiting Chicago and St. Louis. Geological Survey: Buys scientific instruments and supplies through chief field purchasing office in Denver. Bureau of Reclamation: Buys principally in the field; main procurement office in Denver. Office of Education: Some field buying, mostly from Seattle branch. National Park Service: Buys various materials. Alaska Railroad: Consolidated purchasing and shipping unit in Seattle. Hospitals and Institutions: Most of purchases made direct.

SCANDALS MUST BE AVOIDED

Secretary Ickes, however, does not hold that he is charged merely with making the motions of administering the relatively moderate activities such as might be inferred from a stereotyped description of departmental routine. He is quoted as regarding himself as the custodian in effect of public property: parks, water powers, mineral resources—the treasures of the public domain. Guardianship of our public lands, he has expressed it, discovering, appraising, developing our national resources. The way he has already handled his responsibilities has caused him to be known as "Honest Ickes."

Moreover, the New Deal may go into developments on a bigger scale than the department has ever before visualized. Already operations have either been started or projects have been proposed for power developments in no less than five different regions. These developments, with their radiating networks of possible transmissions, spot the continent from coast to coast and border to border. Nobody can say with assurance whether even this is the end of revolutions or only the start. But whichever it is, Ickes' courage is good and he will not be blocked or stampeded.

Ickes' fitness for a place on the Cabinet of the New Deal is manifest. He is anything but a novice. For a lifetime he has been outstandingly a liberal, progressive and revolutionist. Men of his breadth are peculiarly hard to label because they do not stay put in hard-and-fast compartments. If asked to label Ickes, however, all would unhesitatingly attach to him the label of the New Deal. Certainly no badge of party regularity would ever stick on him. He was an ideal selection for the secretaryship and he has the entire confidence of the President

The Department of the Interior, in a special sense, calls for more than revolution—it demands reliability. It is inevitable that a branch of government entrusted with the possession of public properties, and now more recently entrusted with the expenditures of almost inconceivably colossal public moneys, should be the potential breeding ground of scandals. If there is any one department of which the director should be of irreproachable devotion to the public welfare, and tested powers for public protection, it is the Department of the Interior with the newly organized Public Works establishment.

Not even the United States Mint is more in a position of responsibility, for the Mint can at least be put under lock and key; but how can we padlock a whole continent? The protection of our public resources and the billions appropriated for public works, is solely the character and the capacity of the administrators. We have real reasons for a feeling of security because such administration is headed by "Honest Ickes." For surely he is both fearless and beyond reproach.

For more than thirty-five years he has been in the thick of public combat, under the white lights of a publicity that beats even more mercilessly upon the political arena than upon the throne. We may well believe that if there had been spots of badness or weakness in this thirty-five-year record, they would have been broadcast to the world—ruthlessly! Even those who have no particular love for revolution *per se*, if forced to a choice, prefer to take their chances with an honest revolutionist than a question-mark reactionary.

INTEREST IN EDUCATION

The Department of the Interior has many divisions, all important; but one especially appeals to me as having great latent possibilities—the Office of Education. As the head of this division, Secretary Ickes has selected George Frederick Zook—age 48—formerly president of the University of Akron.

Working his way through the University of Kansas by driving a hearse, he has taught modern European history at Kansas, Cornell and Penn State. He was a war-time propagandist under George Creel, a division chief in the Office of Education before he went to Akron. Methodist and Rotarian, Dr. Zook kept more free of local politics than most municipal university presidents. Because he never told how he voted, he was called "Poker Face" by his professors and by Akron politicians. Dr. Zook did not seek his United States job, nor did his friends seek it for him.

Dr. Zook moved with his wife and adopted son to Wesley Heights, Washington suburb. He plays golf twice a week, is noted for length off the tee. Daily he steers his Buick to the office where he works at a desk usually clear of papers. Dr. Zook knows President Roosevelt, but not as yet very well. Since he took office in July it has become apparent to him as much as to anyone that the New Deal has scarcely touched Education. Commissioner Zook went up to New York, told a Teachers College conference not to expect Federal funds for teachers' salaries (*Time*, August 14). Recently he wrote in the Washington *Star*: "The Depression hit schools later than it did the business community. It will linger with schools longer than with business and trade. This year, therefore, will probably be the most difficult year of the Depression so far as schools are concerned."

Though many a conference has voted to urge federal aid—notably one at Teachers College which went so far as to advocate a dole for all pupils until they find employment—the United States Government regards the difficulties of the schools as purely local problems. Commissioner Zook can offer no cash help. But, like a kindly, keen-eyed, plump-faced uncle, he may give advice, put at education's disposal a vast amount of statistics. Dr. Zook said on taking office: "We have a product to sell to the people. If we are to be successful, it must be so organized and so displayed as to make the people desire it more than some ephemeral pleasure done up in a tinseled package." Commissioner Zook has gone about organizing his product as follows:

TEACHING ABOUT THE NRA

Dr. Zook would gear the Office of Education to be a powerful liaison service between the schools and the new agencies of the government. This month the office's *School Life* (paid circulation 10,000—largest of any government organ) describes for teachers the "Children's Code" (child labor ban), tells how school districts may apply for Public Works funds for building. *School Life* asks: "Can you name the ten new Federal agencies whose long names have shrunk to initial letters? Do you know the purpose of each of these ten weapons Congress has given to the President to fight the recovery campaign?" As an aid to teachers in telling their pupils about them, it presents "thumbnail sketches" of NRA, AAA, PWA, CCC, FCOT, FERA, TVA, RFC, FFCA, HOLC, with a map of Washington showing their locations.

A code for teachers was submitted to NRA last

month by the American Federation of Teachers. It was rejected on the ground that teachers are government employes. Nevertheless, Commissioner Zook cautiously announced that the Office of Education is studying the "implications" of a code, with some recommendations to NRA in view. Meanwhile pedagogues were ostentatiously anxious to help NRA by expounding it in the classrooms. The National Education Association, which works hand-in-glove with the Office of Education, announced a program by which teachers would reinterpret textbooks, explaining to children why such maxims as "Competition is the life of trade" and "A penny saved is a penny earned" are at present invalid.

Whether or not NRA is of immediate benefit to Education, Dr. Zook predicts it will widen education's bounds. The child labor ban will put 100,000 new pupils in the high schools. And the increase of leisure will increase the demand for adult education, by which teachers may "interpret social trends and . . . reemphasize the fundamental significance of education in our social development." Further, NRA should bring an increased interest in, and revaluation of, history, civics, government and economics (at present studied by only 3 per cent of all high-school students).

When Dr. Zook became Commissioner he announced that he wished to bring experts frequently to Washington, to confer and make available to all the nation their combined ideas. He exclaimed: "I would like to see our conference room occupied by one such conference every week!" Since then Commissioner Zook has sponsored various gatherings, to consider this question.

WHOM TO SEE

For the benefit of business men who visit the Department of the Interior in connection with the expenditure of the $3,000,000,000 Public Works money, I want to say a word about Emil Hurja (pronounced hur-ya). Incidentally, it is rumored that he represents Postmaster-General Farley. If so, this is interesting because Farley has been crazy to get hold for his followers of some of those millions but "Honest Ickes" would not let him in the door. Therefore watch out!

Emil Hurja was born of Finnish parents some forty years ago in upper Michigan. He went to Alaska, got a job sweeping out the office of the Fairbanks *Daily Times*, later earned enough to put himself through the University of Washington. He first turned up in Washington as secretary to Frank Sulzer, one-time delegate from Alaska. Last year he was an early rider on the Roosevelt bandwagon, got himself chosen to the Chicago convention as an Alaskan delegate. Manager Farley, impressed with his ability to forecast political trends, to find out what voters were thinking, took him under his wing. Most of last year's Farley predictions were based on Hurja calculations. After March 4, Postmaster-General Farley took Mr. Hurja to Washington with him, made him his right-hand man on patronage. Tall, stout, full-faced, Democrat Hurja quickly became a power among job-seekers. Following Jim Farley's formula ("For Roosevelt before Chicago") he did most of the picking and choosing. Then he was put into RFC as personnel officer. In commenting on this *Time* stated as follows:

General Farley's toughest job has been to get Secretary Ickes to see reason in the matter of Democratic appointments. Mr. Ickes loudly declared that there would be no politics in his Public Works Administration. Democrats have been ruthlessly brushed aside from his office. Adroitly Mr. Hurja was steered back and forth across Secretary Ickes' path. Like Jim Farley, Mr. Ickes was impressed with the man's dynamic ability, his easy manners, his poise. Last week he made Mr. Hurja his Public Works administrative assistant, gave him a cubby-hole office in which he began to interview job-seekers.

Well aware that he had apparently surrendered on patronage, Secretary Ickes declared: "Mr. Hurja had not applied for a position here and he was not suggested by anyone. . . . I am confident he will be useful. As Secretary of the Interior I have passed on personnel matters myself. I have done the same as Administrator of Public Works. I shall continue to be my own personnel officer."

However—notwithstanding these comments, I still believe that "Honest Ickes" will continue to watch the Treasury. Brother Hurja is destined to have hard sledding.

"Honest Ickes" lives at 1327 Thirty-Third Street, Washington, D. C.

CHAPTER VI

"MOLEY'S FRIEND"

ALTHOUGH nonspectacular and quiet, I personally feel that Cordell Hull, Secretary of State, is the most experienced revolutionist in the Cabinet. He, however, has specialized more on international problems than on industrial. He is an internationalist and to a certain extent a pacifist rather than a baiter of bankers and employers. He feels that if each nation and individual had a fair opportunity most problems would solve themselves. To the high tariff Republican, Cordell Hull is the "worst revolutionist" of the bunch; although he would feel insulted to be called even a "pink." Personally I am fond of him and feel he has the right goal even if he is ahead of his times.

Cordell Hull is from Tennessee and his selection for Secretary of State was a natural one for two reasons. First, because he is a good Democrat and has been a close personal friend of President Roosevelt since the President ran as Vice President on the Cox ticket some years ago. Secondly, and this is what was given to the press at the time of the announcement, because Cordell Hull is the best posted man in the Democratic party on tariffs. This may or may not be true, but without doubt Mr. Hull has given much time to the study of all forms of federal income of which receipts from tariffs is an important factor. Underlying these two reasons is the desire of the administration to control Congress.

Cordell Hull, who was Senator at the time of his appointment, is in a position materially to help the President along these lines. Without doubt, this desire on the part of President Roosevelt was a deciding factor in the selection of Senator Hull as Secretary of State, although the desire to have the benefit of his experience as well as to reward faithful Democrats may have been a consideration.

One important question which faced the Department of State on March 4, 1933, was the question of what should be done with the debts which foreign nations owe the United States government. Of course, to a certain extent this is a matter of negotiation between the Roosevelt administration and these foreign countries; but practically the real problem is to get the approval of Congress to the plan upon which these foreign governments and the administration may agree. If there is one thing Democratic Congressmen have thus far disliked, it is the idea of canceling the foreign debts! Many Democratic leaders have taken the position that they would not even discuss the matter! Hence, it is of the greatest importance that the new Secretary of State, who would be in charge of these debt negotiations, should be able to swing Congress to the administration's point of view. Considering all phases of the question, Senator Hull is probably the best man to be Secretary of State in order to accomplish this special task.

HIS ANCESTRY

Cordell Hull was born October 2, 1871, in Overton (now Pickett) County, Tennessee. His father was William Hull, a farmer near Carthage, Tennessee. Cordell Hull was brought up to earn his own way and he used to raft logs down the Tennessee River. His mother was Elizabeth Riley, and he was one of an average-size family. Both his parents came from ancestors who served in the Revolutionary War. These ancestors came from Virginia and North Carolina to Tennessee. His great-grandfather, Jesse Hull, was in the War of 1812. Cordell Hull married Mrs. Frances Whitney of Staunton, Virginia, in 1917. They have no children. Not only were most of the people of Tennessee in those days Democrats, but Cordell Hull was brought up in an atmosphere which was distinctly southern if not of an anti-northern nature. From boyhood he instinctively learned to distrust, if not fear, northern people and northern influences. This training, or rather environment, of his youth has doubtless influenced his entire life and has probably cost the North many billions of dollars. But this fact gives his Democratic friends confidence in him and, when he approves heartily a foreign debt settlement, his associate Democrats will feel that it is just and not alone in the interest of Wall Street and the country's bankers.

After graduating from the public schools and the National Normal University at Lebanon, Ohio, in 1899, Cordell Hull went to Cumberland University at Lebanon, Tennessee, from the Law Department of which he graduated two years later. He started practicing law in the humblest possible way in Tennessee after he was admitted to the bar in 1891. The law business was dull in his community, and it is always difficult for a young man to get started in a profession. For want of something better to do, he became mixed up in state politics and in 1893 was elected for two terms to the lower house of the Tennessee legislature.

When Cordell Hull was 27 years old the Spanish War broke out and he enlisted in the 40th Tennessee Volunteers. He served in Cuba with the rank of captain and had an honorable record. He has always been of a serious nature. Temperamentally he is somewhat of the Coolidge type. He does well the job given him to do and does it quietly without any blare of trumpets. On the other hand, fate and good fortune seem to be with him and he has always naturally been promoted from one position to another. He is distinctly of the executive and office-working, and not of the spectacular speech-making, type. To Wall Street and the vested interests he is decidedly a revolutionist.

After Cordell Hull returned from the Spanish War, the Governor of Tennessee appointed him Judge, which position he held until he was definitely elected in 1903 Judge of the Fifth Judicial Circuit of Tennessee. This position he retained until he resigned during his race for election to the Sixtieth Congress in 1907. At that time Judge Hull was one of the youngest judges on the bench, but he always handled himself with dignity and was always recognized for his thoroughness and honesty. Most Tennessee colonels still refer to him as "Judge." His sense of integrity was well illustrated by the way he resigned from his position on the bench before he knew whether or not he would be elected to Congress. While talking with Tennessee people, both Republicans and Democrats, I learned that they all respect Cordell Hull, even though they feel he may have a distorted view as to the purposes, motives and ambitions of northern people.

CONGRESSIONAL RECORD

Cordell Hull entered Congress as a fairly young man. He took the job seriously, modestly minded his own business, but attended carefully to the tasks presented to him. As a result, he was reelected to the Sixty-first Congress, the Sixty-second Congress, the Sixty-third Congress, the Sixty-fourth Congress, the Sixty-fifth Congress and the Sixty-sixth Congress. The Harding landslide in 1920 put him out of office for two years, but he was back again in the House to serve in the Sixty-eighth Congress beginning in 1923. He again was reelected to the Sixty-ninth Congress, the Seventieth and the Seventy-first Congresses. Thus his acquaintance with both the personnel and the history of the House of Representatives is exceptionally valuable. There are few Democrats who have the personal knowledge and background that Cordell Hull has in connection with Congressional legislation and what can and cannot be done with a Democratic Congress.

On November 4, 1930, Cordell Hull was promoted to the United States Senate, where his term of office was to expire March 3, 1937. He was elected to the Senate by 154,131 votes against his opponent who received only 58,654 votes, thus giving him a plurality of nearly 100,000 votes. This is a considerably larger majority than his associate Senator Kenneth McKellar of Memphis ever received. Senator McKellar was elected to the United States Senate November 7, 1916, by a majority of 25,498; was reelected in 1923 by a majority of 80,323; but secured on his last reelection in 1929 a majority of only 55,070. It will be seen, therefore, that Cordell Hull entered the Senate with both the longer legislative record and also as the more popular Senator from Tennessee. When all the southern Senators are weighed in the balance, it might be said that—with the exception of Senator Glass of Virginia—Senator Hull was the leading southern Democratic Senator.

Cordell Hull performed another service to the Democratic party which should not be forgotten. At the time of the Republican landslide in 1920, he accepted the chairmanship of the Democratic National Committee, which job no other prominent Democrat was willing to take. This position he held from 1921 to 1924, when control was taken over by Raskob and the New York interests. I say that the Democratic party owes Hull a debt of gratitude for doing this, because the party was without friends or funds when he assumed the position. The country was in the throes of the business depression and the tremendous collapse in commodity prices which followed the war-time boom. Even President Wilson had been reelected in 1916 by almost the barest possible majority and the Democrats had merely held on by their teeth until 1920, when a Republican victory was inevitable. Hull was the only respectable Democrat who was willing to assume this position which no one wanted. The party was saddled with a debt, he lacked even funds for a decent office and clerical hire. He immediately became the butt of a successful and arrogant Republican organization. During these trying circumstances, however, Cordell Hull remained patient and courteous and endeavored to deal justly with all conflicting interests.

FATHER OF THE INCOME TAX

Let us now drop back a few years in Cordell Hull's history. For some time prior to the war, it was evident that Congress must have some means of securing necessary revenue other than from tariffs, stamp taxes, etc. For constitutional reasons, the federal government cannot raise money by real estate taxes and certain other customary forms of taxation. Therefore, it was necessary to resort to a distinctly new source of revenue. From the earliest days, a tax on incomes—both corporate and personal—was considered. All such legislation, however, was strenuously opposed by northern interests—especially by the banking and industrial interests of such powerful states as New York, Pennsylvania, Illinois, Ohio, and the New England states. Some of these states even today have no state income tax legislation. Gradually, however, individual states adopted income taxes as a source of revenue. Finally, a determined step was taken to have the federal government adopt income taxes as a source of revenue.

In the early part of this century, it became recognized that income taxes could be assessed in a practical and satisfactory manner by the federal government only by an amendment of the Constitution. Hence a campaign was started to bring about such a revolutionary amendment and Cordell Hull was one of the revolutionists in this campaign. Finally, an amendment was passed by the Sixty-first Congress on July 18, 1909, and was

declared to have been ratified by three-quarters of the
states in the proclamation of the Secretary of State,
dated February 25, 1913. Incidentally, all states ratified excepting Connecticut, Florida, Pennsylvania,
Rhode Island, Utah and Virginia. The amendment is
now known as the Sixteenth and reads: "The Congress shall have power to lay and collect taxes on
incomes, from whatever source derived, without appor-
tionment among the several states and without regard
to any census of enumeration." The enactment of this
amendment gave Cordell Hull his opportunity. He accepted the responsibility and went to work.

Everybody in Washington gives Hull credit (or
blame, according to the point of view) for the income
tax system which was inaugurated in 1913. Without
doubt the system as originally planned was just and
necessary. Few Congressmen visualized the great World
War and the tremendous events which have since tran-
spired, when devising the federal income tax system. If
these events had been visualized at that time, it is de-
batable whether or not three-quarters of the states
would ever have ratified this Sixteenth Amendment.
Many political leaders believe that if such ratification
had not been obtained in 1913, it never would have
been obtained; while others claim that the exigencies
of the World War would have forced such a ratification.
The fact remains that the simple income tax system,
devised by Cordell Hull in 1913, became expanded
within three years beyond all dreams and expectations.
Whether the enactment of this amendment in 1913 was
fortunate or unfortunate will always be a subject for
debate.

In August, 1914, the World War broke out. At first, there was no idea of the United States getting into it. Even President Wilson was re-elected in 1916 under the slogan "He kept us out of war." Gradually, however, the pressure became stronger and stronger for the United States to enter the conflict. This pressure was especially strong in the North, including the great industrial and financial states of New York, Pennsylvania, Illinois, Ohio, Massachusetts and Connecticut. Delaware, the home of the duPonts, was also bringing great pressure on our government. Finally, with the sinking of the *Lusitania,* this pressure could no longer be withstood and Congress, with the approval of President Wilson, declared war upon Germany. The fat was then in the fire. Already a conflict was raging between the industrial interests of the North, which were making huge profits from the war, and those more humble interests represented by the rank and file of the Democratic party. It was this feeling "between those who have and those who have not" that caused a revision of the income tax system and the enactment of the Federal Estate and Inheritance Taxes of 1916. Both these acts were prepared and engineered through Congress by "revolutionist" Cordell Hull.

It was in connection with this income tax legislation that Cordell Hull reflected his southern training and environment. Although he handled the matter conscientiously, from his point of view, doubtless the income tax law would be of an entirely different nature had it been designed and amended by northern financial interests or if a Republican administration had been in office during the World War. I am not here saying that what happened has not all been for the best. It might have been impossible for a Republican administration, with its capitalistic and dictatorial traditions, to have enacted and so successfully operated a national draft system and the collection of such huge amounts of taxes. To many it seems providential that the Democratic party should have been in power at that time; they believe that only the Democratic party could have "sold" the war to the American working people. On the other hand, it may be unfortunate that this income tax legislation could not have been made a nonpartisan and nonsectional affair.

STUDENT OF TARIFFS

Cordell Hull is—as above stated—a student of tariff legislation. It is doubtless true that his interest in using income taxes as a source of federal revenue became a necessary result of his desire to lower federal tariffs on imported goods. As a practical matter, the federal government was in dire need of more revenue, and higher tariffs seemed absolutely necessary unless some other source of revenue became available. Hence, Hull and his Democratic associates who were interested in lowering the tariff on imported goods were forced to consider income taxes. Republicans have always referred to Hull as a "free trader," and he was said to be the "only free trader" left in the House during the Seventy-first Congress. He, however, resents this indictment and calls himself a Jeffersonian Democrat—in favor of a tariff, but a tariff for revenue only. Therefore, it is important for all who have dealings with the

State Department to realize that the new Secretary of State is not only a revolutionist as to northern industrial and financial interests, but also believes in a tariff for revenue only.

No manufacturer—especially in normally Republican states—can expect any sympathy from Secretary Hull in connection with the protective tariff. In 1910 when the Payne-Aldrich Bill was being discussed, he described it as "a miserable travesty, an ill-designed patchwork and a piece of brazen legislative jobbery." He fought it every inch of the way through both the House and the Senate. In 1932 when the Hawley-Smoot Act was before Congress, he flayed this legislation as "utterly disastrous to our trade." He is probably today the most revolutionary proponent of a tariff for revenue only, even though there has developed a large protective complex amongst the Democrats of the South. This especially applies to the Democrats of the Carolinas, Georgia and Alabama which are fast becoming industrial states. It is for this reason that most manufacturers view with alarm having Cordell Hull sit at the head of President Roosevelt's Cabinet. Rightly or wrongly, these manufacturers believe in protection as the basis of American industrial prosperity. This belief was a primary reason for the action of the commodity and security markets in the early part of the Roosevelt administration.

On the other hand, Cordell Hull is not a revolutionist of the college professor type. In 1910 he saw that the only practical way of getting the tariff reduced was to provide some other source of revenue, and consequently he went to work in a practical way to enact income tax legislation. Today he sees that the only practical way of reducing tariffs is through the enactment of trade reciprocity treaties; in fact, he wrote the reciprocity tariff plank into the Democratic platform of 1932. He will use his power of negotiating an adjustment on the war debts with a concurrent purpose of lowering the tariff and "freeing foreign trade," to use his own expression. Whether or not Secretary Hull is doing this in the best interests of the country is a question which only the future can decide. He is a man who had not traveled extensively and before March 4, 1933, had few world contacts.

HULL'S REVOLUTIONARY IDEALS

"The business of all nations," he says, "is on an artificial basis."

Condemning what he describes as "the blind, selfish, and dumb economic leadership of this country since 1920," he asserts that "its type in other countries should be summarily thrown out of power and a leadership substituted which, while disclaiming economic internationalism, would challenge economic nationalism and pursue a sane, liberal, middle course in the conduct of our domestic and international economic affairs."

"The strangulation of international trade," he adds, "from what would be a normal level under the pre-war ratio of increase of nearly $55,000,000,000 down to $12,000,000,000 by extreme tariffs, quotas, embargoes and exchange restrictions, constituted the greatest single cause of the panic, while its restoration is an indispensable prerequisite to the redistribution of gold, monetary stabilization everywhere and the payment of external indebtedness, both public and private, by all countries."

In accordance with these views Mr. Hull may not consider war debts the crux of the depression problem, although he does not minimize their importance. Moreover, he believes that the United States government, like all creditors, public and private, should always be considerate toward its debtors.

In suggesting means for relieving conditions, Mr. Hull holds that "reciprocal commercial treaties based on mutual tariff concessions and, as nearly as possible, the unconditional favored-nation policy if other governments will agree, would greatly supplement the usual legislative method of tariff readjustment."

That these ideas should be applied realistically was the burden of a statement Mr. Hull issued after his appointment as Secretary of State had been announced. Outlining his views on February 24, in his first pronouncement made in the light of his approaching service in the Cabinet, he said:

"There should be sane and realistic international co-operation, keeping in mind our traditions and our Constitution, to aid in preserving the peace of the world. This policy is vital. This nation, henceforth, must play its full part in effecting the normal restoration of national economic relationships and in world commercial rehabilitation, from which alone business recovery in satisfactory measure can be hoped for. . . . The policy of international readjustment assumes that all fundamental domestic remedies for trade improvement also will be pursued."

While Mr. Hull brings to his office the mind of a student, he contributes also the experience of a politician. His friends say that the representatives of foreign governments will find him a considerate, painstaking negotiator, with a breadth of view that can comprehend both sides of a question.

Tall and lithe, a true son of Tennessee, with intellectual features set in Grecian mold, Mr. Hull has reserve and natural dignity along with that friendliness which makes him one of the most approachable of men. Almost austere, his appearance is softened by kindly eyes. His speech is deliberate and his style somewhat literary and oratorical. But he always has a clear idea of what he is saying. His dealings are straightforward and direct. He is considerate, frank and sincere.

Mr. Hull lives quietly. He does not care for formal social functions and, since he is not wealthy, they will probably be few, so far as he is concerned, during his term as Secretary of State. Also he cares little for sports, and it is not likely that he will be seen on the golf links or along the bridle paths in Rock Creek Park, where many of his predecessors have gone for relief from pressing affairs.

LOOKING AHEAD

I go into these details regarding Secretary Hull because there never was a time in the history of the United States when the actions of the State Department have such a direct bearing upon the industrial, financial and labor interests of the country. The Department of State has always held an important position; but its work heretofore has been almost exclusively confined to negotiations of a super-political nature. Questions relating to the protective tariff and other allied problems, in which big business has been so greatly interested, has been a matter for only Congressional action. Hence, these business interests have beset their Senators and Representatives with appeals for and against tariff legislation. Today, however, the situation is entirely different. Business interests are flocking to the State Department, which is now negotiating reciprocity treaties to provide lower tariffs, in exchange for concessions on war debt obligations.

The futures of most industries and many communities are largely in the hands of Secretary Hull at the present time. He, with the assistance of his friend, Judge Moore, is engaged in plans for lowering our tariffs, which action may make or break certain industries and communities. It is, therefore, important for business and financial interests to understand thoroughly Secretary Hull's inheritance, environment, training, prejudices and beliefs. He is in an important position with tremendous power to wreck or make American business. He is honest, studious, painstaking, patient and unselfish. However, he is absolutely convinced in his own mind that the protective tariff is a scheme of the Devil's. There is, however, one satisfaction, namely that he is just as much opposed to having foreign countries enact tariffs against American goods as to have the United States enact tariffs against foreign goods. He has never had practical experience as a diplomat, but has read every decision handed down by the World Court and "can recite by heart" every trade barrier the world over. Like Coolidge, he quietly listens to all you say, but has little to say in return. It is said that when you ask Secretary Hull the time of day, instead of telling you, he silently exhibits the face of his watch to you. This is the man with whom business men will have to cope.

As to Secretary Hull's world views, I can simply quote his own statement which follows:

"The mad pursuit of economic nationalism or aloofness—every nation striving to live unto itself—has proven utterly empty and disastrous. The practice of the half-insane policy of economic isolation during the past ten years by America and the world is the largest single underlying cause of the present world panic. . . . Economic disarmament and military disarmament are patently the two most vital and outstanding factors in business recovery.

"The absurd attempt of every nation to live unto itself and aloof from others by erection of trade barriers has resulted in a breakdown of international confidence, credit, finance, exchange and trade and is gradually pushing the world into bankruptcy. No human imagination can describe the utterly chaotic and dislocating effects of this veritable network of restrictions of every kind for obstruction, discrimination and impediment to the natural movement of capital, goods and services back and forth between nations. The most hopeless derangement and disorganization of our international financial, credit, exchange and trade situation has inevitably resulted. How can any person not blinded by provincialism or selfishness fail to recognize the indispensable necessity for practical international cooperation to clarify and liberalize these extreme complications before we can hope for that degree of balanced prosperity here at home that the welfare of the American public requires?"

Secretary Hull stated on war debts: "However important they may be, they are not a major cause of the panic nor are they a major remedy. . . . Each important country before seeking separate and preferential consideration of their claims for further [debt] reduction, should first indicate their attitude toward the more fundamental program of tariff cuts."

To assist Secretary Hull in running the State Department two names are prominent[1]—William Phillips and, until recently, Raymond Moley, to whom I have already referred. Mr. Phillips is a long-time career diplomat. As envoy he has represented the United States in the Netherlands, Belgium and Canada, served two years (1922-24) as Undersecretary of State. He is a protocol (procedure) expert. Judge Moore—a long-time friend of Secretary Hull, has taken Professor Moley's place. Robert Walton Moore, 74-year-old Virginia bachelor, is an old-time Democrat. "Judge" Moore, whose honorary title is due to his looks, sat in the House for twelve years (1919-31) as Representative of the Virginia district just across the Potomac from Washington. He served on the Foreign Affairs Committee. He is fond of orating on historical subjects. One of his first acts as Assistant Secretary was to ac-

[1] Those desiring further details as to the State Department should secure from the Government Printing Office or from the Superintendent of Documents the latest *Register of the State Department*, a book of 386 pages selling at $1.25 per copy.

cept an invitation from the Alexandria (Va.) Kiwanis Club to speak on "The Constitution as an Inspiration for Better Citizenship." Secretary Hull will have a fellow Tennessean to work with in the person of Norman Hezekiah Davis, President Hoover's Man-About-Europe, chairman of the United States delegation to the Disarmament Conference. Finally in November, 1933, Francis Bowes Sayre, President Wilson's son-in-law, was appointed Assistant Secretary of State. Mr. Sayre was once assistant to the president of Williams College from which he graduated in 1909. In 1917 he went to Harvard College to teach in the Law School with Professor Felix Frankfurter. He has also served the State of Massachusetts by being its Commissioner of Correction.

"Moley's Friend" lives at Carleton Hotel, Washington, D. C.

Chapter VII

"YOUNG HENRY"

ONE member of President Roosevelt's Cabinet who perhaps as much as any other has been called a revolutionist is the young Secretary of Agriculture. In fact, in the early weeks after he took office he was watched with apprehension and even fear by conservatives in all parts of the country. There was no social experiment, however revolutionary, which it was felt he would not be capable of trying should he take it into his head to do so. Like all such bogies, this picture of Secretary Henry Agard Wallace was a gross distortion of what admittedly has some basis in fact. Secretary Wallace is a revolutionist but one whose idealism is soundly American. His roots are firmly fixed in the tradition of generations of forefathers who have served this nation well and have consequently earned the right to criticize its shortcomings.

WALLACE'S BACKGROUND

Mr. Wallace comes from a dynasty of dirt farmers, men who have cared enough literally about the soil of America to fight for it. In his present office he holds a position which his father, as Secretary of Agriculture under President Harding, held before him. He is a grandson of "Uncle Henry" Wallace, a member of

President Theodore Roosevelt's Country Life Commission and in his day the idol of prairie men throughout the West. With this heritage of blood and environment, one can realize that "Young Henry's" radical tendencies are not those of an impractical theorist nor a parlor Bolshevist. Moreover, he is intensely earnest and honest.

I had not had the privilege of meeting Mr. Wallace until I saw him at his office in Washington a short time after he had assumed the portfolio of Agriculture. What impressed me immediately, and what I carried away as my outstanding memory of our conversation, is his intense sincerity and burning idealism. While one may differ from Mr. Wallace on programs and policies, one has only to see him to be won by his candor and simplicity of manner. Coupled with his passion for social justice is a first-rate scientific make-up. Because he possesses these two qualities and because they are reasonably well balanced, I feel that this country need have no apprehensions over Mr. Wallace and the conduct of his office as Secretary of Agriculture. He has detailed ideas carefully worked out for the solution of the various aspects of the agricultural problem confronting the United States today. Yet he is the first to admit that the entire farm relief program is "as crude as the first automobile of thirty years ago."

He goes even further and admits that some of the things he wants to put into practice are frankly experiments, but this does not in the least weaken his essential position. He believes that the government must of necessity cast aside its ancient policy of laissez faire and "rugged individualism" and take a scientific hand in achieving a balanced social state. He is like the President in his willingness to experiment either with or against his own preconceived ideas: He is a revolutionary experimenter rather than a revolutionist.

"As our economic system works," he said recently, "it seems the greater the surplus of wheat in Nebraska, the longer the bread lines in New York. In a complicated world system of exchange it seems to be necessary to maintain a balance between different groups of producers if we are to avoid suffering. Our surplus of food crops seems to have had as disastrous an effect upon national well-being as crop shortages used to have upon the isolated communities of a simpler age."

FRANKNESS VS. TRADITION

Another quality that has aided in building up this *enfant terrible* is his habit of plain speaking. The average politician weighs his words in the scales not of what he wants to say, but of how they will be heard. He cuts and trims them to fit the pattern of his audience. Recently, when Secretary Wallace was preparing an address on the farm problem, a friend dropped in at the office just as his secretary brought in a draft of the speech. Mr. Wallace tossed the copy across the desk and asked his friend to read it. When the latter had finished, he told Wallace that it was an admirable speech, but suggested that it should be tempered here and there, the language modified for fear it might sound too harsh and vigorous.

"Why can't I say it that way?" shot back Mr. Wallace. "I am tired of this idea of not saying what you mean just because it does not sound polite." Another story is told of Mr. Wallace which bears out the fact that he is not at all afraid of the word "revolutionist" and concerns an address he delivered before some local chapter of the Daughters of the American Revolution. After a vigorous denunciation of some of the evils of American economic conditions today, he concluded his address with the simple but significant statement: "And above everything else remember, ladies, that after all you are daughters of a revolution."

In brief, Mr. Wallace has no use for tradition or conservatism if those words are merely masks to conceal accumulated evils and social maladjustments. At this point, however, let me make it clear that "Young Henry's" social economics and willingness to experiment have not carried him toward any Fascist or Communistic goal. He believes that conservatism can be preserved, but only if we are willing to make certain major changes and above all to see clearly our own shortcomings and stupidities and take immediate steps to cure them. He admittedly is not hopeful that this will be done, because, as he says, the "administration's emergency program is the last ditch in the attempt to preserve capitalism in the United States." Consequently, those who fulminate most sharply against what they think are Mr. Wallace's dangerous doctrines should pause and realize that at any rate he is offering them not in an attempt to destroy but to preserve our American institutions.

In this sense, the American revolutionists of 1776 were engaged in a similar struggle. As Mr. Wallace explained to me more definitely his ideas, I appreciated the unselfish patriotism which actuates him. I felt that he might reply to his detractors and critics by paraphrasing Patrick Henry's famous words, saying: "If this be revolution, make the most of it."

THE FARMER'S FRIEND

Mr. Wallace knows how to be partisan. I have described him as a man with a perspective sufficiently broad to see the whole of our economic problem at one time. This is true, but at the same time Mr. Wallace is first and last a friend of the farmer. He conceives his job at Washington to be that of militant leadership in behalf of our agricultural industry and its workers. In his own words, "This department will make good for the farmer or I will go back home and grow corn."

"Young Henry's" loyalty to farmers has been unwavering, but he was not in office many months before he had an experience common to all men who offer themselves in the public service. He learned that those whose interests he had most at heart could turn on him—or at any rate some could. Generally regarded as the administration's most revolutionary advocate of currency inflation, Secretary Wallace went into the Cabinet insisting on currency reform. After six months of sobering and often somewhat disillusioning experience of hard work as a Cabinet member, he went to Chicago where he delivered an address aimed at the Farm Belt's cries for inflation. It took courage to deliver the sort of speech "Young Henry" made.

In it he reiterated his fundamental attitude toward controlled inflation but admitted that cheap money is no magic cure-all for cheap wheat or other farm products. In the course of this speech he said, "Waving wands will not dissipate real economic problems. . . . Price-pegging may have its uses but resort to price-fixing without control of supply is fraught with danger." Among the voices of disapproval from the farming sections was that of the Farmers' Union of his own state, Iowa.

If there was any evidence needed as to Secretary Wallace's essential integrity both as a public official and as a man, this Chicago address furnished it. In that speech he dispelled at once all suspicion of demagoguery, on the one hand, or lack of personal courage, on the other. Eastern conservatives breathed easier and western radicals realized that here was a leader, not a politician—that in Secretary Wallace were the seeds of statesmanship and not of class prejudice. He has ideals, energy and courage. It is a real inspiration to talk with him.

HIS FATHER'S POLICIES

No account of Secretary Wallace's career can be given unlinked to that of his father, Henry Cantwell Wallace, who came to Washington in March of 1921 and gave three strenuous years of unselfish service in the Cabinet of President Harding as Secretary of Agriculture. He died in 1924, one of the best beloved men in Washington, and was buried from the White House, mourned by his associates regardless of party. The elder Wallace had a high reputation among midwestern farmers as editor of *Wallace's Farmer* (now combined with the *Iowa Homestead*). This mouthpiece of farming sections had been founded by a still earlier Wallace —"Young Henry's" grandfather—and had a powerful influence in the agricultural West.

Consequently President Harding's choice was a popular one when he named the man whose son twelve years later was to carry on the work which the elder Wallace began. Political parties have never meant a great deal to the Wallace family—not at any rate as against their loyalty to their fellow farmers. The reason why "Young Henry" holds office under a Democratic President while his father was a Republican can be traced from the fact that the farm reform policies of Wallace senior were steadily opposed by a certain bloc in the Harding-Coolidge Cabinet headed by the then Secretary of Commerce Hoover.

Secretary Hoover, honestly differing from what he considered the unsound and radical program of the Secretary of Agriculture (which included the McNary-Haugen Bill as a means of dumping farm surpluses abroad), was responsible for the defeat of the Wallace program. "Young Henry," who devoutly and sincerely shared his father's views, came out militantly for Roosevelt in the 1932 campaign and is credited with having been a major factor in swinging Iowa into the Roosevelt column on election day. It, therefore, was a gracious act on President Roosevelt's part to reward Henry with this honor.

"Young Henry" was born on a farm in Adair County, Iowa, October 7, 1888, and is the eldest of six children. After the usual public school preparation in primary, grammar and high-school grades, he matriculated at Iowa State College of Agriculture, one of the land-grant colleges established by an act signed by President Lincoln. He received his degree in 1910 and immediately joined his father and became a fledgling member of the staff of *Wallace's Farmer*. Here for a decade he studied and wrote and thought about farm problems. In 1914 he married Miss Ilo Browne of Indianola, Iowa, and settled down to the life of a practical agriculturist. The Wallaces have three splendid children—Henry B. Wallace, age 17; Robert B., age 14; and Jean B., age 12 years.

These ten years of association with his father in the editorial rooms of the magazine was a fruitful training period for the young man. Then early in 1921 his father went to Washington as Secretary of Agriculture and "Young Henry" joined the editorial staff of *Wallace's Farmer*. He continued to hammer home to his thousands of farmer-readers the same policies which his father was enunciating in Washington in behalf of farm relief. But always he approached these problems as a scientist and not as a crusader.

As an economist and statistician myself, I can particularly appreciate one talent which he early developed and that was the ability to forecast economic trends. Before turning to broad economic events, however, he had applied himself scientifically to research in the breeding of corn. Soon after getting through college he began to experiment—and it is interesting to note that he is still experimenting in this subject twenty years later—with high-production corn. He familiarized himself with all the current theories and finally succeeded in producing a seed corn with its strains definitely fixed and refixed each year. It has proved its worth, yielding four to ten bushels per acre more than the common variety.

Then, with his "Hi-bred" corn a recognized success, he turned to the field of economics. In those days he developed a statistical method to a high degree of utility and employed it in the correlation of weather cycles and crop production, and the monthly charting of the relative returns of hog-feed corn and corn sold as grain. Developing his studies, he found it possible to anticipate many phases of the depression long before it began. As early as January, 1919, in an article on the farming depression in England following the Napoleonic Wars he discussed the collapse of inflated prices and the persistence of high fixed prices which resulted in profound agricultural depression.

He came to the conclusion that the World War had created an almost identical set of economic facts and that the reconstruction period would be a repetition of that following the Napoleonic Wars. Bearing out his forecast, in 1920 came the first agricultural collapse. Another thing Secretary Wallace did as an editor during the closing war years when prices were high: He continually dinned into his readers' ears the earnest and insistent advice that then was the time to pay off debts. This surely was good advice, and if it had been followed the farmers would have no abnormal troubles today.

Furthermore, at this time he was beginning to point to a fact which he has reiterated more and more frequently in connection with his stand on international economic problems during recent years—namely, that the United States had changed from a debtor to a creditor nation and that our foreign trade was in grave danger. It was at this time and for this reason that he came out in behalf of the revolutionary program of removing the tariff so that foreign countries might trade with us. He also urged that we preserve our export market by lending money abroad. This was in order that foreign nations might buy goods. Finally, he trumpeted a blast in behalf of canceling the war debts.

THE PRESENT SECRETARY'S PROGRAM

Now we come down to the present year and to "Young Henry" as Secretary of Agriculture. A welter of words swirled around the Farm Act once it was enacted. It was praised as the most farsighted and heaven-sent piece of remedial legislation ever conceived by the mind of man. It was damned as the most vicious class-ridden measure which ever saddled some people's burdens on other people's backs. But it was part of our National Recovery program and as such it deserved the support of every good citizen. And in my talk with him Secretary Wallace summed up the reasons why he supported this measure. I came away from our conversation convinced that he is honestly attacking the most serious problem confronting the United States to-day and that he is entitled to a fair hearing and a fair trial of his program. What he told me was undramatic in its nature—it was quietly expressed. It had no emotional appeal. It was a simple presentation of what at least to him seems a sanely practical plan. He said this:

"In the solution of the farm problem it is important that we restore farm purchasing power by every means at our command. But it is also important that, in our desire to see prices go up, we do not deceive ourselves concerning the true nature of the market. In the long run inflation will not increase the purchasing power of Europe for our surplus farm products. Reciprocal tariffs will not by themselves be sufficient. Agreements with the processors, no matter how skillfully they may be supervised, will help only a little *if we disregard the fundamental necessity of cutting our acreage to fit the fact that we are now a creditor nation.*"

Now what of this huge Department of Agriculture which this youngest member of the Cabinet has under his direction? What are the duties of the Secretary of Agriculture and what is the scope of activities covered? In some ways this department throws its direct functions over a wider field and into more nooks and corners of the country than any other federal department. Its various bureaus—animal industry, dairy, plant, forest, chemistry and soils, agricultural economics, home economics, just to mention a few—touch directly the lives and welfare of farmers from Maine to California.

The romance of manufacturing—the dramatic growth of such industries as the automobile and aviation, for example—has so great a hold on the American interest that we are likely to overlook the fact that we are still an agricultural nation. What happens to the farmer more directly affects what happens to everyone else than any other single influence in our economic well-being as a people. So let us rivet this fact down where it will not escape in the shifting emphasis of economic values—*ours is an agricultural nation.* In order for the manufacturer to prosper, the farmer must prosper. In order for the East to prosper, the West must prosper.

Because this is so, the responsibilities of the Secretary of Agriculture are basically of the utmost importance. His duties under the Constitution are "to promote agriculture in its broadest sense." And it is in the "broadest sense" that Secretary Wallace is endeavoring to carry out his task. Let me repeat once more what I hope every page of this chapter has emphasized by implication—Secretary Wallace is not a politician, not an officeholder. He is what I would like to term a scientific idealist and already the imprint of his personality upon the affairs of the department reveals this fact. He is trying to make the Department of Agriculture the servant of the farmer and indirectly of every citizen in the nation—a servant which metamorphosed becomes at once a laboratory, a schoolhouse, a friend and an adviser. All these rôles does the department play in behalf of the man who perhaps more than any other individual may be called the "forgotten man," the American worker of the soil.

Secretary Wallace is the youngest man in the Cabinet. He has just crossed his forty-fifth milestone. He is filled with the zeal of service in behalf of a better, a happier nation. He is absolutely sincere. He is utterly fearless. Not a business man, he may be said to suffer from whatever practical experience he lacks in that direction. Perhaps the best characterization of his devotion to his ideals lies in a remark I heard about him the other day:

"What grips me most of all about Henry," this friend said, "is that you know he would cut off his hand for an abstract ideal and cut off yours too, just as readily."

Maybe it's time this country had a few more such men!

"Young Henry" lives at Wardman Park Hotel, Washington, D. C.

CHAPTER VIII

"CAPTAIN DERN"

I F YOUR idea of a proper Secretary of War includes the stentorian voice of the parade-ground drill sergeant and the gold-lace blazonry of the drum-major, then George Dern has revolutionized one idea at least. He is a stalwart, well set-up figure of a man, martial enough in physical stature as becomes a former football captain; but his manners are gentle and kindly. He has none of the arbitrary traits which you mean by "military." Quite the contrary; he is genial, human and affable, with a warmth of sincerity and complete lack of pomposity and swagger.

Stopping off in Nebraska—his old home—on his way from the Governorship of Utah to the Secretaryship of War, Mr. Dern stated with complete frankness that he was unfamiliar with war. He further stated that he hoped uninterrupted peace would make such familiarity unnecessary. When informed that he was being considered for the post of Secretary of War, Governor Dern smilingly disclosed his military experience as playing in a cadet band. On this point, the University of Nebraska *Alumnus* prints as follows:

As the bass grunted "ump" and young George tooted "pah," little did he realize that his first experience with army regulations as a second altoist in the university cadet band would eventually lead to an appointment as Secretary of War in the Roosevelt Cabinet. Not that George Dern, ex '97, would claim any direct connection between the two! The average person would probably be more inclined to attribute the appointment to his achievements as Governor of Utah and to his intimate acquaintance with President Roosevelt while both were governors of their respective states. They do, however, mark the two occasions of his active participation in the military organization.

A SUCCESSFUL BUSINESS MAN

Possibly the most significant characteristic of the present group of Washington revolutionists is their diversification. What they have in common is merely the spirit of the New Deal. Otherwise their differences are radical. George Dern, for illustration, was a successful big business man. I do not affirm this of all the present Cabinet—for such a statement would be most untrue—as the run-of-the-mill revolutionists are indifferent business men! Reliability, punctuality and efficiency; solvency, fact-finding and fact-facing; clocks, calendars and arithmetic—above all, arithmetic; these are words of an unknown tongue to the conventional revolutionist. Not so with George Dern. He built and ran a fine business of his own before tackling the business of a state or the affairs of a nation. He made his money *before* he went into politics!

Before placing any side-lights, let us sketch this career in outline. George Henry Dern was born in Dodge County, Nebraska, September 8, 1872, the son of John and Elizabeth Dern. He was graduated from Fremont (Nebraska) Normal College in 1888 and attended the University of Nebraska in 1893-94. He married Charlotte Brown of Fremont, June 7, 1899; children—Mary Joanna (Mrs. Harry Baxter), John, William Brown, Elizabeth Ida and James George. He has fine robust health and is bringing up his family to be useful citizens.

He began mining in Utah in 1894: treasurer, Mercur Gold Mining & Milling Company, 1894-1900; general manager, Consolidated Mercur Gold Mines Company, 1900-13; various other mining and metallurgical enterprises since 1913; vice president and general manager, Holt-Christensen Process Company (owner Holt-Dern roaster patents); director, Pleasant Grove Canning Company; director, First National Bank of Salt Lake City; director, Mutual Creamery Company; director, First Security Trust Company.

George H. Dern was a member of the Utah State Senate, 1915-23; member State Council of Defense, World War; Governor of Utah two terms, 1925-32 inclusive. He is a member of American Institute of Mining and Metallurgical Engineers and Delta Tau Delta. He is a Mason (K. T., 33°, Shriner). Clubs: Chamber of Commerce, University, Alta, Rotary, Country (Salt Lake City). He is the joint inventor, with Theodore P. Holt, of the Holt-Dern ore roaster.

If revolutionist means to you a man more concerned with public prosperity than with his own financial and political fortunes, then Dern is a revolutionist. This is plainly written in his record as Governor of Utah and in his preceding annals as state senator. One trait he possesses in common with President Roosevelt: Dern has never hesitated to oppose not only foes but friends—men in his own financial and social circles. He compelled the passage of revolutionary legislation: Workmen's Compensation Act, State Income Tax, Corrupt Practices Law, Public Utilities Act, State Mineral Land Leasing Act. Time and again he has thrown his strength into causes which were apparently in conflict with his own personal advancement. The conservative vested interests of Utah have always feared him.

George H. Dern has made rather a specialty of making headway against apparent handicaps. Utah is traditionally a Republican stronghold. Nevertheless, Democratic Dern was elected Governor by a margin of 10,000 votes in the same year that Coolidge carried the state nationally with a 30,000 majority. Four years later Governor Dern was reelected, increasing his majority to 31,000, with Hoover taking the state nationally. Furthermore, Dern is a Congregationalist in Salt Lake City, which is controlled by Mormons! Some record! He was a Democratic governor with a Republican legislature. It is not likely that he finds anything especially disconcerting in being Secretary of War after a record as staunch champion of international agreements to settle world controversies. If he is criticized for pacifism by the big-army crowd, he may find comfort in the reflection that many times before has he been on the receiving end of criticism.

PERSONAL CHARACTERISTICS

Criticism rose to its height when Governor Dern fought for his tax revision program against mighty opposition. He drew the antagonism of powerful interests and set against himself many a business or personal friend. He stood by those whom he regarded primarily as the public. He pushed through the right program, as he saw the right, even though he incurred thereby the resentment of his own industry—mining. The Workmen's Compensation Act was similarly repugnant to the personal associates of Senator Dern, but he strove for this enactment unfalteringly. The soundness of the compensation legislation has now been generally conceded. The tax legislation, tangled in the coils of depression, has not now equal acceptance. It is probable that George Dern would again unhesitatingly go through with these or any other measures in which he believed, quite regardless of the cost in personal popularity. Yes, this man has in him much of the stern stuff of which revolutionists are made.

As already narrated in our summary, George Dern was a Nebraska boy, born on a farm at Hooper (near Fremont), the second son of John and Elizabeth Dern. He may still be described as a Nebraska farmer in the sense that he now owns three farms around Fremont. He was educated in the Fremont High School and the University of Nebraska, where he captained the 1894 football squad. Though familiar with dirt farming, the pay-dirt which had greater appeal to him was in mining. He went to Utah and started business in the Mercur Gold Mining & Milling Company's bookkeeping department. This was a property owned largely by George's father, who had sold his Nebraska farm. The company was on the upward trend through application of new processes of low-grade ore treatment. Then in 1900, numerous mining properties were put together into Consolidated Mercur Gold Mines Company. George Dern rose to assistant general manager, rose again within a year to manager, and remained manager until 1913.

By this time, two characteristics had cropped out. In the first place, it was clear that Dern had a pronounced streak of liberalism. He was genuinely concerned that something be done for the improvement of working and living conditions of his workmen. Especially in those days, a manager of mining properties who took any such attitude as that was an out-and-out revolutionist. It is understood that certain stockholders took him to task—and from some acquaintance with stockholders we can well believe this—charging that he was more interested in miners than in dividends. History does not record Manager Dern's reply, but inferentially we may judge that he gave efficient attention to both personnel and profits. The properties flourished and the family grew wealthy.

Besides this active interest in workmen's welfare, the second outcropping of character was a real interest in business. With some other mining experts, Dern worked out improved processes and equipment for treating ore. The Holt-Dern roaster, for example, was developed to treat low-grade silver ores, and it has been used by silver producers all over the world. Now all this is very revolutionary, indeed. Seldom have revolutionists been competent to produce successful technical equipment, and still more extraordinary, make their achievements a commercial success. Dern is that rarest of species: a welfare worker with a payroll—a tax reformer with a tax bill.

FRIENDSHIP WITH ROOSEVELT

His appointment to the Roosevelt Cabinet may have been due in part to the President's personal friendship, but that can easily be overemphasized. Dern brings to the Cabinet elements of real strength. He is an appointee on merit. It should be weighed that the Roosevelt administration has been embroiled in business as violently and completely as the Wilson administration was finally immersed in war. Secretary Dern is a business man, a seasoned and successful entrepreneur. If there is any one type a depression Cabinet needs it is the business type. I have respect for the gentlemen of the Brain Trust and for revolutionists of all shades in the chromatic scale of reform. To keep the balance, however, and wage a real fight against the stern realities of depression, there is need also for a Brawn Trust.

By "brawn trust" I mean men who have farmed on farms, mined in mines, and know black ink from red ink. I mean men who have signed payroll checks as well as cashed them; who have kept costs and looked balance sheets and income statements in the face. Some men of this type, business men of proved capacity, must be on hand if the New Deal is ever going to get anywhere in dealing with this generation. It is a business depression and the business viewpoint is needed to cope with current conditions. Feeling this strongly as one of the necessities of the situation, I contend that if George Dern does not do another thing, he can earn his place in the sun just by forecasting from hard experience the things that will work and the things that will not work.

Again, Secretary Dern contributes to Cabinet balance in a geographic way. He knows the Middle West by birth and the Mountain States by adoption. We all have our sectional loyalties, but in our hearts we know that the interests of the nation are best served not by an All-Eastern team or an All-Western team but by an All-American team. Secretary Dern has dug in the soil of Nebraska, mined in the Rockies, fought out the Colorado River Pact which distributed that river's flow among five states in its drainage basin. Washington needs a few revolutionists like that if we want a truly American revolution.

Temperamentally, the Secretary of War has assets of cordiality and affability, useful in these days of stress, as the country has learned from the President's own gift of easing the strain with a human smile of friendliness. The Secretary is an ardent reactionist and standpatter as a family man of the old school, and the Dern home life is delightfully nonrevolutionary. Mrs. Dern emulates her husband in lifelong interest in questions of economics, sociology, politics—in gracious hospitality to people, to ideas.

Heretofore the Secretary's favorite recreations have been outdoor sports. He has found relaxation in roaming among the scenic beauties and grandeurs of the West. Presumably his hours for recreation have been curtailed by the responsibilities of an establishment so vast and involved that no mere summary can touch upon even the chief essentials. We can undertake herein only the briefest résumé of the activities of the vast War Department.

HOW THE DEPARTMENT BUYS

The War Department is one of the biggest of the government buyers.[1] It has been filling the living requirements of a personnel equivalent to a city of about 150,000 population. In addition it must provide the great array of technical materials essential to a military establishment. There has more recently been added the requirements of the Civilian Conservation Corps, with a personnel of possibly 300,000. The quartermaster's annual expenditures, heretofore averaging about $120,000,000, will doubtless rise considerably above that figure.

The procurement policies of the War Department differ somewhat from those of the Navy, where purchasing is largely centralized. Nevertheless, the Assistant Secretary of War has supervision over both the purchase of materials and manufacture in the government's own arsenals and plants. Significant from a business viewpoint, the Assistant Secretary is the official charged with the war-time mobilization of materials and industrial organizations.

The business organization of the department heads up in the Quartermaster Corps. Under the Quartermaster-General this branch buys the greater part, at least 60 per cent, of military requirements. Special technical items are procured by the branch which will

[1] See *Methods and Procedure in Federal Purchasing*, by Monteith and Burack.

make exclusive use of such material. Standard supplies and supplies common to two or more branches are procured by the Quartermaster's Corps. This category covers about 10,000 different items.

In procurement plans the United States is districted into four areas. Each area has a central purchasing bureau to procure local requirements. These regional departments are located: Brooklyn, Chicago, San Antonio and San Francisco. Business men desiring to sell nationally to the Quartermaster's Corps, will usually deal separately with several procurement agencies, all handling the respective bids and awards independently. In assigning purchases to be made by local agencies, the policy of the Quartermaster's Corps is governed by considerations such as the following: primary source, storage costs, transportation costs to destination, breaking bulk vs. decentralized procurement.

By act of August 7, 1789, the War Department was created to provide for national defense. Until 1798, when a separate Department of the Navy was established, the War Department had charge also of naval affairs. Until the creation of the Department of the Interior in 1849, the War Department was charged with the supervision of public lands, military pensions and Indian affairs. Historically there is a group relationship among these three divisions. The parent department was War, a part of whose activities was later transferred to Navy and Interior.

In 1920 under the National Defense Act, the War Department was fundamentally reorganized as to the broad policy of national defense. Under this act, the Army of the United States consists of three branches:

(1) the regular army; (2) the National Guard of each state; (3) the Organized Reserves (Reserve Officers Corps and Enlisted Reserve Corps). Resources are further strengthened through military training in civilian camps and in schools and colleges. The primary work of the War Department is concerned with the army as above defined. Under the supervision of the department, however, are all matters relating to fortification and defense of United States borders, coasts and overseas possessions.

The department's nonmilitary duties are numerous. It supervises civil government in insular possessions. It improves harbors and rivers for navigation and commerce. It engages in projects for the control of floods and prevention of obstructions in the Mississippi and other navigable rivers. It sets up harbor lines, bridges navigable rivers, operates carriers on inland, canal and coastwise waterways, and builds terminal facilities. In both its military and nonmilitary functions, the department conducts technical and scientific research. It is charged with supervision of the United States Military Academy at West Point. It cooperates in the New Deal's Civilian Conservation Corps.

HOW ORDERS ARE EXECUTED

The program of the army is originated, perfected and executed by the General Staff Corps. The chief of this corps is adviser to the Secretary of War in all affairs concerning the military establishment. Army officers head the component bureaus of the department and engage in their military duties. Several of the bureaus are occupied with nonmilitary functions. In the aggregate, the work of the War Department represents an enterprise of remarkable magnitude and diversity, measured even by purely industrial standards. It is big business.

It has been said that Dern himself might have been better pleased had he been appointed Secretary of the Interior rather than Secretary of War. Moreover, it is probable that his appointment was more acceptable to the pacifist-minded than to the militarist-minded groups. Why, then, was he placed in the War Department? How is the War Department viewed in the light of the New Deal? Though I have no shadow of sanction to presume to voice the views of the administration on this point, certain inferences can be drawn from known administrative tendencies and trends.

Here is my analysis of current conditions in the light of recent world history. The administration need fear only one thing: Fascism! The President knows that he can keep control of his own Washington revolutionists and their comrades throughout the country. He is the crowned king of the liberals and has nothing to fear from these loyal subjects. The radicals of this country will neither revolt from Roosevelt nor ruin his reign by running amuck. His real danger is an uprising of oppressed conservatives. That is the cloud in his sky, and already the cloud has grown bigger than a man's hand. If the conservatives are attacked too ruthlessly and persecuted too relentlessly, they will counter-attack.

What will be the form of that counter-attack? It will be a fascist demonstration by the conservatives under their own chosen leader. Contrary to some mistaken public ideas, fascism is not a move toward liberalism. Rather it is the last resort of despairing conservatives. To grasp the full import of the Washington situation, you must understand this point clearly. It is the key to much that otherwise will seem a paradox and an enigma. You must remember that fascism comes only as a reaction from extreme radicalism.

The way to make a socialist grow pale is to talk to him about fascism. The way to make the face of any liberal crease with lines of worry is to threaten his progressive program with a "back-fire" of fascist dictatorship. It is really a movement toward "the right" and away from the red end of the social spectrum. The President knows this. He realizes that if Wall Street and the conservatives are driven into utter desperation, there can be but one reaction. They will try to set up fascism under a dictator of their own choosing. Who such a dictator might be, whether Al Smith or some other popular hero or some unknown warrior, cannot be foreseen at this stage.

Such a move would inevitably result in a titanic contest. It would precipitate a crucial question: *Where does the army stand?* Would the army go with Roosevelt and the liberals? Or would it go with the conservatives? In the Italy of Mussolini and in the Germany of Hitler, and in every other kindred movement, the real issue turned on the question of who could control the army. In appointing his Secretary of War, it appears from outside analysis that Roosevelt did not dare to trust anyone who had been with the army. He did not want anyone obsessed with army traditions, connections, clannishness. He wanted someone who (1) would be loyal to him, (2) who had social vision, (3) who had executive ability.

In short, he wanted a Secretary of War who would save the army for the government and not let the army go to the support of Wall Street and the conservatives against Roosevelt. If the conservatives as a desperate effort should attempt to set up their own dictator to administer fascism, what about that army camp across the Potomac at Alexandria? That was the rub! The whole decision might rest on getting the support of the army; for the navy in this particular crisis might play only second fiddle. From that viewpoint, therefore, Secretary Dern, with the aid of Secretary Swanson, can be pictured as the President's insurance policy against being overthrown by a fascist uprising under a dictator chosen by the conservatives to lead them out of the last ditch.

That, in a hurried sketch, is the development which must suggest itself to anyone who will acquaint himself with contemporary trends. I earnestly hope there need not eventuate a contest such as I have outlined, though its potentialities are clearly revealed. If, however, such a show-down develops, Secretary Dern— we must admit—would not be a "bad bet." A perusal of his career shows that when fighting is required to accomplish a desired result he is a fighter of no mean abilities. He fights without sapping his energies by rancor or bitterness, and thereby fights the more effectively. As a leader of men, he is what is admiringly called "a natural."

Moreover, if the veil of the future holds any more

world wars in which the United States would be involved, we can be sure of one thing. They will be increasingly fought in the dual field of military strategy and industrial efficiency. Scientific and technical progress is revolutionizing warfare and carrying the machine age into battle. The armies of the future will be reckoned not alone in manpower, but in "horsepower," for they will be kept in action by the supporting armies of industry.

In other words, the revolutionizing of warfare may revolutionize the rôle of Secretary of War. He will be the commander of two sectors: combat and supply. The Blue Eagle as a bird of battle is well pictured as a two-fisted fighter. We see the Blue Eagle clutching in one talon the lightning bolts of military force, but in the other talon he holds the gear-wheel of industrial output. Not a bad emblem for our Secretary of War to hang above his desk if I have correctly drawn the character of this man and correctly analyzed the revolutionary conditions into which he has been thrust.

"Captain Dern" lives at 3301 Rittenhouse Street, Washington, D. C.

Chapter IX

"BIG-NAVY CLAUDE"

A̲T FIRST glance, Secretary Claude A. Swanson seems the complete opposite of a revolutionist. He shows no trace of the old-style swashbuckler, storming the vested interests and blasting the status quo; nor does he in the least resemble the bloodless revolutionist of the modern Ph.D. school. His type is neither the trust-buster nor the brain truster, but a gentleman of Virginia pure Democrat, without apparent tinge of the progressive, the bolter, the maverick or the coalitionist. From the gallery, he would be picked as the arch-symbol, not of revolution but of regularity.

The essence of revolution, however, is to revolve. It is not the fireworks which make the revolution, but the practical turn of the wheel. In this respect, Secretary Swanson contributes to the composite psycho-photo of the Cabinet; and he contributes the countenance of a true revolutionist. Ever since the World War, the fifteen-year reactive swing of the pendulum of public thought has been toward limitation of navies. The present Secretary's entire half-century of public life places him squarely on the side, not of militarism or imperialism, but of adequacy of naval strength. In that new direction he now pushes with ardor; and no long-haired howler or ruthless college professor could press forward with more indomitable zeal and fire.

Provided one has the revolutionist's single-mindedness and indestructibility, a bearing of dignified courtliness is an asset. Claude Swanson rounds out the Roosevelt Cabinet. He adds to its elements of maturity and poise a real balance and proportions. He also brings to the Cabinet a splendid background of experience, a panorama of personal contacts with men and events, reaching over nearly fifty years. With his aid, the Cabinet is not dependent alone upon files, records and other second-hand chronicles, but has at hand the direct information and wisdom of a man who has helped to *make* history as well as to study it. Moreover, this career has been steadily in public service of widening radius: four years Governor of Virginia, twelve years Representative, twenty-two years Senator—and now member of the "economic war" Cabinet.

Secretary Swanson's Virginia is a maritime state. It is the home of Hampton Roads, a big harbor for vessels of war; the Norfolk navy yard; the Newport News Dry Dock and Shipbuilding Company, where numerous warships have been built. This man from the seaboard state of Virginia has long been a naval specialist and enthusiast. During the latter stages of the World War, he was chairman of the Naval Affairs Committee of the Senate. In that capacity he met the Assistant Secretary of the Navy, Franklin D. Roosevelt. Thus began a friendship which has culminated in the reunion of two men who have given the navy their personal devotion. We have a Secretary whose mastery of our naval affairs in their international relationships is unmatched. Behind him is the support of a Chief Executive who has served personally in the department of which he now becomes ex-officio the Commander-in-Chief.

WHAT OTHERS SAY

As a side-light on the character of this lifelong naval specialist here is an illuminating little anecdote. It shows that a revolutionist can fight for a cause effectively without rattling either the saber of the militarist or the statistics of the professor. The story is told by a famous Republican, George Wharton Pepper, formerly member of the United States Senate from Pennsylvania:[1]

"The Navy and the Army have their supporters and their detractors on both sides of the aisle. One of those to whom the Navy owes most is Senator Swanson, of Virginia, a consistent advocate of reasonable naval preparedness." Mr. Pepper then refers to the struggles of the Senate Committee on Naval Affairs, a committee on which Senator Swanson was the ranking Democrat and Senator Pepper the ranking Republican. President Coolidge and the House, Mr. Pepper points out, were opposed to beginning work on certain 10,000-ton cruisers, the building of which had previously been authorized. He relates:

"We had the task of maintaining our position against both the President and the House, but the soundness of the Senate view was finally recognized and the appropriation was made. Some of the public comment on my part in this work convinced me that it is often

[1] From *In the Senate*, by George Wharton Pepper, page 87. University of Pennsylvania Press, 1930.

necessary to be charged with bloodthirstiness and a militaristic spirit to secure even the minimum requisites of national defense."

That quotation gives one viewpoint on Secretary Swanson as stated by a resident of the Atlantic region. Here is an expression from the Pacific Coast, in an editorial of the Los Angeles *Times*:[1]

Plans of Secretary of the Navy Swanson to gain the treaty ratio for the United States Navy, either by building up to the Treaty of London limits or by inducing other nations to reduce their strength, is apt to be generally approved. The plans involve no inconsistency with the position of the United States at any time in the past. The Naval Holiday was a guarantee of this nation's good faith in seeking general disarmament, but the slowness of other nations to follow suit constitutes a new fact in the situation.

This new fact seems to require a change in policy. If it is true, as naval experts assert, that the Navy will be 135 vessels short by 1936 of the strength permitted by the London Treaty, some method of equalization becomes highly desirable. Which method is to be adopted, as Secretary Swanson remarks, is a problem for the State Department.

Such action on our part, of course, constitutes no threat to any other nation and cannot be construed as a preparation for war. It is a simple defensive measure. The United States Navy is the first line of defense of the United States, a nation with one of the longest coast lines in the world with a necessity for keeping open its ports. A Navy adequate to the defense of that coast line and of our commerce, in proper proportion to the other fleets of the world, is necessary in a world which cannot yet rely upon treaties to maintain the peace.

Whether parity with the London ratios can be reached by

[1] March, 1932.

the reduction method is a question to which positive answer cannot be given but it seems improbable that efforts in this direction will be successful. It would be the sensible and logical method, particularly in view of the dislocation of the world's economic system which makes naval expenditure burdensome upon everyone. The world, however, does not run on logical lines. Costly as the Navy is, it is relatively cheap insurance, and this country cannot afford to let its insurance lapse.

swanson's background

In one respect, the Secretary can claim spiritual kinship with traditional revolutionists: In his impressionable youth he saw and felt around him the miseries of human sufferings and economic maladjustments. He was born March 31, 1862, on a farm near Swansonville, Pittsylvania County, Virginia. Therefore, his boyhood was cast in a place and time torn by all the post-war reactions of depression and deflation. He takes up our current problems with the poise and philosophy of one who has seen the country rise from a desolation scarcely less profound than this chaos of the 'sixties. By teaching school when sixteen years old he earned enough to put himself through one session at Virginia Polytechnic Institute. Then by working as a clerk in a Danville store he saved the money for three years of college at Randolph-Macon. He there got his A. B. degree at about the same age as those who do not have to work their own way.

A year later, Claude Swanson obtained his law degree at the University of Virginia. The next seven years were spent in the practice of his profession at

Chatham, Virginia, which is still his home town. Chatham is in Pittsylvania County, in the Fifth Congressional District, about fifty-five miles south of Lynchburg. Chatham has a population of about 1,100, with no foreign-born. It is a 100 per cent English-reading, residential town in an agricultural community. Local activities: tobacco warehouse, cedar-chest and cigar factories; Chatham Hall School for Girls; Hargrave Military Academy.

The political career of the Secretary can be summarized as follows: nominated and elected or reelected to the following Congresses: Fifty-third, Fifty-fourth, Fifty-fifth, Fifty-sixth, Fifty-seventh, Fifty-eighth, Fifty-ninth. Candidate in the Democratic primary for Governor of the state of Virginia. Nominated, and elected in November, 1905.

After Mr. Swanson was elected Governor of Virginia he resigned his seat in Congress and was inaugurated February 1, 1906. He served until February 1, 1910. After a four-year term as Governor of Virginia, retirement is the rule. However, on August 1, 1910, Governor William Hodges Mann, his successor, appointed him to fill the vacancy in the United States Senate occasioned by the death of Senator John Warwick Daniel, for the remainder of Daniel's unexpired term ending March 3, 1911. He was reappointed by Governor Mann from March 4, 1911, until the meeting of the General Assembly of Virginia, which elected him to fill the unexpired term beginning March 4, 1911, and ending March 3, 1917.

Swanson was nominated by the Democratic party as its candidate for the United States Senate and elected without opposition at the election held November 7, 1916. He was reelected without opposition for the term beginning March 4, 1917, and ending March 3, 1923; reelected again for the term beginning March 4, 1923, and ending March 3, 1929; reelected again without opposition for the term beginning March 4, 1929, and ending March 3, 1935.

At the time of his appointment to the Cabinet, Senator Swanson was ranking Democrat of the Senate Committee on Foreign Relations and the Committee on Naval Affairs. For a score of years he has been identified with naval legislation. He was a delegate to the London Naval Conference. He has been a lifelong student of international conditions, and has visited Europe many times, taking part in the meetings of the Interparliamentary Union. In connection with his dominant interest in naval affairs, his chief diversion has been reading and study on world problems.

QUITE A POLITICIAN

President Roosevelt's success in securing the prompt passage of his many emergency measures shows that revolutionists, no less than reactionaries, can aid their progress by political experience. The enactment of the legislation for the gigantic recovery program is a fine illustration of how political talents can be used in an emergency. Secretary Swanson adds to the resources of the administration with respect to political acumen and powers. By both his experience and his native gifts, the Secretary of the Navy is a genius in analyzing the politics of a situation. Among the famous lines at-

tributed to him, are the following barbed shafts of
ironic wit:

"I detest political cowardice. It takes a lot of courage
to sit on the fence, and to get shot at from both sides!"

"Stay on the fence as long as you can, then drop
down on one side, run fast, get to the head of the pro-
cession, and eventually you will be credited with having led all along!"

"When in doubt, do right!"

My delving into the career of Secretary Swanson has
given me respect for his life of public service even
though he is laughed at by some. In order, however,
that this review of the Secretary's biography may not
sound too much like an uncritical eulogy, I introduce at
this point a note of relief by quoting from a *timely*
magazine. Its smiling copy-writers tapped out the following characteristic blast of iconoclasm:

Claude Augustus Swanson, 70, got into the Cabinet only
when his Senate Colleague from Virginia turned down the
Treasury. Behind his appointment lay the following political
situation: Senator Swanson is up for reelection next year;
Harry Flood Byrd was getting ready to beat him for re-
nomination; by side-stepping into the Cabinet, Senator Swanson makes way for Harry Byrd to enter the Senate immediately by appointment, neatly saves his own old face.
  Clerking in a grocery store gave Claude Swanson the money
to go to Randolph-Macon. There his close friend was James
Cannon, Jr., now the political religionist. He was long (1893-

1905) a member of the House. The Jamestown Exposition
was the biggest event of his governorship (1906-1910).
Twenty-three years in the Senate made him No. 1 Democrat
on the Naval Affairs Committee. A Big-Navy man, he was
sent as a delegate to last year's disarmament conference at
Geneva, made his big speech in praise of battleships. In the
Senate he wears frock coats and high wing collars, declaims
his speeches, mixes his metaphors and keeps both ears to the
Virginia ground simultaneously. Admirals expect him to give
them a free hand in running the Navy.

Running the navy should be a real assignment. Well
may any Secretary leave most of the technical administration to his admirals. In equipment and supplies,
the navy commonly uses over 50,000 different items.
Its living requirements alone correspond to those of a
city of about 100,000 population; and in addition there
is the vast volume of technical and professional equipment—ships, armament and ammunition. The Navy
Department is one of the largest of the procurement
agencies of the government. It maintains ten or more
plants for shipbuilding, repair or manufacturing.

HOW THE NAVY BUYS

Within the naval establishment, five procurement
agencies are set up under the direction of the Secretary of the Navy, viz: Solicitor for Navy Department:
buys or charters vessels; draws contracts for equipment involving installation. Bureau of Yards and
Docks: controls all matters that concern the navy's
public works. Bureau of Ordnance: buys arms, ammunition, gun forgings. Marine Corps: buys its own

requirements except for public works. Bureau of Supplies and Accounts: with above exceptions, has charge of procurement of all supplies and equipment for the naval establishment.

Many business men who seek a market for their products in the navy in a national way may find the demand for supplies concentrated in the Bureau of Supplies and Accounts, where annual purchases average about $80,000,000. Local requirements are filled through field agencies, calling for about $40,000,000 additional —or total bureau purchases of about $120,000,000 annually. The Bureau of Supplies and Accounts is under direction of the Paymaster-General of the Navy.

The Department of the Navy was established April 30, 1798. Prior to that time naval affairs had been under the supervision of the War Department, which was established in 1789. Today the Secretary of the Navy directs an establishment of immense scope. His official duties include those assigned to him by the President who is Commander-in-Chief of the navy.

The Department of the Navy carries on many activities of a technical and scientific character. The Naval Observatory derives official time and keeps astronomical records. The Hydrographic Office serves the needs of navigation by sea and air. The Naval Research Laboratory promotes the development of aviation and radio communication. The Department of the Navy patrols North Atlantic steamship lanes on watch for icebergs and other perils to navigation. It has conducted explorations and expeditions, in the annals of which appear names of such scientific fame as Louis Agassiz, Asa Gray and John Muir.

In the Department of the Navy are: the Marine Corps, "the soldiers of the sea"; the Compensation Board, dealing with costs of vessels built at private shipyards; the Aeronautical Board and the Joint Board, representing the Navy and War Departments in common problems and policies; and many important bureaus. The Department of the Navy receives the reports of the Governor of the Virgin Islands, and coaling stations of American Samoa and Guam.

In briefest bird's-eye view, those are some of the chief activities of the department. The bare summary of official duties covers page upon page; and a mere reading thereof will give one an overwhelming sense of the magnitude and complexity of the operations assigned to the Secretary of the Navy. The navy offers problems of extreme professional difficulty, often complicated by international considerations of the utmost gravity. All that Secretary Swanson has learned from years of naval and world affairs, he can use to the full on a score of fronts. It is a job that calls for more than revolution—for information.

NEW NAVIES AND NEW DEALS

What, then, is the revolutionary concept of the Navy Department as envisaged in the peculiar perspective of the New Deal? It is essentially a world perspective. The New Navy is our chief essential in implementing all relationships with other nations. The New Deal is a régime of experiment. Some of these experiments may dictate that the United States should develop policies of internationalism. In that case, if we are led to assume more world authority and responsibility, the importance of the navy's rôle is clearly apparent.

If results of experiment persuade us to take the other fork of the parting of the ways, and we temporarily swing from involvement to isolation as our basic policy, then again the navy is necessary. It will be the chief assurance that our "splendid isolation" shall be surrounded with adequate *insulation*. In other words, a good navy as the sword of the seas is truly a two-edged sword, indispensable alike whether our policy shall prove to be increasing participation in world problems or further withdrawal.

The foregoing viewpoint is not inconsistent with the desire for world peace, which surely is an objective of the New Deal. The President has reiterated his ideals of international neighborliness. What, then, do good neighbors want with big navies? One answer is that the navy of the United States is not a pace-maker in any international race whether of armament or of disarmament. A renowned analyst of world conditions[1] has stated his views that by cutting down the naval program the United States would have no effect whatsoever in enticing other nations to reduce. Neither would enlargement of our program, he says, spur other nations into greater naval building. Other nations are watching solely one another, runs this argument. The United States is strictly on the side lines and not in the game as either a menace or an exemplar.

Moreover, the Big Navy program which revolutionist Swanson has so much at heart is thus far still on paper. As such, it would serve to improve the "trading

[1] See *Can America Stay at Home?* by Frank H. Simonds.

position" of the United States in international discussions and could be revised either upward or downward. If carried into execution, it will become an important item in the program of public works, providing employment, stirring business through purchase of materials. At least this is what I am told and I pass it on without comment.

The functions of a Big Navy program in the far-flung activities of the New Deal is summarized by Secretary Swanson as follows: It is a potential source of employment and stimulus to business. It gives the United States an added supply of concessions for trading uses in international dealings. It gives other nations no real incitement to armament. It would enable us to make more effective either isolation or involvement—whichever may be our final choice.

In choosing a Secretary of the Navy, then, it would appear that the President would seek primarily a man of unbounded enthusiasm for the navy *per se*, acquainted with its technical requirements, conversant with its world relation. Preferably the ideal Secretary of the Navy under the New Deal would not be a fire-eater or saber-rattler, but a man sufficiently schooled in international relationships and sufficiently aloof from militarism, imperialism and jingoism to treat world neighbors respectfully without loss of self-respect. Finally, the requisite type of man for the new job would not be an unknown explosive but a well-proved, seasoned and tempered veteran, a responsible revolutionist.

So far as those specifications have been correctly inferred, Secretary of the Navy Claude A. Swanson measures up acceptably to the qualifications required. Of his fidelity, devotion and singlemindedness to the navy as he sees it there can be no question. Of the breadth of his experience and studies there can be no criticism. It might perhaps be a fair inquiry whether in the calamitous event that the navy should be called into violent action, the rôle of Secretary would call for a man of more might. Then an executive rather than a politician would be needed.

It must be remembered, however, that above the Secretary there stands as Commander-in-Chief of the navy the President himself. It happens that the President himself is personally versed in this arm of the service. With such backing we need have no apprehension that, come what might, the navy would have anything but full understanding, complete sympathy and supreme power. So far as revolution affects the navy, under the present secretaryship things are revolving satisfactorily.

"Big-Navy Claude" lives at 2136 R Street, N.W., Washington, D. C.

Chapter X

"THE CHIEF EXECUTIONER"

EVERY successful organization needs some one to do the disagreeable jobs. An orchestra would be of no use if it were made up of all first violin players. Therefore, although Dan Roper cannot play a first violin, he is a necessary part of the New Deal orchestra. He is the executioner of the administration. When the President or some member of the Brain Trust has a disagreeable thing to do, they send for Dan Roper. Moreover, Dan does it so nicely that the unfortunate victim thanks the administration even after being decapitated. Of course, Mr. Roper does not pretend to know all about the newfangled ideas of the New Deal. Surely he is no revolutionist by nature; but he is a good soldier and obeys orders.

ROPER'S BACKGROUND

Daniel C. Roper, Secretary of Commerce, is an old Democrat war horse, who started in as a member of the South Carolina legislature in 1892-93. At the close of that session he came to Washington and from 1893 through 1896 served as a clerk of the United States Interstate Commerce Committee. He, therefore, early in life was initiated into the technicalities of interstate commerce problems. During his services as clerk to this

committee, extensive hearings were held on bills to
perfect the work of the Interstate Commerce Commission, especially in connection with the "long-haul"
and "short-haul" provisions of the Interstate Commerce
Act. At the close of the administration, Mr. Roper entered private life and was a life insurance broker from
1896 to 1899. It was during this period that he married
and began his home life which has been so happy ever
since.

In 1899 the lure of government service again became
attractive and Mr. Roper accepted a federal appointment as a special agent of the Census Bureau. His
task was to determine the feasibility of measuring cotton production by a count of the cotton bales turned
out at the ginnery. This was an exceedingly difficult
task and required ten years of research: from 1899 to
1909. During these years he also aided the Census
Bureau in perfecting its system of reports on the world
distribution of United States cotton. In connection with
this study, Mr. Roper visited the cotton manufacturing
centers of Europe and America. Later he extended these
studies to other fibers relating to the production and
manufacture of cotton. This extended his research to
cover all the textiles. These ten years of service gained
for Mr. Roper an exceptional knowledge of the Census
Bureau, which is one of the important divisions of the
Department of Commerce.

When the Democrats again came into control in 1910,
Oscar W. Underwood was given the task of revising
the tariff. He appointed Mr. Roper as clerk and statistician of the Ways and Means Committee of the House
of Representatives. In this work Mr. Roper secured

an excellent knowledge of the foundation of American foreign trade. He formed contacts and secured information on imports and exports which especially fits him to supervise the Bureau of Foreign and Domestic Commerce, which is now an important division of the Department of Commerce. Even after retiring as Commissioner of Internal Revenue and entering private life, Mr. Roper kept up his statistical research in the public's interest. In 1926, for instance, he collaborated with Howard Elliott and George Soule in an investigation of reclamation projects for the Department of Interior. Moreover, he has always been a writer for business journals and political science publications.

While with the Ways and Means Committee, Mr. Roper became acquainted with Albert Sidney Burleson, then representing the Austin, Texas, district in Congress. Mr. Burleson had already been acquainted with Mr. Roper's study of cotton production. When Mr. Burleson became Postmaster-General in March, 1914, he appointed Mr. Roper First Assistant Postmaster-General. Mr. Roper handled, constructively and satisfactorily, the appointment of postmasters from March, 1913, to August 1, 1916. This experience with the Post Office Department gave Mr. Roper an extensive acquaintance with administrative matters and further extended his contacts centering at Washington and spreading out over the entire United States. He accomplished this work so satisfactorily that he resigned in 1916 to become, at the request of Colonel E. M. House, director of the Organization Bureau to reelect Woodrow Wilson in the 1916 campaign. It was in this campaign that I became personally acquainted with

Mr. Roper and was impressed with his industry, loyalty and modesty. I was especially interested in a book which Mr. Roper wrote at that time, entitled *The United States Post Office*.

POST OFFICE AND INTERNAL REVENUE EXPERIENCE

This book by Daniel C. Roper is the classic of the United States Post Office and should be read by all who expect to do business therewith. The book gives the history of the Post Office Department, its past record, present condition and potential relation to the new world era. It fills nearly four hundred pages with highly interesting details of the structure, purpose and operation of the Post Office Department. It shows what the Post Office Department means to Americans, how it is operated and what its future may be. Few citizens have any conception of the large and complicated business carried on by merely one of the government departments. Mr. Roper did not confine himself either to history or present conditions, but peered into the future in a most interesting way. In this connection it may be said that he used as a frontispiece for his book a picture of an airplane which he believed would revolutionize mail service. This indicates his vision of air mail which he is now seeing developed by the air mail lines honeycombing the nation.

Mr. Roper is both a good executve and an exceptionally good politician in the best sense of the word. He has a keen, native political mind. He is, however, of an unselfish type so far as his personal interests are concerned. He is not always looking out for Roper, although many believe that he is always looking out for the Democratic party! This is well illustrated in the way that Mr. Roper resigned from the Post Office Department on July 31, 1916, in order to take over the organization work of the campaign for the reelection of Woodrow Wilson. Although distinctly modest, and always personally keeping in the background, he was an important factor in that campaign when Charles Evans Hughes was defeated by Woodrow Wilson. Yet, to show how peculiar Washington is, Mr. Roper had never met Mr. Hughes until after the election. At a Washington function at which the two men were present, in 1917, Mr. Roper was introduced to Charles Evans Hughes, the defeated Republican candidate, as "the man who defeated you."

In view of the reelection of President Wilson, on March 22, 1917, Mr. Roper was appointed by the President as vice chairman of the Federal Tariff Commission, which had just come into existence. The appointment was for a ten-year term at $7,500 annual salary. When, however, the War Revenue Act was enacted in 1917, William G. McAdoo, then Secretary of the Treasury, sent for Mr. Roper and urged him to resign from the Tariff Commission and accept the office of Commissioner of Internal Revenue. This Mr. Roper did in October, 1917, and for nearly four years concentrated on War Revenue Tax Work, during which time he collected and turned into the Treasury $11,500,000,000.

The War Revenue acts, going deep into the nation's pocketbook, had to be interpreted and enforced; and yet there had to be that element of human sympathy and understanding behind the collection that would not in any way mar the effectiveness of this extreme measure of government. Individuals and corporations were called upon to do unheard-of things in the way of making known their innermost secrets to Uncle Sam; great opportunities for favoritism and bias came up continually. Throughout these trying times Mr. Roper sat in his big office with always an open ear for anyone's troubles, but never could anyone get into private conference with him on matters of taxation. The force under his command grew from a few hundred clerks to over five thousand at Washington and nearly ten thousand men out in the field. From an office collecting a few million dollars each year in excises and stamp taxes, the Internal Revenue Bureau became the chief collecting agency of the government touching every phase of income in America, gathering in vast inheritance taxes, in addition to a vast horde of war "nuisance" taxes.

ROPER AND PROHIBITION

In January, 1920, national prohibition became effective and its enforcement was placed under the Treasury Department. Although Mr. Roper was noted for "falling in line and taking orders," he balked at the plan of having the Treasury Department enforce prohibition. He insisted that the enforcement of prohibition should come under the Attorney-General's Department. At the first hearing before the Appropriations Committee of the Senate (January, 1920), Senator Mark Smith, of Arizona, asked this question: "Mr. Roper, how many men will it take to enforce the prohibition law?" The reply was: "Senator, that depends upon how much assistance you and I as citizens are going to contribute toward the enforcement. If we are to rely solely on enforcing officers, we shall not be able to get enough men or money to do the job." Secretary of the Treasury McAdoo (who is now Senator from California) was then both personally and politically dry, and therefore, as a favor to his chief, Mr. Roper fell in line. It is interesting, however, in the light of subsequent developments to record that Mr. Roper was one of the original Democrats from a southern state to say that liquor would be controlled only through educational work and not through prohibition.

On April 1, 1920, Mr. Roper resigned as Commissioner of Internal Revenue and planned to retire from public life. This showed good judgment as on March 4, 1921, the Republican administration came into power. In the fall of 1921, Mr. Roper organized a law firm in Washington specializing in matters before the federal departments. This firm had considerable success in its work before the Revenue Department in connection with tax adjustments. During all this time, however, Mr. Roper had been faithful to the Democratic organization. He was active in the 1920 and 1924 campaigns when Cox and Roosevelt ran against Harding and Coolidge, and when Davis and Bryan ran against Coolidge and Dawes. But when Smith and Robinson ran against Hoover and Curtis he was inactive, due to the action of the Houston Convention. He has been especially allied with the southern McAdoo branch of the party rather than with the northern New York branch. This explains why Roper went to Roosevelt with McAdoo in the campaign of 1932. Without doubt, Senator McAdoo was a factor in having Mr. Roper become a member of President Roosevelt's Cabinet on March 4, 1933. During these latter campaigns, Mr. Roper's specific work has been in connection with the raising of funds for the party and in harmonizing its different elements.

Daniel C. Roper has been useful in many ways other than merely political. He has always been a respected member of the Methodist Church and was active in the General Conference of the Methodist Church which met at Dallas, Texas, in May, 1930. He is a thirty-third degree Mason and a member of the Phi Beta Kappa, and the Sigma Alpha Epsilon. He is a member of the University Club of Washington and the Chevy Chase Club. He was also a member of the Sixth Ecumenical Conference in 1931. Mr. Roper has served as trustee of Duke University and was an important factor during the period of the reconstruction of the university after it received its large grant of funds following the death of Mr. Duke. He has also served as a member of the Board of Trustees of American University and has recently served as the chairman of the Reorganization Committee of the American University. It is, therefore, evident that Mr. Roper has a distinct interest in religious and educational affairs and hence can be appealed to on civic and welfare grounds as well as political.

Daniel C. Roper was born in Marlboro County, South Carolina, April 1, 1867. His father was Wesley Roper and his mother Henrietta V. McLaurin, both being direct descendants of the Jamestown colonists. The family was distinctly a southern family with traditions evidenced by Mr. Roper's middle name which is "Calhoun." He, therefore, was brought up both in a southern social atmosphere as well as in a southern industrial atmosphere, as his father was a cotton planter. This means not only that the Department of Commerce, during the present administration, will have as its head a man with first-hand knowledge of southern conditions, but one who will probably be partial to southern interests. Heretofore the Department of Commerce has been operated largely by northern interests. For a Secretary of Commerce, Presidents have usually turned to large cities in the North. President Wilson selected William C. Redfield of New York City; President Harding selected Herbert Hoover of California; President Coolidge selected his friend Whiting of Holyoke, a large paper manufacturer of Massachusetts; while President Hoover selected first Robert P. Lamont and later Roy D. Chapin of Detroit who was connected with the Hudson Motor Car Company.

Not only was Mr. Roper born and brought up in the South, but his education was distinctly southern. After attending the grade schools in Marlboro County, he entered Wofford College where he spent two years. He then transferred to Trinity College and graduated

with the class of 1888. Trinity College later became
Duke University, at Durham, North Carolina. With
this institution Mr. Roper has constantly been identified, serving in 1928 as President of the Alumni Association. While at Trinity College, young Roper planned
on being a teacher and actually started out by teaching
school. But he broke down in health and returned to
the farm. It was during this period of resting on the
farm that he became interested in local politics and
was put forward as a candidate for the South Carolina House of Representatives in 1891, three years after
his graduation from college.

As stated, he served in the legislature for two years,
after which he went to Washington where he served until 1896 as clerk for the Senate United States Interstate
Commerce Committee. In 1896 Mr. Roper returned to
private life where he remained until 1899. On Christ-
mas Day, 1899, he married Miss Lou McKenzie of
Scotland County, North Carolina, who has surely made
him a good wife. They have had eight children, each
of whom has been given a good education and had the
privilege of choosing an Alma Mater. May, the oldest
daughter, graduated at Randolph-Macon College for
Women at Lynchburg, Virginia; James Hunter attended Trinity for one year and later graduated from
the University of Michigan; Daniel C. Jr. attended
George Washington University at Washington and received his diploma from Bowdoin College, Maine;
Grace graduated at Vassar; John Wesley is a graduate
of the United States Naval Academy; Harry McKenzie
finished at West Point; and Richard Fred was a member of the class of 1929 at Duke.

The Ropers have an open door at their home for all Democrats, especially those from the southern states. True gracious southern hospitality and native charm are found in the Roper home. The parents still believe that children are the only worth-while assets and that a happy family circle is worth more than real estate, stock certificates or bank accounts. It is said that Mr. Roper's home life with his large family of children has been an important factor in training him to get on so well with other people. While he was Assistant Post-master-General he had about three hundred thousand postal employes immediately under him, of which he personally appointed over sixty thousand. Furthermore, it should be said in this connection that Mr. Roper made an honest attempt to remove the Post-Office Department as much as possible from politics and establish efficiency based on civil service standards. He has always been known as a man with a heart, willing to listen patiently to one's troubles with a sympathetic understanding that has enabled him to settle differences.

PERSONAL CHARACTERISTICS

Mr. Roper is not a rich man and perhaps cannot even be classed as well-to-do. His salary never exceeded $7,500 a year and he had, as has been seen, a large family to support in Washington. Such money as he has accumulated was made after he retired on April 1, 1920, as Commissioner of Internal Revenue, when he formed the firm of Roper, Haggerman, Hurrey & Parks, with offices in the Transportation Building,

Washington. Although the firm was supposed to make contact with all Washington departments, it specialized in tax adjustments. While it was necessary for this new firm to deal exclusively with a Republican administration in connection with tax adjustments, yet it was successful and received large fees. The reasons for this were twofold. First, because the law was new and, having been compiled hurriedly, contained inconsistencies and loopholes; and second, because such assessments as were in dispute had been made under the Roper management. Therefore, corporations and individuals came to the Roper firm for help in their adjustments. On the other hand, Mr. Roper has always had a reputation of honesty and fairness so far as is possible in an active political life, and even the Republican administration which came into power in 1921 gave a careful ear to Mr. Roper's requests and explanations.

President Roosevelt cannot be charged with wanting a revolutionist when he selected Mr. Roper as Secretary of Commerce. He may have desired to reward a faithful Democrat, but he also recognized that Mr. Roper has certain characteristics which would be of great value to the President in helping him clean house. Mr. Roper has experience, training and an ability to harmonize opposing interests. In fact, the President would be justified in giving the three following reasons for selecting Daniel Calhoun Roper as Secretary of Commerce: First, he is an executive and an organizer. Second, he has been long in public life, and has had experience in drafting and interpreting economic legislation. Third, he can be depended upon to obey orders. Further—and this is important—he is inspired by the ideal of national service.

In dealing with any member of the President's Cabinet, it is essential to know his personal characteristics as well as his background. Therefore, now for a few more personal words regarding Mr. Roper. He is a man of good character—honest, kindly, tolerant. He is a Christian, being active in the Mount Vernon Place Methodist-Episcopal Church South of Washington, D. C. He has always been a staunch prohibitionist and his home life has been of the best. He is not personally ambitious, as many feel Herbert Hoover was when he was Secretary of Commerce. Mr. Roper cannot be either bribed or frightened so far as his personal advancement is concerned. No criticism can be made of him in this connection, and President Roosevelt can absolutely be sure of a loyal and unselfish worker in the Department of Commerce. For this reason, Secretary Roper's advices at Cabinet meetings are impartial and helpful from any points of view.

Daniel Calhoun Roper, however, is distinctly a party man; next to his God and family, the Democratic party and its traditions have an important part in directing his life and actions. He will give respectful attention to the pleas of a Republican or of a Republican state; but in rendering a decision Secretary Roper cannot help but consider first the welfare of the Democratic party. As the welfare of the Democratic party ultimately is dependent on the welfare of the nation as a whole, to this extent the requests of Republican interests will be given careful consideration, *but only from this point of view*. In approaching Herbert Hoover when he was Secretary of Commerce, it was well to state in a tactful way how the cause presented would benefit Herbert Hoover in his great desire to become President of the United States. No such appeal will be of use in dealing with Secretary Roper. It is, however, only fair to say that Secretary Roper can be influenced by Democrats in whom he has confidence and by arguments as to the effect of any decision on the future of the Democratic party.

AN UNPLEASANT TASK

During Herbert Hoover's period as Secretary of Commerce, and even after he became President, the Department of Commerce was greatly overextended. Whether Mr. Hoover made these extensive developments primarily for his own personal aggrandizement or to help the business interests of the country is still a subject of debate in Washington. At any rate, President Roosevelt had his eye on the Department of Commerce in connection with his desire of cutting government costs 25 per cent. Secretary Roper assumed his present position with this understanding. The customary attitude of a member of the President's Cabinet to "fight for his babies" and work for larger appropriations for his department will not be the case with the Secretary of Commerce. This revolutionary attitude naturally causes resentment within the department. To have Secretary Roper side with Lewis Douglas, Director of the Budget, and with Swagar Sherley in cutting down expenses is disheartening to men who have given their lives to the Department of Commerce. This is especially true at a time like this when these faithful employes cannot go out and get a position in business.

Congress has given the President authority to merge, abolish or shift functions of independent agencies and bureaus. This authority will be exercised by the President and Secretary Roper especially in connection with the Department of Commerce. Some functions will be discontinued entirely and others severely curtailed. This applies to the trade attachés whom the department has placed throughout the world and who, the Department of State claims, overlap the State Department attachés. It is also believed that the department's field offices throughout the United States will be curtailed, if not abolished. On the other hand, it is rumored that the transportation interests of the government, including the Interstate Commerce Commission and the Shipping Board and the Air Service, may be placed under the Department of Commerce. The present independent Radio Commission and other independent bodies may ultimately find themselves under the control of Secretary Roper.

As to Secretary Roper's personal ideas and policies little has been said. His whole life and training have been to carry out orders rather than to determine policies. Early in his administration, however, he seemed mostly concerned in helping the President and the railroads—rather than American business men. This brought forth various newspaper comments of which the following editorial from the Washington *Post* is an illustration:

The new Secretary of Commerce, Mr. Roper, may be excused for over-emphasizing the importance of foreign trade in the American economic system, but he should remember that the Department of Commerce is devoted to the stimulation of American business at home as well as abroad. The public is now anxious to hear what plans the new Secretary has for the stimulation of domestic commerce.

"In foreign commerce," says Mr. Roper, "there must be buying as well as selling. No nation can successfully market its goods abroad if it stubbornly persists in refusing to let in a remarkable volume of the products of other countries." This is distinctly the foreign-trade point of view. Secretary Roper's words may be paraphrased from the domestic-trade viewpoint with equal potency:

In domestic commerce there must be buying as well as selling. No nation can successfully market its goods at home if it stubbornly persists in refusing to give jobs to its own people. It is to be hoped that Secretary Roper neglected the latter viewpoint only because he was talking to exporters.

The relationship of domestic and foreign trade should be kept in mind. One school of thought advances the theory that international trade is all-important in promoting domestic trade. Since domestic trade amounts to about 90 percent of all American business and foreign trade amounts to only about 10 percent, this theory has the aspect of trying to make the tail wag the dog. The other school of thought insists that preference should be given to domestic trade, because of its vital importance, and that foreign trade should be cultivated as a desirable adjunct to domestic business, but should not be permitted to injure domestic trade or employment.

Foreign commerce will improve when normal business is resumed within national boundaries. It cannot be revived by admitting cheap-labor foreign goods without disastrous consequences to American labor. Let attention first be concentrated upon restoration of the 90 percent domestic market. Any other policy will not square with President Roosevelt's dictum of putting "first things first."

ROPER AND THE NRA

Although Daniel C. Roper is Secretary of Commerce, he refers most of the revolutionary questions to his assistant, John Dickinson. This man is a graduate of Johns Hopkins, a graduate student at both Harvard and Princeton. Dickinson has won a reputation as being one of three or four leading authorities in the United States on the subject of administrative law, that is, the law relating to the authority and duties of administrative boards and commissions. His volume on *Administrative Justice and the Supremacy of Law* is regarded as a standard treatise. For many years he was a member of the Committee on Public Administration of the Social Science Research Council, an agency promoting research and teaching in the field of public administration. He has taught economics and government at Harvard, and has made several economic surveys, notably a survey of the garment industry in New York City, launched under the auspices of a commission of which Governor Lehman was chairman in 1925. He was at one time a law partner of Senator W. G. McAdoo.

In politics, Dickinson has been a lifelong Democrat and often has spoken before the Democratic gatherings. One of his recent addresses before the Democratic Women's Club of Philadelphia was printed as a pamphlet. While a member of the Harvard faculty, in 1926, he took the stump in the Bay State to fight against repeal of the Direct Primaries Act. He occupied the same platform with Senator George W. Norris of Nebraska in a speech which he delivered at Worcester. He is a friend of Professor Felix Frankfurter.

Mr. Dickinson holds that there is close relationship between law and economics, and believes that business will have increasing need of the help of the legal science in solving many of its problems. Commenting on the fact that he was a lawyer, he said in an interview on assuming his duties as Assistant Secretary of Commerce: "I suppose many people might think it unusual for a lawyer to be named Assistant Secretary of Commerce. As a matter of fact, I welcome the opportunity to serve under Secretary Roper in the Commerce Department because, in my opinion, there is a very close and intimate relation between law and economics. The many activities which by common consent the Government is having to undertake to meet the present depression are economic measures, but in their formulation and drafting they enlist imperatively the interest and experience of the lawyer. It has been my good fortune, in my legal studies and practice, to have worked mainly in the border line between law and economics, so that I welcome the opportunity to carry on this work in such close proximity to the biggest and most fundamental problems of our time. The Department of Commerce is the economic clearing house of the nation and under Secretary Roper's administration will seek to be of fundamental assistance to the economic life of our people as a whole."

John Dickinson represents the Department of Commerce on the Brain Trust as Tugwell represents the

Department of Agriculture and as Douglas represents the Treasury Department, and as Moley represented the State Department before his resignation.

Willard L. Thorp, an authority on industrial statistics, the Amherst professor who now heads the Bureau of Foreign and Domestic Commerce, points out that his great goal is adequate and reliable statistics. Upon assuming office he is reported to have said:

"No scientist would dream of carrying on an experiment without providing for the most detailed observation of its results, and we are in the midst of a great economic experiment. Much of this information has a usefulness far beyond the individual industry. It is essential to the Government in order to direct properly the economic life of the nation. Most of the codes provide for the collection of statistics by trade associations or other designated agencies. These provisions, however, do not abrogate the ultimate authority which the Industrial Recovery Act vests in the President to require statistical reports. In at least one instance where the code did not set up a statistical agency, this principle has been re-stated in the Executive order in which approval was given, where the following clause appears:

" 'And it is hereby approved on the condition, compliance with which is hereby required, that reports shall be furnished from time to time to the Administrator by each employer of the industry, setting forth information on wages, hours of labor, and such other matters in such form, manner, and detail as he may require.'

GOVERNMENT RESPONSIBLE

"The present situation, therefore, is that authority for the collection of statistics has been given specifically to the Code Authority, but that the Government has not relinquished its ultimate responsibility in the matter. There are two essentials to successful operation of an industry as an economic unit. The first is knowledge; and the second is power. For the first time, the Government is giving positive support to the gathering of information concerning each industry. The National Industrial Recovery Act states that the President may require the making of reports and the keeping of accounts. The codes of fair competition provide for the collection of statistics, and failure to report is a violation. Many code authorities are instructed to set up systems of standardized cost accounting and the members are required to cooperate. Furthermore, Code authorities are given permission to investigate and recommend improvements in trade practices within their industries."

"The Chief Executioner" lives at 3001 Woodland Drive, Washington, D. C.

Chapter XI

"THE REVOLUTIONISTS' ATTORNEY"

STRIKING swiftly in unexpected places, death has often played a dramatic rôle in the affairs of our nation. Last March, on the eve of the inaugural of Franklin D. Roosevelt, Senator Thomas J. Walsh of Montana was hurrying to Washington to take his place in the new Cabinet as Attorney-General. Suddenly stricken, he died on the train which was bearing him to the Capital.

STORY OF APPOINTMENT

Confronted at once with grief over the loss of one of his closest personal friends and with the necessity of finding quickly a man who could temporarily take the place of "Tom" Walsh, President Roosevelt did not hesitate. A long-distance telephone call to Homer S. Cummings in Connecticut resulted in Mr. Cummings' agreeing to fill the breach and accept a temporary appointment as Attorney-General. Naturally Mr. Cummings was pleased at this compliment and it was easy later to prevail upon him to take the post permanently.

It happened that Mr. Cummings was already slated for a post—that of Governor-General of the Philippines—a position offering the sort of opportunity he particularly welcomed. But he obeyed his chief and started immediately for Washington. On the day before the inauguration exercises, the following brief statement was issued from Mr. Roosevelt's headquarters:

"Mr. Roosevelt had expected to announce today the selection of Homer S. Cummings of Connecticut to be Governor-General of the Philippines. Because of the untimely death of Senator Walsh, he has asked Mr. Cummings to assume the post of Attorney-General for a few weeks before going to the Philippines."

Cummings is still in Washington and the administration of Philippine affairs is in other hands. There may have never been any question in the President's mind about the permanence of the appointment. Now that sufficient time has elapsed in which to make an appraisal of Mr. Cummings' administration of the office, there is little doubt but that the Attorney-General's portfolio will continue to be held by this Yankee lawyer of Scotch ancestry. Although the appointment is far from satisfactory to conservative constitutional lawyers, they would rather have him than some real revolutionist in the post.

In some instances Mr. Roosevelt has turned to men outside the active political arena and placed responsibility and confidence in them by making them members of his Cabinet. He has, however, leavened these selections with other choices representing more direct political experience and training. Mr. Cummings falls within this latter group because he has been an active worker in behalf of the Democratic party for many years. Along with a lot of other young idealists in 1896, he took Bryan as their leader and fought and bled behind his standard in that epochal campaign year.

A GOOD SPEAKER

Advancing through various positions of power and influence in party councils, Mr. Cummings has at other times received more than passing consideration for promotion. The Connecticut delegation to the Democratic Convention in 1920 and again in 1924 were solidly behind him for the presidential nomination. That he should ever be a presidential candidate seems almost inconceivable to many in Stamford and Greenwich, Connecticut. They insist that the Connecticut delegation simply used his name as a stop-gap preparing to trade later. But the facts are as given here. Cummings can make a wonderful speech on any subject with the least preparation imaginable. He also has the gambler's courage which is useful at times. Hence some of the "Cummings for President" boosters may well have been in earnest.

Meanwhile, Mr. Cummings goes about his daily work as head of the legal department of the government without giving any thought or attention to what may lie in the future. He is patient. He believes in doing the day's work and letting what lies ahead wait until it comes to hand. And he surely is a worker— early and late. Furthermore, he feels that a great opportunity has come to him and he is truly anxious to please his chief.

There are times when those of us who are not members of the legal profession suspect that the administration of our laws is not all that it should be. We see passion and prejudice enter the portals where justice alone should reign supreme. We see red tape and bickering technicalities replace a straightforward attempt to deal fairly and swiftly on the merits of the particular case. We tend to become cynical of our courts and of our attorneys.

It was during President Hoover's administration that the famous Wickersham investigation was made of our courts and police departments. In the report, which made a public sensation at the time, considerable space was given to the conduct of police and district attorneys toward prisoners. A shocking amount of "third degree" brutality was uncovered and revealed by the commission. Prominent in the report was the statement that district and state attorneys often go to any extreme to convict a prisoner and that the tendency of the prosecutor's office is to win the case rather than to see justice done.

STATE VS. ISRAEL

In the course of this Wickersham report a glowing encomium of Homer S. Cummings was made for the manner in which he had conducted the office of state's attorney for Fairfield County, Connecticut, a post he had held a few years earlier. A specific case in which Mr. Cummings had prominently figured was mentioned in detail and it quickly became famous in legal circles from one end of the country to the other. This was the case of *State vs. Israel.* I mention it here for the reason that in his handling of this case Mr. Cummings showed most strikingly a fine perspective on the duties of his office.

Sometimes a single episode will reveal a man's character and do more to present an accurate picture of his entire personality than a lengthy chronicle of his achievements can tell. In the case of *State vs. Israel* Mr. Cummings stands revealed as a man singularly qualified to uphold the responsibilities of the office of the Attorney-General if his interests continue purely and solely in the cause of justice rather than technicalities. In the great constitutional questions accompanying the New Deal, it may be far better to have an Attorney-General of Cummings' type than one who is always worrying about the technicalities of the law.

The case in question involved the murder of a priest in Bridgeport, Connecticut. A young man, Harold Israel, was arrested and charged with the crime. What seemed like conclusive evidence pointing to his guilt was in Homer Cummings' hands. A number of eyewitnesses identified Israel as the man they had seen fleeing from the place of the murder. Israel himself confessed to the crime, under police examination. A ballistic expert testified before the coroner that the bullet found in the head of the priest had been discharged from a revolver found on Israel when he was arrested.

It looked like an air-tight case. The conservative lawyers were all against Israel. A confession, expert testimony as to the bullet and the revolver, and a number of eyewitnesses able to identify the prisoner—were all against Israel. Not one prosecuting attorney in a thousand would have gone further. It was the sort of case in which the politician type of district or state's attorney would have delighted. It was made to order. But this was not State's Attorney Cummings' idea of his responsibilities. Certain things about the case struck him as a bit odd. He began to check up. The results were astounding.

First he found that Israel's mentality was extremely low and that he had yielded supinely to the police investigation and confessed in order to put an end to the questioning. Knowing that the most treacherous of evidence is that of eyewitnesses, Mr. Cummings conducted a rigid examination of all the witnesses. He found so many discrepancies in their stories that it was quite clear they were honestly but definitely in error. Last of all, he demonstrated that while the bullet came from a gun like the one Israel owned, it actually was not fired from that particular revolver.

Armed with this evidence, Mr. Cummings went before the court and presented himself in the amazing rôle of a prosecutor asking that the man's life be spared. The court, after a careful consideration of Mr. Cummings' facts, agreed that the case should be *nol prossed* and the defendant released. The Wickersham report said of this case: "The Israel case is a notable illustration of the proper discharge of the prosecutor's duty." Yet if Cummings had followed the letter of the law and had failed to interpret the evidence in the light of common sense, Connecticut would have had on its hands a Sacco-Vanzetti case with serious consequences.

Our institutions, particularly our legal system, are in fairly safe hands when such a custom becomes more universal. We need more of this sort of zeal for equity and justice on the part of our legal profession. The less of the weasel-like maneuvering, whereby technicalities take the place of issues and eloquence replaces a dispassionate presentation of the facts, the better.

CUMMINGS' BACKGROUND

Homer S. Cummings was born in Chicago, Illinois, on April 30, 1870, the only son of Uriah and Audie Schuyler Stille Cummings. The Cummings family was of Scotch descent. Biographers believe that one of their ancestors was John Cummin, regent of Scotland and rival of Robert Bruce for the crown of that kingdom. At any rate, Homer's friends kid him about this and he seems to like it.

Uriah Cummings, who was considered one of the highest authorities on cement in this country, was a resident of Stamford at the time of his death on November 10, 1910. Homer received his early education at Heathcote School, Buffalo, New York. He was graduated from Sheffield Scientific School at Yale University in 1891, and then entered Yale Law School where he was graduated with a degree in 1893. He had a good chance to enter the cement business, but he did not.

In August of the same year he went to Stamford and entered the office of State's Attorney Samuel Fessenden. On January 1, 1895, the law firm of Fessenden, Carter and Cummings was organized. In 1900, Mr. Cummings withdrew and practised alone for the following nine years. On September 1, 1909, the firm of Cummings and Lockwood was formed. Mr. Cummings' partner was Judge Charles D. Lockwood, Judge of Probate for the Stamford district. Another partner in that firm was the late George Pratt Ingersoll, former Minister to Siam.

On July 1, 1914, Mr. Cummings was appointed state's attorney for Fairfield County. He voluntarily resigned that post after holding it for slightly more than ten years. On his resignation he was given a testimonial dinner at Bridgeport by the Fairfield County Bar Association, at which George W. Wheeler, Chief Justice of the Supreme Court of Connecticut, was the principal speaker.

Mr. Cummings first became interested in the Democratic party in 1896, and has always retained that interest in his party's welfare. He was mayor of Stamford in 1900, 1901, 1902, 1904 and 1906. During 1902 he was president of the Mayors' Association of the state. In 1908 he started a four-year term of office as corporation counsel for Stamford. From 1903 to 1911, he was president of the Stamford Board of Trade.

In 1896, the year of his first political venture of any serious nature, he was candidate for secretary of state. In 1902 he was Democratic nominee for the office of Congressman-at-large, receiving the highest vote on his party's ticket. In 1910 he was the unanimous choice of Democrats in the General Assembly for United States Senator; and in 1916 he was again a candidate, losing the election by only a narrow margin of votes.

Mr. Cummings was a delegate-at-large from Connecticut to the Democratic National Conventions of 1900, 1904 and 1924, and an alternate in 1920 and

1932. From 1900 to 1924, by successive appointments, he was a member of the Democratic National Committee, resigning his committeeship on December 1, 1925. In 1913, he was vice chairman of the National Committee, and held that post until February 26, 1919, when he became chairman of the National Committee. He was national chairman of the party until July 20, 1920.

As temporary chairman of the Democratic National Convention at San Francisco on June 28, 1920, Mr. Cummings delivered the keynote address. He was then nominated for the Presidency of the United States by Charles F. Crosby, United States attorney, representing the Connecticut delegates. He received only twenty-seven votes at the convention and was naturally disappointed. He was, however, never beaten although down and continued to labor for his party's interests.

In the conflict which raged between Alfred E. Smith and William G. McAdoo, Mr. Cummings always took the part of Mr. McAdoo. In fact, he never became a Smith man. Therefore, when Smith attacked Roosevelt in 1932, Homer Cummings strongly defended the Governor of New York against Al Smith. Probably this was one reason why Roosevelt desired to reward him with the office of Attorney-General. While opinions differ as to his ability as a constitutional lawyer, all are agreed that he has a lot of common sense, can make a splendid speech and has fair political acumen. Furthermore, he has always put the goal ahead of the technicalities of the law.

Mr. McAdoo went to the 1928 convention an avowed candidate and it was generally understood that Mr.

Cummings would be quite acceptable to Mr. McAdoo as second choice; but neither the first nor any other choice could withstand the Smith steamroller. In the most recent campaign Mr. Cummings worked night and day in behalf of the Roosevelt candidacy both before and after the Chicago convention which nominated him in June, 1932.

During the war period, Mr. Cummings was appointed by Governor Holcombe of Connecticut as a member of the State Council of Defense, and was active in its deliberations, and worked through the duration of the war. He has given freely of his time and name to all local causes.

HOME LIFE

Mr. Cummings now makes his home in Greenwich. His first wife was Miss Helen Woodruff Smith. They had one son, Dickinson Cummings. This marriage was dissolved by divorce in 1907. In 1909 he again married, this time Miss Marguerite T. Owings, of Indianapolis. This marriage also did not prove a happy one and a divorce followed. In 1929 he married Miss May C. Waterbury of Stamford.

Mr. Cummings is a member of the New York and Washington bars and is also a member of the American Bar Association and the Fairfield County Bar Association. In the higher courts of Connecticut and adjoining jurisdictions, as well as in the United States Supreme Court and other federal courts, he has been counsel in many celebrated cases involving large monetary interests and important questions of law. He has had a fair degree of success and made friends rather than enemies.

He is a member of the First Congregational Church and is a director of the First Stamford National Bank. He belongs to the Metropolitan Club, the National Democratic Club of New York, the Congressional Country Club of Washington, D. C., the University Club of Bridgeport, the National Arts Club of New York, Woodway Country Club, the Stamford Yacht Club, Masonic orders, Odd Fellows, Elks, Eagles and Knights of Pythias, and many other social or fraternal organizations.

President Roosevelt has many splendid qualifications for the Presidency, but probably none greater than his ability to surround himself with men who will help him. In Homer Cummings the President has exactly the sort of man he wants. A liberal and an idealist, he is nevertheless a practical expert in politics. He knows the Democratic party inside out. He may be looked upon as halfway between the viewpoint of Secretary Ickes, on the one hand, and Postmaster-General Farley, on the other. He combines the former's liberalism with the latter's knowledge of the political "ropes." Furthermore, it would have been risky for the President to have appointed some high-brow lawyer who would have put his own reputation as a constitutional lawyer ahead of the people's welfare. Roosevelt has to have as Attorney-General some one who will forget himself—and his own reputation—and fight for the President and his revolution.

Yet in the eyes of Connecticut Republicans, Homer is not looked upon as a revolutionist. Certainly he is not the overconscientious kind like Miss Perkins. Rather he may be more of the opportunist group which follows its leader. However this may be, he suits the President and cooperates with the President as to the character and timeliness of his opinions and investigations. He is especially loyal in defending the President as to the constitutionality of the Roosevelt revolutionary program. However, Cummings will not push himself into the limelight to steal thunder from his chief. He is playing the President's game whether you like it or not. And the President knows he can always depend upon Homer S. Cummings.

"The Revolutionists' Attorney" lives at Hamilton Hotel, Washington, D. C.

Chapter XII

"THE NEWCOMER"

ON MARCH 4, 1933, the curtain rose in Washington on one of the most momentous scenes that ever opened the drama of any administration since the founding of the Republic. The nation was on the edge of an economic and financial collapse. Banks were closing in every state. Panic was in the air. People went about their daily tasks—if they had any—uneasily, apprehensively. Every eye was on Washington, on the new President and his friends. Who influenced this smiling chief executive who seemed to shoulder burdens of appalling gravity with a light-heartedness which reassured even as it amazed?

If you ran an anxious eye down the cast of characters which peopled the Washington stage in March of 1933, you would nowhere have found the name of the man who, within a space of less than a year, was to assume responsibilities second only to the President himself. Had you mentioned the name "Morgenthau" to any old-timer in Washington, you would have been met with: "Why, of course! He was Wilson's ambassador to Turkey in 1916."

For it was from Henry Morgenthau, Jr.'s father that the present Secretary of the Treasury gained his first interest in public affairs. Like another "Young Henry" —Henry C. Wallace, Secretary of Agriculture—among

230

the Washington revolutionists, the youthful Morgenthau was early inspired by his father's example. The elder Morgenthau, as chairman of the Finance Committee of the Democratic National Committee in 1915, had made a significant impression on President Wilson. The following year the President appointed him ambassador to Turkey and he served during that most difficult period following America's entry into the World War.

ROOSEVELT'S FRIEND

At this time Franklin D. Roosevelt was a somewhat obscure young assistant Secretary of the Navy. The young Morgenthau was only three years out of college, beginning to interest himself in agriculture as a gentleman farmer in New York State. This was after his return from Texas, where he had spent some months on a large ranch. Returning to New York, with physical vigor, he determined to follow the calling of his forebears. Farming was in his blood, for back in Germany his people had tilled the soil. He therefore turned his back on his father's successful real estate business and began to comb New York State for the sort of farm he wanted.

Young Morgenthau found not one farm, but three. In Dutchess County, in the neighborhood of the Roosevelt estates along the Hudson, he bought three old, well-watered farms back of Fishkill Hook, fourteen hundred acres in all. Today the place is a prosperous establishment with 250 acres, mostly of Macintosh apple trees. Half of them are now bearing and last year were reported to have yielded 20,000 bushels. Dairying is also an active industry at the Fishkill farm, with a large herd of registered Holsteins and Jerseys.

Soon after he had acquired this property, America entered the World War. Unable to pass the army entrance examinations because of his eyes, young Morgenthau secured a position in the Navy Department with the rank of junior lieutenant. But as soon as hostilities were over he was ready for the peaceful plowshare again. The years slipped along—peaceful, post-War years. Marriage, children, a consuming interest in his agricultural pursuits. Henry Morgenthau, Jr., seemed destined to a life quietly rural and remote. Already, however, the strings of destiny were drawing him slowly to the important rôle he was eventually to play, treading in the footsteps of Alexander Hamilton at a time when the nation needed a strong man in the Treasury. Near by were the rolling ancestral acres of another gentleman farmer—Franklin D. Roosevelt. One can picture the scene on a summer morning now years ago. Two men leaned against the fence on a New York State farm, chewed straw, and talked about spraying apple trees.

One was broad-shouldered and blond, a man with a hearty, infectious laugh. His forebears had inhabited the shores of the Hudson for two centuries. The other was slender, dark, and younger. His parents were the first American-born generation of a family which had long tilled the fields of a European countryside. Both were good Americans, with a mutual interest in trees. So the friendship flourished.

Their paths were quietly converging. Trees were

perhaps the first tie between Franklin D. Roosevelt and Henry Morgenthau, Jr. But as the families became acquainted, the rising young Assemblyman, now candidate for the governorship, could not fail to notice the growing influence of his dark, slim friend. When Mr. Roosevelt was elected Governor, he named Mr. Morgenthau head of an Advisory Commission on Agriculture. The commission proved to be a live agency, and Mr. Morgenthau took an active part, financing some of the operations himself. The result was recommended legislation on taxation and appropriations, much of which was written into law.

AS CONSERVATION COMMISSIONER

When Mr. Roosevelt came up for reelection, he was able to read a long program of accomplishment—highways, agricultural credit corporations, aids to agricultural education, health. Here indeed was a feather for any candidate's cap to display to the people. Achievements of the Advisory Commission were deeds recognizable as performed for the public weal, revealing figures that showed a substantial saving for the public purse. When Governor Roosevelt entered his second term Mr. Morgenthau continued his previous duties and was given official public office as well. He was appointed Conservation Commissioner with functions that Governor Roosevelt watched over with a loving eye. Thus, for the second time, they were talking trees— this time officially.

Meanwhile, Henry had acquired ownership of *The American Agriculturist*, which he conducted for years in behalf of the American farmer. It became an important journal in the long battle of the farmer to secure his just rights. Even as I write, comes the news that, under the pressure of the terrific burdens of the Treasury, Mr. Morgenthau has decided to let *The American Agriculturist* pass out of his hands. In thus disposing of it, he acts consistently. No nominal ownership interests him. He must be passionately involved and concerned with whatever he puts his hand to.

During these long years in which President Roosevelt was being groomed by events for the tremendous task he was to assume in 1933, the tie between the two men became indissolubly riveted. Few Presidents have commanded such personal affection as surrounds Mr. Roosevelt. Few of the President's devoted friends and supporters are as whole-souled and as single-purposed in devotion as is Henry Morgenthau. With him it is a fierce, unquestioning loyalty. One might easily determine this in a single glance at the burning dark intensity of the man.

GOVERNOR OF THE FARM CREDIT ADMINISTRATION

Let me bring the story down to 1933 and to the White House. I have said that Henry Morgenthau's name was nowhere on any roster when the new administration took over control. Yet unmentioned as his name was, there remained one place in Washington where, without any question, his name was already written indelibly—and was being held for the proper moment to release it. This place was the tablet of President Roosevelt's mind.

It was not long before the President acted. On March

26, 1933, the following news story appeared in every paper in the country:

WASHINGTON, March 26.—President Roosevelt moved today to consolidate and reorganize all agricultural credit agencies of the Federal Government and to abolish the Federal Farm Board. He announced that he would send to Congress tomorrow an executive order to effect these changes.

Henry Morgenthau, Jr., of New York, will be appointed to head the new unified farm credit bureau which will take over the activities of the following Federal agencies:

Federal Farm Board.

Federal Land Banks.

Joint Stock Land Banks.

Intermediate Credit Banks.

Agricultural Credit Corporations set up by the Reconstruction Finance Corporation.

Crop Production Loan Bureau of the Agricultural Department.

Loan Bureau of the Department of Agriculture to aid local agricultural associations.

As governor of the Farm Credit Administration, Henry Morgenthau, Jr., found thrust upon him the responsibility of administering $4,500,000,000 of Federal funds—land loans, intermediate credit loans, agricultural marketing loans, and emergency loans. In addition there was the task of refinancing farm mortgages. Morgenthau took off his coat and went to work. After he had appraised the scope and nature of the task, he outlined in explicit language his conception of it—a conception which he later moved steadily forward to realize. He said:

"What do I consider my job? Well, as I see it, it is twofold: first, to get the farmer out of debt; and second, to place him eventually in control of the federal machinery with which this is to be brought about. The Federal Land Banks last year cost the government about $950,000 to operate and they paid their own way only to the extent of about $350,000. There is no reason on earth why that $350,000 cannot be increased to $950,000 and the banks be made to pay their own way." Continuing, he said: "In our specialized economic system farming is a life vocation. It is more than a trade. I think it is entitled to the dignity of being called a profession. It takes study and constant alertness as well as intelligence and experience to practice it successfully. I am entirely confident that the task of providing food, clothing materials, and the other products of the soil that go into manufacture to meet human wants will remain in the hands of the professional farmer—the man who makes it his life work and prepares for it. I think the farmers will remain a very substantial portion—probably not less than a fourth—of our whole population. Those who process and handle farm crops and those who derive their living by selling materials and services to the farmer will be an army equally large.

"Agriculture is, and will continue to be, our dominant industry. It is from the soil that we live. The farmer is competent to manage his own affairs if we give him a chance. When he has been clamorous about the management of national affairs he has had good reason to be. When we adopt a national economy that strips the farmer of his possessions we can expect to hear from him. If we didn't, the nation would be in a bad way. The farmer has more than once interposed his ideas and his force to save our form of government and to save our industry. Industry and labor must recognize that the farmer is at least an equal partner in the cooperative effort that makes up national economic life and national government."

COMBINES BUSINESS AND VISION

Mr. Morgenthau dug in and was oblivious to everything except the welfare of the farmer. His was the job of finding markets for the wheat and cotton stocks piled up by the Farm Board in its attempts to stabilize the prices of these commodities. In addition, some disposal had to be made of the great quantities of commodities accepted by the board during the past three years for its loans, now totalling $182,000,000, to cooperative marketing associations. His first pledge on taking office was that under his direction the government was to be taken permanently out of stabilization operations. These, in his opinion, had done more to hinder the purposes of cooperative marketing than any other factor short of the collapse of prices of all farm commodities. Two months later the Farm Board was definitely out of stabilization and its commodity purchases were completely liquidated.

Henry Morgenthau, Jr., besides revealing a capacity for getting things done, showed a strict sense of responsibility for the government's money. Loans by the Farm Board, if made at all, he announced on becoming chairman, were to be made according to sound banking practice. One of his first discoveries was that the board was continuing to pay interest on large debts in New York, although it had sufficient funds to pay them off. He called in the person responsible, and, on learning that such matters had. always been decided by the members of the board in session, gave instructions that henceforth the financial division was itself to be responsible for conducting the business of the board on a business basis.

The momentous year 1933 moved toward its close. The situation was improving throughout the country, but only slowly, hesitantly. The spirit that carried business upward seemed in full flush until July. By autumn, however, it had again subsided. The focal point centered more and more around the nation's financial policies, around our contemplated program regarding the dollar at home and abroad, our rapidly approaching and imperative need for gargantuan expenditures out of the national Treasury.

SECRETARY WOODIN'S ILLNESS

For months Secretary of the Treasury William H. Woodin had been a sick man. It was an open secret that President Roosevelt had become his own Secretary of the Treasury. As the summer passed and autumn approached, Mr. Woodin faded more and more out of the picture. He had been a surprise choice for the post and his appointment was more a source of puzzlement than it was either of approbation or disapproval. He had taken hold of the job, however, in a quietly efficient manner and he had the President's respect and confidence. Now, however, those on the inside at Washington knew it was only a question of time when Secretary Woodin would resign. Speculation buzzed as to his successor. The names of many men were mentioned.

Finally, in November, the President acted—and it was to Henry Morgenthau, Jr., he turned. His appointment was first that of acting Secretary of the Treasury; but with Mr. Woodin's resignation at hand, on New Year's Day the President officially designated his New York State neighbor and friend as successor.

Mr. Morgenthau moved his belongings from the somewhat antiquated office which he had occupied as chairman of the Federal Farm Board into an upper room at the sunny end of the Treasury Building. If some in Washington were surprised when President Roosevelt named Mr. Morgenthau back in March for the post of financial guide to the American farmer, that surprise grew into amazement when Mr. Morgenthau assumed the key position of financial guide for the entire nation. Tongues buzzed—and among the various opinions expressed it must be admitted that not all were favorable. "They" said:

"Is this new chap a financier? Why, he's just a farmer—and a gentleman farmer at that. He has no stamp on him at all, no alliance with Wall Street or Big Business or anything! What does he know about money? What is this country coming to, anyhow?" Let me also quote here the typical Republican viewpoint. The speaker has been a close observer in Washington affairs over a period of years. I have regard for his judgment as to how the congressional leaders feel. This man told me:

"Now, if we are to call a spade a spade, I have got to say that Mr. Morgenthau is no more schooled in national and international finance than I am trained in marine engineering. The truth is that Mr. Roosevelt is his own Secretary of the Treasury. He gives his orders to Morgenthau, who does as he is directed. In the old days he would have been labeled a 'yes-man.' He is not even that. He does as he is told. He is the intimate friend of the President. Many leaders did not give Mr. Woodin a very high rating as Secretary of the Treasury; but he had much more background and understanding than has his successor, Henry Morgenthau, Jr."

Against this sort of judgment on Mr. Morgenthau, is the much more prevalent feeling that the President knew his man. It is said that President Roosevelt knew what the public did not—that Mr. Morgenthau was the silent partner in many of his father's financial adventures. His name does not appear in the directorates of his father's companies; but he has been a close student of their problems and in his own right he assumed a careful custodianship of no small responsibility. Hence the President asked the man who once told him so much about orchards to keep the nation's books and collect its bills. Dollars, of course, do not grow on trees; but even to grow apples takes a knowledge of the use of dollars.

FACED A SEVEN BILLIONS DEFICIT

Consider for a moment the magnitude of the task which confronted the new Secretary of the Treasury on that morning not so very long ago when he first sat behind the broadest desk in all Washington. The Treasury Department was on the threshold of assuming the heaviest burdens which any administration had undertaken under the strain of the nation's emergency. It was the Treasury's task to find ten billions of dollars during the first six months of 1934 with which to combat the depression and to retire maturities. Furthermore, the Treasury had to deal with a deficit of seven billions of dollars in this fiscal year and with one of probably two billions next year. It must maintain the government's credit in the face of a contemplated public-debt total by June 30, 1935, of almost thirty-two billions of dollars. These figures indicate faintly the magnitude of the responsibility the President has intrusted to his friend and neighbor.

Mr. Morgenthau has been on the job but a comparatively short time. It is impossible, therefore, to do more than indicate tendencies. Time will test the answers. I was interested in what one highly trained and expert Washington observer had to say about the way Mr. Morgenthau is running his department. After commenting that the newcomer did not fit into the position smoothly at first, this observer said: "Morgenthau now has begun to find himself. . . . He is gradually knitting together a more compact, less wieldy Treasury Department. He sometimes shows signs of being elaborately inarticulate, but he has one great asset in his favor—Roosevelt trusts him implicitly."

His talent, I am told, is not the scholar's, but the organizer's. He has the gift of coordinating the efforts of a large and complex group and concentrating them on one objective. After the objective is won, it ceases to interest him. When he had brought order out of the farm-mortgage confusion last year, he turned over the smoothly running new Farm Credit Administration to his deputy assistant and took on the difficult job of organizing trade relations with Russia. It is obvious that President Roosevelt had his eye on him and that the White House decision to promote him to the Treasury was made on the basis of the Morgenthau record. Once more let me offer you Mr. Morgenthau's own words to show that he has a profound realization of what is involved in the Treasury post. Mark well how appropriately these words designate him as one of the real revolutionists in the President's Cabinet.

"The Treasury," he said, "is the point, of all points, where the government and the citizen come closest together. You may say this, that the Treasury is going to be run in the interest of every citizen and with fairness to all. The principle of approach is that all are to be treated alike. Selfish wealth has been allowed to evade its obligations to the common welfare for the last time. All the skill of its clever lawyers is not going to do it any good now. The special-privilege class in this country is abolished, so far as the Treasury is concerned. For the first time in years the internal revenue forces concerned with income-tax violations have a free hand. They had been putting away rich gangsters and passing by 'respectable' offenders. They had been called off so often that they had almost lost their punch. They are a fine group of men who want to do their duty, and they are tickled to have a chance at last. Under this administration they can go after any tax-evader in the land without asking any man's permission."

PERSONAL HISTORY

These are the highlights of the man and his career so far. To complete the picture, it is necessary to sketch in some of the more formal biographical facts to serve as a background and help make more understandable Mr. Morgenthau's achievements. He was born in New York City on May 11, 1891, which makes him the youngest member of the Cabinet in years, as well as in point of service. No reference to his childhood is adequate without commenting on the strong influence which the father had on his son during these formative years. Henry was the only boy in a family of four children, and this fact further accented his father's interest in the boy's education and training. The family was in what would be called reasonably affluent circumstances, but an unostentatious simplicity and thriftiness marked their manner of living. Morgenthau, senior, unlike some fathers, had the wisdom to encourage thrift and a certain Spartan discipline in his son in regard to money and its uses. He himself had known what it was to carve out a career and fortune through his own unaided efforts.

Born in Germany in 1856, Morgenthau, senior, was only eleven years old when his parents came to this country. He attended public schools in New York City and was graduated from Columbia in 1877. He then embarked on a business career which carried him steadily upward and in which real estate proved the corner stone of his success. Young Henry followed in the footsteps of his father as to his early educational training. He was graduated from the public schools, but instead of completing his education at the university from which his distinguished father was graduated, he turned to Cornell University at Ithaca, New York.

When he matriculated here in 1909 it was with the avowed intention of studying architecture. He had decided upon this with the approval of his father, both agreeing that a knowledge of architecture on Henry's part would prove of direct value, should he link his business career to his father's real estate interests. Before the end of the first term, however, Henry found himself spending more time over at the School of Agriculture than over a draught-board and blue prints. Just at the time he completed his first year, in 1913, his health broke down. Never strong as a boy, he had always been obliged to favor himself physically. Now, however, a crisis loomed and a family council quickly came to the decision that Henry's health was of far more importance than his education at Cornell.

He was packed off to a Texas ranch to recuperate, and the next two years he made a successful fight to recover his health, returning robustly eager to go on with his education. He spent one more full year at Cornell in 1912-1913, during which time his interest in agriculture increased into enthusiasm. It was during this period that he met Professor George F. Warren, the much-discussed prompter of the nation's gold-buying program. Professor Warren made a deep impression on Henry, and there is no question but that in later years President Roosevelt's interest in Professor

Warren was emphasized by Mr. Morgenthau's admiration for the Cornell professor.

After establishing himself at Fishkill farm, Henry married Miss Eleanor Fatman, of New York City, on April 17, 1916, thus culminating a romance of several years' standing. His wife, a charming and cultured woman, has shared his tastes and interests most harmoniously. Three children have been born to them— two sons and a daughter. The oldest is also named Henry, a quietly studious youth of seventeen. His brother, Robert, is fourteen years old, and Joan, the youngest, is eleven. Mr. Morgenthau's Washington home is a beautiful stone house with a deep bit of woods behind it, out Rock Creek way. It looks like an abode of ease, but the head of the house breakfasts daily at an early hour and is on his way to the Treasury office before many of his staff have yet awakened.

Mr. Morgenthau dislikes pomp and ceremony in his official activities, as he does in his private life. Consequently, there is an air of quiet informality about the Treasury office, which makes him reasonably accessible to callers. He gets through a vast amount of work in a day, and has the reputation of being mentally "on the job" all of the twenty-four hours. In this he lacks a little the resiliency of his chief, who is so marvelously well able to shake off the responsibilities of office when he does relax. With Mr. Morgenthau, however, earnestness and sincere application to the work engross him. Whether or not he is able to stand the strain, readers may be sure that Henry Morgenthau, Jr., is taking himself and his job in deadly earnest. He surely is a serious revolutionist.

"Is it your understanding," he was asked, "that Dr. Warren takes an interest in monetary questions in the hope of helping agriculture?"

"In the hope of helping humanity," briefly answered Mr. Morgenthau. And that might fairly be said to be the basic revolutionary principle of this forty-three-year-old newest member of the Washington revolutionists.

The "newcomer" lives at 2447 Kalorama Road.

Chapter XIII

"BIG JIM"

IT IS admittedly difficult to picture James Farley in the rôle of a revolutionist. Any such characterization of the genial Postmaster-General would be straining a bit at the facts. Jim Farley is one of the "regular" members of the administration and upon his broad shoulders has fallen the burden of comforting many old-line party leaders and workers. These men, disappointed and bewildered by the Perkinses and the Wallaces, the Johnsons and the Richbergs, have turned for solace to at least one administration official who has some regard for the traditions of party and for the principles of political rewards first laid down by Andrew Jackson.

FARLEY'S TASK

Jim Farley has in some respects had to be the whipping boy for the administration. He has been viewed with suspicion by the reform element and he has been viewed with reproach by the "regulars." When the twelve lean Democratic years came to an end on March 4, 1933, there was a stampede of the faithful to Washington. Jobs, jobs, jobs—that was the one cry which went up from thousands of throats. And it was upon Jim that the hungry hordes of office-seekers descended. If ever he had need for the imperturbable good-nature which has always marked his dealings with men, he needed it then. He stood like a rock amid the swirling whirlpool of requests, of pleas, of insistences.

Finally, the tide subsided and the miracle had been accomplished whereby the administration in general, and Mr. Farley in particular, emerged unscathed. In fact, he holds the record of giving fewer jobs to "deserving" Democrats than any administration, either Republican or Democratic, since Andrew Jackson reannounced that ancient adage, "To the victor belong the spoils." Furthermore, Mr. Farley was still smiling and there was no evidence that his reputation had been even slightly damaged in the eyes of those who might be expected to be most critical—the office-seekers themselves.

The point of all this is important. It may be summed up in the observation that "Jim" Farley knows human nature. Where visionary idealists, with the most ambitious and roseate plans for utopian programs of political and economic reform, go astray is on this very reef of human nature. Blueprints and copy-book maxims of the millennium are one thing. But taking human beings just as they are, studying them, fusing them in a desired direction—that's a task for another sort of leader. And Jim Farley is that sort.

It is a curious twist in the fabric of our national political structure that the one man more responsible than any other that Franklin D. Roosevelt became our President at a time of great national emergency—is James A. Farley. Not only did Jim Farley carry the banner of Roosevelt almost single-handed to the floor of the Democratic Convention in June of 1932, but he kept it there upright amid the thundering battle and fury of votes and ballots until Roosevelt was finally acclaimed the victor.

Long before Chicago, however, Jim Farley had cherished the vision of Franklin D. Roosevelt in the White House. While Mr. Roosevelt was Governor of New York—and more than a full year before any open campaign in his behalf was even thought of—Jim Farley was planning a campaign to "sell" Roosevelt to the American people as their next President. To go back even further, it was Mr. Farley who in 1928 prevailed upon Al Smith to press Franklin D. Roosevelt into heading the New York state ticket that year, not that Al Smith needed any urging. Whatever differences have more recently developed between these two great Democratic leaders, they have not altered their essential respect for each other's ability. In any case, Jim Farley made certain that everything he could do to push the Roosevelt candidacy for Governor was done —and done well. Then when victory rested on the Democratic standard-bearer, Mr. Farley began definitely dreaming dreams and making plans.

REASONS FOR SUCCESS

Two years later, in 1930, Roosevelt swept New York State in his campaign for reelection by a majority of 732,000 and it was then that Mr. Farley uttered the terse but accurate prophecy: "We have elected as Governor the man who will be the next President." While Roosevelt's personal magnetism and charm have been

an invaluable aid in making him one of the most successful vote-getters in the history of American politics,
yet the President will be the first to agree that "Jim"
Farley has had not a little to do with the overwhelming totals which election night returns have unvary-
ingly presented.

The secret of Jim Farley's success is not one possessed by the ordinary politician. Mr. Farley is not a
silver-tongued orator, albeit he can deliver an adequate
speech. He is not given to moving men in masses. *With
Jim it's one man at a time.* The effect is like one of
these endless chains which every so often appear—the
recipient tells ten others. When Jim Farley leaves a
man, that man is not only a loyal and devoted friend
of Farley's, but he does not stop until he has lined up
his own friends likewise. I have seen it and I know it.

This is exactly what Mr. Farley has always done in
upper New York State. He left New York City and
the other big cities alone and he concentrated on the
rural vote. He knew, as no other man in New York
in a generation had known, the rural point of view in
those small upstate towns. They had been without
Democratic prominence since the days of David B.
Hill. No matter who was governor they got the small
end of the stick. Jim Farley capitalized this fact and
won.

So, when some of us are inclined to focus our
thoughts on those in the President's official family who
are now doing such splendid work toward making this
country a better place for *all* of our people to live in, let
us not forget Jim Farley. Let us remember that Miss
Perkins, Henry Wallace, Harold Ickes—or any of the

other Cabinet members who find the calcium light of public interest focused on them—would not have had a chance to expound their revolutionary creed were it not for Jim Farley and his unadorned courage and splendid vision.

I stress this point, not because Jim Farley needs any defense, but because in any division of the honors surely a generous share should go to the one who combines—in such a remarkable way—both the visionary and the practical man of action. If further evidence of where Jim Farley stands in the political scheme of things is necessary let it be remembered that Tammany never has had any use for Farley nor he for Tammany.

RELATIONS WITH TAMMANY

The New York City Democratic organization, which in its structure Mr. Farley has emulated in his own up-state county organization, has consistently opposed Mr. Farley and his candidates whenever opposition was practical. The manner in which Tammany sidetracked Mayor Joseph V. McKee, who was in Farley's camp, in favor of O'Brien after the former had done so excellent a job following Mayor Walker's forced resignation, is evidence that Farley and Tammany are not in the same boat. Furthermore, the New York mayoralty fight of 1933 was the direct result of this action.

After all, this country is governed by the party system. Until the time comes when we abandon this method of running the affairs of the nation, must we

not be willing to accept the party system with its implications? We surely saw the evils of the party system
under the Harding administration, when the spoils system was carried crudely and blatantly to extremes and
where in specific episodes it became criminal. In de-
ploring this aspect of politics, however, we should not
lump under one heading all phases of patronage and
spoils.

As I have pointed out, Mr. Farley, in his position
as Postmaster-General, believes that during the past
quarter of a century the Democrats have not had a
fair deal and he is setting out to remedy the lack by
giving them a new deal. I have examined many of the
appointments for which Mr. Farley has been responsible. I think it can be maintained that, on the whole,
they rank fairly high and show an earnest desire to
make merit and personal qualifications as paramount a
test as party loyalty.

In fact, Mr. Farley is sensitive to the fact that he
went into office with the eyes of the entire country upon
him as the man who had 150,000 jobs at his disposal.
He has leaned over backward to make sure that his appointments could be scrutinized by hostile as well as
impartial eyes. When appointments which appear unfit
seem to have been made, some other person has usually
been the culprit. Jim Farley may not be a saint, but he
is a good citizen.

If my readers are cynical on this subject, let them
remember one thing: what concerns Jim Farley more
than anything else during these next four years is to
develop a militant party. He is vitally anxious to make

no "breaks" which the Republicans can capitalize. So that, four years hence, President Roosevelt will be sweepingly reelected. To do this all party scandals, such as nearly wrecked the Republicans in the Harding administration, must be avoided. Under these circumstances it is not reasonable to believe that so capable a strategist as Mr. Farley will make any blunders of a major political nature.

PERSONAL HISTORY

No career in American politics has been more meteoric in its rise to power than that of James Aloysius Farley. His story is a saga in the annals of that sort of individualism which so many people are today decrying. He owes his success to his own undiluted energy, initiative and everlasting perseverance. Examine him for any single outstanding talent and it is difficult to put one's finger on what has built up his career. It is rather a combination of commonplace qualities, developed to an unusual degree. It was said of Napoleon that he "had the thoughts of the veriest grenadier but he thought them with unprecedented force." In a sense this applies to Jim Farley, who feels that he is merely an average citizen, that he knows the psychology of any small-town voter because he himself is that small-town voter.

Mr. Farley is from the village of Stony Point, Rockland County, New York. He has been a Democrat since boyhood, using as his political text the life and works of Samuel J. Tilden. Unlike Tilden, he went to neither

Yale nor law school, for he was the second of five children of a widowed mother and at eleven delegated to help support the family. But as a boy he carried a torch for William Jennings Bryan, and in the strongly Republican county of Rockland it was not his fault that the Democratic consensus was limited to his own village.

He grew up to a determination to make that county Democratic, and began the job as a crack first baseman on the county ball team. Those were the days of Charles F. Murphy, last of the iron-handed bosses of Manhattan. The ways of Tammany held an intense interest for the young ruralite. Tilden, too, had studied the Wigwam, and the upshot was the smashing of the Tweed "ring." Jim Farley saw a political lesson in Tammany—a sort of latter-day embodiment of Andrew Jackson philosophy of politics with a personal tone and as a business.

Farley joined Tammany Hall to watch the wheels go round. When, in due course, he began selling gypsum for a building trades concern, he followed the Tammany pattern of copious and continual contacts to further his acquaintance. He came to be sales manager of the gypsum firm and boss of Rockland County, New York, climbing to the latter through the town clerkship and the post of town supervisor.

His home life is ideal. He married Elizabeth A. Finnegan at Haverstraw, New York, in 1920, and three children—two girls and a boy—have blessed their union. He is a good Catholic and neither drinks nor smokes.

RELATIONS WITH SMITH

Thus, with an infinite capacity for getting about and seeing people, a sincere handshake and an infallible memory for faces, Jim Farley became a figure in state politics at thirty. In 1918 he led Rockland County to make a surprisingly good showing for the victory ticket headed by Alfred E. Smith for Governor. Mr. Smith was defeated in 1920, but the Rockland County chairman called to assure him that he would be reelected two years later. Mr. Farley was largely responsible for Mr. Smith's announcement in 1922 that he would be a candidate again.

The governorship went to Mr. Smith by a record plurality, and Jim Farley was elected to the Assembly. Farley, however, was repudiated next election for his vote for repeal of the State Enforcement Act, and has never held elective office since; he has, he says, no desire to do so. He threw himself into the Smith cause again in the convention of 1924, and Mr. Smith rewarded him with the chairmanship of the State Athletic Commission. People began to say Jim Farley knew more folks in the state than "Al" himself; while physicians said he had the strongest physical constitution of any man they knew. "Nuf said."

Boxing in New York is intricately tangled up with politics, and the energetic Stony Pointer moved to New York City, left his gypsum firm and organized his own building materials company, which has since swallowed up six others. In 1928, at Houston, the big blue-eyed fellow from New York met more people and toiled ceaselessly for his candidate. He verged on the Tilden record that year with the secretaryship of the Democratic State Committee. Tilden had been chairman.

Jim's loyalty to Al Smith did not make him blind to the fact that the crest of Smith's public career was reached in 1928. Right behind Smith and moving vigorously forward into the public eye strode Franklin D. Roosevelt who accomplished an unprecedented feat in 1928. This feat was riding into office on a wave that everywhere else throughout the country had been a tidal wave of destruction to the Democrats, but which in New York State had landed Roosevelt in the capitol at Albany.

I have already narrated how Farley took hold of the Roosevelt cause in 1928 and carried it unwaveringly forward until that moment when, at the Coliseum at Chicago, in June of 1932 Roosevelt stood before cheering thousands with one arm around Jim Farley's shoulders, then and there acknowledging the debt he owed to the man who had faith in him when no one else was more than mildly interested in the future of another Roosevelt.

MAKER OF MEN RATHER THAN POLICIES

Farley is willing to let the creative accomplishments of the administration rest for the most part in other hands. He is content with the assurance of the warm friendship of his chief. He knows that after all the shouting and tumult have died away it will be up to him, more than to any other man, to direct the future campaigns of his leader and of his party. He is saving his strength and reputation for this task.

So it is that a rural county "boss" of metropolitan savor comes to have national prominence and power. Today, at only forty-five, of commanding height, if of thinning hair, this first of the Roosevelt men has the same genial knack of being honestly and warmly helpful that he had back in Rockland County, New York, where he learned his primary lessons in American politics. From personal experience I have seen him go out of his way to do little favors which few of his assistants would bother about. Unfailingly genial, he is as convinced that no one can resist him for long as he is convinced of his facts. His vivid green-ink signature is known the country over, forever hammering at the forging of a strong and united Democracy.

It should not be thought that, because he has been the field marshal of the Democratic party's fighting forces, Mr. Farley has allowed this fact to interfere with his official duties as Postmaster-General. It happens that under our party system the Postmaster's portfolio is often given to the key man in the party who is to be responsible, directly or indirectly, for the bulk of the patronage distribution. It will be remembered that Will Hays served the Republicans as chairman of the Republican National Committee and, like Mr. Farley, took over the post of Postmaster-General when President Harding assumed office. Farley is no shirker. He is closely attending to post office affairs in a really hard-headed business way.

Thanks to the civil service and the faithful records of many "career men," the Post Office Department is now singularly free from the sort of inefficiency and politics that would inevitably mark it if it were to be permitted to become a football of favoritism at the hands of either party. I have considerable respect for the men who have occupied the office before Mr. Farley —men like Hubert Work under Harding, Harry S. New under Coolidge, and Walter F. Brown under Hoover. They have all done splendid jobs. At the same time, it is my opinion that Mr. Farley's record and personality are such that, before the four years of his office tenure are up, he will bring the Post Office to the highest pitch of operating efficiency that the department has ever known.

Mr. Farley's career and personality have interested me extremely because in them seem combined the best qualities of the old-time political "boss" coupled with the zeal and devotion of a modern crusader. He has taken the Tammany technique, squeezed much of poison out of it and made it serve his purpose. He has given us, almost single-handed, an idealist as President. He has ushered into office the man who stands for the revolution, the man who has surrounded himself in his administration of the Presidency with other revolutionists.

Because of what he has done let us not too hastily forget Jim Farley and give these other Washington revolutionists all the credit. The others may be the makers of revolutions—Jim Farley is the maker of revolutionists. Because of this, in the final analysis, he may be appraised the greater crusader for the New Day in American life.

"Big Jim" lives at Mayflower Hotel, Washington, D. C.

CHAPTER XIV

WHOM TO SEE AND WHERE FIRST TO GO

WASHINGTON is a gold mine of resources. It is the greatest field for profit as well as for service in the United States. Washington abounds in opportunities for the student, the professional man, the business man, the manufacturer and the merchant. Officials of states, counties, cities and towns may secure tremendous aid from Washington sources. Such people should visit Washington more often, establishing contacts for the benefit of themselves and others. "The harvest certainly is great but the reapers are few," and these few are mainly large corporations and professional lobbyists. The truly forgotten man, who is the average business man, is often the one who does the forgetting. Surely, ninety-five per cent of the business men of this country forget the privileges and opportunities offered by Washington and its revolutionists.

A whole book could be written on the sources of information in Washington, and it would be of inestimable value to every banker, manufacturer and merchant. The greatest bulk of such information is obtainable from the Commerce Department, the Agriculture Department, the Interior Department and the Labor Department; but all the departments have their libraries and files. Employes are prepared to give information to those who are interested in the specific lines that their department covers. For instance, if you have any goods which could be used for equipping, feeding and maintaining the great forts, camps or barracks, you should visit the War Department. If the ships could use any of your products, you should visit the Navy Department. The Post Office Department is a tremendous purchaser of supplies. This, in fact, applies to every one of the departments.

As the ten executive departments probably have 90 per cent of the information and control 85 per cent of the business at Washington, this book is confined primarily to a discussion of the heads of these ten departments. In addition, however, to these departments, I am mentioning many more commissions and boards in the chapter next following. Furthermore, when visiting these do not fear any revolutionists. Those whom you meet are not interested in any special political system. All they want is to hold their jobs. The "outs" are the revolutionists—not the "ins," as a rule.

GETTING ABOUT WASHINGTON

You vote for one Representative and two Senators who go to Washington. In most cases, the job as Representative or Senator is the sole source of income for the individual—in other words, it is his job and you are his employer. Every voter, therefore, has a direct influence with his one Representative and two Senators —especially with the Representative. In the case of business men who employ others, this influence is increased by the number employed: that is, a man's influence at Washington depends upon the votes he can control. There is no reason why any reader of this book need go to Washington with his hat in his hand as a beggar. Your Congressman has far more to fear from you than you have to fear from him. When he campaigns for election he refers to himself as "your servant." Therefore, when you go to Washington take him at his word and see that he treats you accordingly.

On reaching Washington, go first to the office of the Superintendent of Public Documents at corner of North Capital and G streets. There purchase a copy of the Congressional Directory, which will cost you one dollar. This is a most useful book, giving the complete organization at Washington, with the locations of the various offices and the names of department heads. Incidentally, you will find in it a story of the life of your Representative and Senators, as well as details regarding other people you may wish to see. While at this office, it is well to take time to browse around and see what else you can buy in the line of books and pamphlets which may be useful to you. The clerks in charge are helpful and anxious to aid strangers in every way. Tell these men what line of business you are in and what you are especially anxious to accomplish by your visit to Washington.

But do not be content merely to do the special errand for which you have gone to Washington. For instance, if you are in the coal business and are visiting Washington to sell coal to some government cantonment, prison, hospital or other institution, take this occasion while in Washington to learn something about the coal business. Ask the clerk in charge of the Document Room what pamphlets he has pertaining to the coal industry. Look over these books and pamphlets and see if one or more of them would be valuable to you. The same applies to whatever industry you may be engaged in. Of course, in the case of coal this book or pamphlet would be prepared by the Interior Department, which has charge of mining and allied industries; but the document itself might not be available at the Interior Department and you would be obliged to return to the Document Room to secure it. While here, it will be well to secure an index or catalogue of all publications to look over at your leisure, writing later for such books and pamphlets as you desire. I merely am emphasizing that the Document Room should be your first source of information.

From the Document Room you should go to the House Office Building which is directly back of the Capitol. As Congress usually does not go into session until noon, the Congressmen are found in their offices during the forenoon. After you get acquainted with a Congressman, you usually can talk with him in the afternoon by visiting the Capitol and sending in your card. They are often so bored with the routine work of the afternoon that they are glad of an excuse to run out and see one of their own constituents in the anteroom. But it is best first to call upon a Congressman at his private office in the morning. Of course in making these suggestions I am assuming that Congress is in session; even if Congress is not in session, the Congressman's office is doubtless open and some one is there who can perhaps be of real help to you. Therefore, whether Congress is in session or is not in session, you should visit the offices of your Representative and your Senators.

CALLING UPON CONGRESSMEN

When visiting offices in Washington, be careful! In many cases, the secretary with whom you talk in the outside office is the wife or the daughter, or some other close relative, of the Representative or Senator. Under the law every Congressman is allowed a certain sum for clerical help in addition to his salary. Hence it is common for Congressmen to employ their wives or children. Have this in mind when talking with the clerks. If you have some one with you it is important to have this in mind when conversing with him or her while waiting in the outside office. All that you say will probably be repeated to the Congressman you are waiting to see! You will find these secretaries and clerks really desirous of being helpful, even though they may appear bored. This may be due to the fact that it is difficult for the Congressman to discipline his wife and relatives! Perhaps that is why these Washington offices have a different atmosphere from ordinary business offices to which you are accustomed.

When visiting a Congressman, remember that his time is limited. Be to the point and be brief. Tell him who you are, what your connections are at home, and what you are trying to accomplish in Washington. Frankly ask him for advice and help. Probably the most important thing he can do for you is to give you an introduction to the special department which can do for you what you desire. Ask the Congressman to call the department on the telephone and secure the name of the man you should see. Then ask him kindly to check this up by telephoning the man himself and stating that he is sending you along to see him. In order to get by the various clerks who are protecting this department chief from the great American public, it is well to ask your Congressman for a brief note of introduction which you can take along with you.

If possible, secure your letter of introduction to the head of the department; that is, if you are visiting the War Department, secure a letter of introduction to the Secretary of War himself. Although these Cabinet members do not know their individual departments intimately, their function being mainly to serve as advisers and contact men to the President, yet they certainly are held in respect by all the employes from the chiefs down to the colored porters. This is especially true in the case of Miss Perkins, Mr. Ickes and the new revolutionists.

In the Post Office Department—of which the First Assistant is really the head as the Postmaster-General himself has almost nothing to do with the actual running of the department—a letter from Postmaster-General Farley is a golden key. A note or order from the Postmaster-General will create more energy and excitement in the Post Office Building than would the explosion of a TNT bomb. Members of the President's Cabinet are not supposed to be able to give you technical information regarding their departments. The departments are too large and the work is usually wholly new to the Secretary when he assumes office. If, however, you want *action*, get in touch with the Secretary himself. One word from him will cut all red tape and get you results in a few hours, when otherwise it might take weeks or months.

Congressmen, department heads and their assistants are human; they are subject to the same appeals; they have the same emotions and the same troubles. Be patient with them and treat them as you would like to be treated under the same circumstances. Let me also add that in all my dealings with Washington during the past thirty years I have personally never seen any evidence of graft on the part of any department head or his assistant. Evidence which came out in connection with members of President Harding's Cabinet was sad, but I am sure that was exceptional. Naturally, a Washington official is under obligations to those who secured him his position, and he will do more for his friends than for persons he has never before met. Hence the importance of letters of introduction from influential people whom he knows.

STUDY COMMITTEE MEMBERSHIP

The influence which a Congressman has with the various departments in Washington is due to the fact that these departments are absolutely dependent upon the Congressmen for their appropriations. The fundamental urge underlying operations in Washington is the "bread and butter" urge. The primary thing that interests 95 per cent of the people in Washington, from the President down to the humblest scrubwoman, is the job. In the case of a few who have independent resources, the pay of the job is not the important factor. Although all are actuated in part by the desire for service and the pride of accomplishment, yet the vast majority of them are absolutely dependent upon their salaries for bread and butter. Hence they are respectful to the Congressmen who control the appropriations that make their jobs possible. One who has not worked in Washington at the time when the Appropriations Committees are discussing these appropriations cannot realize the fear in the heart of every worker until the appropriation upon which his or her salary depends has been recommended, passed by Congress and signed by the President.

All of the above means that you should ascertain from the Congressional Directory as to what committees your Representative and Senators are members of. If you are fortunate enough to have one of these men, or in fact any Congressman from your state, as chairman of the Appropriations Committee, in either the Senate or the House, you immediately are in a strong position. A letter of introduction from such a man will receive the greatest attention. Even if your letter of introduction is from only a member of the Appropriations Committee of the Senate or the House, it will receive good attention, especially if it is written on the stationery of the Appropriations Committee.

There follows a list of the committee chairmen for the Senate and for the House for the session opening March 6, 1933:

SENATE COMMITTEE CHAIRMEN

Agriculture and Forestry ....Smith
Appropriations ....Glass

Audit and Control .... Byrnes
Banking and Currency .... Fletcher
Civil Service .... Logan
Claims .... Bailey
Commerce .... Stephens
District of Columbia .... King
Education and Labor .... Walsh
Enrolled Bills .... Caraway
Expenditures in the Executive Depart-
    ments .... Lewis
Finance .... Harrison
Foreign Relations .... Pittman
Immigration .... Coolidge
Indian Affairs .... Wheeler
Interoceanic Canals .... Gore
Interstate Commerce .... Dill
Irrigation and Reclamation .... Bratton
Judiciary .... Ashurst
Library .... Barkley
Manufactures .... Bulkley
Military Affairs .... Sheppard
Mines and Mining .... Bulow
Naval Affairs .... Trammell
Patents .... Wagner
Pensions .... McGill
Post Office and Post Roads .... McKellar
Printing .... Hayden
Privileges and Elections .... George
Public Buildings and Grounds .... Connally
Public Lands and Surveys .... Kendrick
Rules .... Copeland
Territories and Insular Affairs .... Tydings

HOUSE COMMITTEE CHAIRMEN

Accounts .... Warren
Agriculture .... Jones
Appropriations .... Buchanan
Banking and Currency .... Stegall
Census .... Lozier
Civil Service .... Jeffers
Claims .... Black
Coinage, Weights and Measures .... Somers
Disposition of Useless Executive Papers.. Green
District of Columbia .... Norton
Education .... Douglass
Election of President, Vice President and
   Representatives in Congress .... Carley
Elections No. 1 .... Clark
Elections No. 2 .... Gavagan
Elections No. 3 .... Kerr
Enrolled Bills .... Parsons
Expenditures in the Executive Depart-
   ments .... Cochran
Flood Control .... Wilson
Foreign Affairs .... McReynolds
Immigration and Naturalization .... Dickstein
Indian Affairs .... Howard
Insular Affairs .... McDuffie
Interstate and Foreign Commerce ...... Rayburn
Invalid Pensions .... Underwood
Irrigation and Reclamation .... Chavez
Judiciary .... Sumners
Labor .... Connery

Library .... Keller
Memorials .... Morehead
Merchant Marine, Radio and Fisheries.. Bland
Military Affairs .... McSwain
Mines and Mining .... Smith
Naval Affairs .... Vinson
Patents .... Sirovich
Pensions .... Gasque
Post Office and Post Roads .... Mead
Printing .... Lambeth
Public Buildings and Grounds .... Lanham
Public Lands .... DeRouen
Revision of the Laws .... Harlan
Rivers and Harbors .... Mansfield
Rules .... Pou
War Claims .... Allgood
Ways and Means .... Collier
World War Veterans' Legislation .... Doughton

You should also study the Committees of Congress from a point of view other than an Appropriations Committee. For instance, if you are endeavoring to secure some action from or to obtain a loan from or to sell goods to the Department of Agriculture or one of its subsidiary boards, then the chairman of the Agricultural Committee of either the Senate or the House, or even a member of one of these two committees, can be of inestimable help. There are about thirty-five of these major committees, each having five or more members. The chairman and the majority of the members of each committee are of the dominant party. With the present Congress, the Democrats are dominant in both the Senate and the House and hence have a majority of each committee. The preceding Congress during the latter part of the Hoover administration operated under a Senate controlled by the Republicans and under a House controlled by the Democrats. Under those circumstances, the Republicans had the chairmanship and the majority of the Senate Committees and the Democrats had the chairmanship and the majority of the House Committees. It is evident that during a Democratic administration a letter from a revolutionist is more influential than one from a Republican.

It will be seen from this that the time you give to a study of the Congressional Directory is well spent. It is important to familiarize yourself with the committees of which your two Senators and all of your state's Representatives are members. I say "all" because if the one Congressman from your district happens to be a new man—especially of the Republican party—it may be better for you to go to some other Congressman of your state who has served a longer term and is of the Democratic party. The first step is to determine the department and the special man in that department who can accomplish for you what you desire. The second step is to study the committees and ascertain what Congressmen or Senator from your state would have the most influence with the department with which you are anxious to do business. If your own Representative has little influence under the circumstances, it may be best for you to go to your Senators. Each of the two Senators from your state is anxious to have your vote and influence at the next election. Hence, they are as anxious to serve you as is your own Representative.

LETTERS OF INTRODUCTION

In view of the service that these Senators and possibly your Representatives can be to you, it may be best to secure from some influential person at home a letter of introduction to the man you want to see, before you go to Washington in case he does not know who you are. It is worth your time and trouble to ascertain who were most helpful in securing the election of the man you are to visit. This information can best be secured by personally visiting the chairman of his party campaign committee for your district for the election of November, 1932. His name can always be obtained by calling up the offices of the state Democratic or Republican committee, according to the party your Congressman is a member of. A letter from the chairman or one of the members of this state committee may serve as a good introduction to a Congressman if it is written by some one the Congressman knows personally. A letter from the Governor or Lieutenant-Governor of the state is always given respectful consideration. The best letter, of course, is from some personal friend of the Congressman whom the Congressman respects or to whom the Congressman is under obligations. The same applies to letters to Senators. By careful inquiry it is always possible to locate some such man whom you or one of your friends personally knows.

Considering the power of friendship, this opens another field of approach to Cabinet members, division heads and their assistants. In addition to carrying to the departments a letter from a Senator or Representative, it is well to have, if possible, a letter of introduction from some one whom the Cabinet member personally knows and trusts. You cannot blame Cabinet members and even division heads for not seeing everyone who calls and for giving scant attention to the vast majority. The demands on the time of these Washington officials is so great that they must absolutely "pick and choose" in order to get through the day's work. They are hard-working people and do not begin to have the time for interviews that Congressmen have, as the latter are usually busier just before an election than they ever are afterwards! Therefore, if you can establish some common point of contact between a Cabinet member and yourself, it gives you both a distinct advantage.

For this reason it is important to study the lives of Cabinet members in order to establish such a point of contact. If you happen to know personally only one member of the President's Cabinet, he will serve for the best possible point of contact for any other member. These Cabinet members not only meet together at the White House Cabinet Meetings twice a week, but they are in constant telephone and social contact with one another. However, if you do not personally know any member of the Cabinet, your next job is to find some high-grade person whom you and the Cabinet member both know. This means that you should ascertain the home city of the Cabinet member and think of some one you know in that city whom the Cabinet member would also know. Another method of approach is to look up what line of business the Cabinet member has been in and with what concerns he has worked and who were his business associates. Look through this list and see if you can find any you personally know. It may be—and this is likely—that the Cabinet member you are desirous of approaching has had a political career. If so, this opens another line of approach.

WOMEN AND CHILDREN

There is the social and family side to the lives of Cabinet members, division heads and all other Washington workers. They nearly all have wives and most of them have children. The wives have friends and the children have friends. A personal longhand note from a child to the father or from some other relative or friend of the man you wish to see is often effective. I am certainly not advising that you secure these letters for any unfair purpose. The fact is that these Cabinet members and division heads are swamped with mail and visitors with requests of every kind. Many of these requests are unjust and are not in the interest of the country. The Cabinet members and other officials must have some quick and easy way of separating the sheep from the goats. Experience has shown that "references" offer the simplest means of classification. It is absolutely essential that some method be adopted by these officials. It has been found that the method above outlined is the most satisfactory in the end even when used by revolutionists.

It is with these objects in view that I have given in this book so many details regarding President Roosevelt's Cabinet and other people of importance in Washington. I have also endeavored to cover the lives of certain key assistants to these officials. Owing to the tremendous pressure on these officials, they are compelled to depend heavily upon the judgment of their personal private secretaries. These often are young people who, although drawing salaries of from only twenty-five to fifty dollars a week, have considerable influence. They are helpful in securing appointments and often trusted by many officials to write entire letters and orders, bringing them to the officials only for signature. I have known cases where the personal secretary of the Cabinet officer practically ran the entire department with expenditures of millions of dollars. This even applied to the entire United States Government when President Woodrow Wilson was ill and Secretary Tumulty was in charge of the White House.

CHAPTER XV

RESOURCES IN WASHINGTON

WASHINGTON is still an undeveloped gold mine, though the city is in the control of so-called revolutionists. Revolutionists cannot upset the multiplication table. Facts are still facts and statistics are still statistics whatever the purpose of the administration. This means that the archives of Washington are still of great value and are growing more valuable every year. This applies to the files of the various departments as well as to the libraries, museums and other mines of resources.

TWO GROUPS IN WASHINGTON

There are two groups in Washington today living entirely apart from each other. Washington is like a man with two distinct personalities. Up to this chapter I have referred mainly to the newer group which has come to Washington and whom I style, in a friendly way, the "revolutionists."

Let me here treat of the older group who do not know that a revolution is in process! These are the scientists, librarians, statisticians and others who think only of their work without any regard to politics. They go to their offices every morning and return home every night with the same habits and thoughts, more or less unaffected by who is President or what are the immediate goals of the administration. To them all we owe a great debt.

Among these nonpolitical groups, I include the *Civil Service Commission*, 7th & F Streets (phone National 0072 and 0075) of which Mr. George E. Campbell is president. Then we have the *United States Bureau of Efficiency* in the Winder Building, 17th & F Streets (phone National 8686) of which Herbert D. Brown is chief. There also should be mentioned the *United States Employees' Compensation Commission* in the Old Land Office Building, 7th & E Streets (phone National 7177) of which Mrs. Bessie Parker Brueggeman is chairman; and the *General Accounting Commission* which has its own office building at 5th & F Streets (phone District 8465), of which J. R. McCarl is the head. There is the *Interstate Commerce Commission* which also has its own building at 18th Street and Pennsylvania Avenue (phone National 7460). This commission rotates as to its chairman and therefore I will give just the secretary's name, George B. McGinty. There is also the *United States Railroad Administration* which is in the Hurley-Wright Building (phone National 7940), and the *Bureau of Standards* connected with the Department of Commerce.

BUSINESS COMMISSIONS

Those desiring financial information should go to the *Federal Reserve Board* in the Treasury Building (phone National 6400). It is well to first ask for Eugene R. Black or his assistant H. Warner Martin. This board is becoming an important institution and is collecting a mass of valuable facts and statistics. The *Federal Trade Commission* is also of great interest to bankers and business men as it now has charge of the "Truth in Securities" Act of 1933, as well as its former duties of supervising fair trade practices. It is located at 2001 Constitution Avenue (phone National 7720) and Charles H. March is chairman.

Business men should also keep in touch with the *United States Tariff Commission*, located in the Old Land Office Building (phone National 3947), of which Robert L. O'Brien is chairman. We all have to visit the *United States Board of Tax Appeals* once in a while, on Constitution Avenue at 12th Street (phone National 5771). Its chairman is Logan Morris; its secretary, Robert C. Tracy, and its clerk, Bertus D. Gamble. It is important that bankers, business men and others should keep in touch with these offices personally and keep their finances in repair. Letters are unsatisfactory. Much better results are secured by both the government and the citizen through personal interviews.

Then we have the *Federal Farm Board*, 1300 E Street (phone Metropolitan 3687), of which Henry Morgenthau, Jr. is chairman. The *Federal Power Commission* is at the Interior Department Building (phone National 1880), of which Commission Frank R. McNick is chairman. The *Federal Oil Conservation Board*, likewise in the Interior Building (phone National 1880); and the *Federal Radio Commission* is in the National Press Building (phone Metropolitan 2180). These commissions are constantly growing in power and importance. They are mostly built up of men of good character who are earnestly working for the best interests of the nation, irrespective of politics.

IMPORTANT BOARDS

Another group of commissions comprises the following: *Veterans' Administration* at Arlington Building (phone National 6740), of which Brig.-Gen. Frank T. Hines is administrator; *Federal Board for Vocational Education* at 1800 E Street (phone District 8388), of which J. C. Wright is director; the *United States Board of Mediation*, 1800 E Street (phone National 8460), of which Samuel E. Winslow is chairman. There also are the *United States Shipping Board* and the *Merchant Fleet Corporation*, which are being consolidated. These can be found in the New Navy Building (phone National 5200). There are also other boards such as the *Panama Canal Board* at the Munitions Building, Constitution Avenue and 19th Street (phone National 4294); the *Joint Board*, Room 2743 Navy Department Building (phone District 2900), and the *United States Council of National Defense*, also in the Munitions Building (phone National 2520), and the *Commission on Navy Yards and Naval Stations* in the Navy Department Building (phone District 2900). Those interested in aeronautics should go to the Navy Department Building, Room 3638 (phone District 2900) or Room 3841 (phone National 5212).

The *Alien Property Custodian* is at the Hurley-Wright Building at 18th Street and Pennsylvania Avenue (phone National 5785). The *Mixed Claims*

Commission is in the Investment Building, 1511 K Street (phone District 4259). The *Tripartite Claims Commission* is in the same building (phone District 8768). But the *International Joint Commission* is in the Old Patent Office Building (phone District 3764) and the *Inter-American High Commission* is at the Department of Commerce at 400 14th Street. There also is a *Boundary Commission relating to the United States, Alaska and Canada,* which is also at the Commerce Building (phone National 5060); while the *Boundary Commission concerning United States and Mexico* has its office in the First National Bank Building, El Paso, Texas. The *International Fisheries Commission* have their headquarters at the University of Washington, Seattle, Washington. The *Inland Waterways Corporation* is located at the Munitions Building (phone National 2520) and *International Highway Commission* in Room 6107 of the Interior Building.

CONSERVATION COMMISSIONS

There are eleven offices which should be visited by those who are interested in maps, planning, parks, monuments and similar developments. These are as follows:

Committee on the Conservation and Administration of the Public Domain at 6342 Interior Department Building (phone National 1880); *Board of Surveys and Maps* of the Federal Government in Room 6206 of the Interior Department Building (phone National 1880); *National Capital Park and Planning Commission* in the New Navy Building (phone National

2520); *Public Buildings and Public Parks* of the National Capital also in the New Navy Building (phone National 2520); the *Commission of Fine Arts* in the Interior Department Building (phone National 1880); *Rock Creek and Potomac Parkway Commission*, Navy Building (phone National 2520); *Washington National Monument Society*, Wm. R. Harr, secretary, 36 Primrose Street, Chevy Chase, Maryland (phone Wisconsin 3193); *Arlington Memorial Amphitheater Commission*, Secretary of War, chairman, 17th Street south of Pennsylvania Avenue (phone National 2520); *American Battle Monuments Commission*, Room 6314 Commerce Building (phone National 5060); *Perry's Victory Memorial Commission*, General Office, Put-in-Bay, Ohio; *National Memorial Commission*, at 923 R Street.

LIBRARIES—MUSEUMS

Whenever I have any spare time in Washington I enjoy going to the *Smithsonian Institute*. This is on the Mall (phone National 1811) and my good friend Dr. C. G. Abbot is at the head. The assistant secretary is Mr. Alexander Wetmore and the librarian is William L. Corbin. Any one of these will be glad to arrange to have you go through the building and will answer questions. Under the direction of the Smithsonian Institute is the *National Museum*, the *National Gallery of Art*, the *Bureau of American Ethnology*, the *National Zoölogical Park*, the *Astrophysical Observatory*, the *Division of Radiation and Organisms*, and the *Bureau Cataloguing International Scientific Literature*. The

United States Geographical Board located in Room 5323 in the Department of the Interior, with Frank Bond as chairman, is doing splendid work. Do not forget to visit the *National Academy of Sciences*, Constitution Avenue and 21st Street (phone District 2614). Under this Academy is the *National Research Council* of which W. H. Howell is chairman.

A pleasant hour can be spent at the *Pan-American Union*, located at 17th Street between Constitution Avenue and C Street (phone National 6635), of which Dr. L. S. Rowe is director-general. In the same building is the office of the *Pan-American Sanitary Bureau* with General Hugh S. Cummings as director. When on 17th Street it is worth while to visit the *American National Red Cross Building*, between D and E streets (phone National 5400), of which John Barton Payne is chairman. Women will be interested in visiting the *Congressional Club*, 2001 New Hampshire Avenue (phone Potomac 5196), composed of women in official life and which has a sort of semi-governmental status.

MISCELLANEOUS COMMISSIONS

The *United States Soldiers' Home* is operated by a board of commissioners, located at the home (phone Adams 9100). Major General Henry P. McCain is governor. The *Puerto Rican Relief Commission* is found in Room 3044 of the Munitions Building (phone National 2520). The *Columbia Institution for the Deaf* is located at Kendall Green (phone Lincoln 2450), and the Rev. Ulysses G. B. Pierce is secretary. The *Colum-*

bia Hospital for Women is located at 25th Street and
Pennsylvania Avenue (phone Potomac 4210) and the
superintendent is Dr. S. B. Ragsdale. The *National
Training School for Boys* is on Bladensburg Road
(phone Lincoln 0197); and the *Federal Employment
Stabilization Board* is in the Commerce Building (phone
5060).

NEW BOARDS

Most of the above boards have been in existence for
many years and have stood up under both Democratic
and Republican administrations. The revolutionists,
however, felt that they must also have some boards to
carry out their work in addition to the Federal Reserve
Board and certain others. I especially have in mind the
Reconstruction Finance Corporation (although it was
organized under the Hoover administration), the *National Recovery Administration*, the *Farm Administration* and the various loaning boards. These boards at
the moment cast a shadow over all of the other boards
and commissions of the government. Therefore, instead
of treating them in a general way, I am analyzing them
according to their functions. Perhaps it would be only
fair to say that the following distribution is an analysis
of the personnel of the revolutionist organization apart
from the old-time group alignment described above.

Super-Cabinet

The President and his Cabinet.
Chief Co-ordinator: Frank C. Walker.

Lewis W. Douglas, the Director of the Budget.

L. W. Robert, Jr., Assistant Secretary of the Treasury.

Jesse H. Jones, the chairman of the Reconstruction Finance Corp.

Henry Morgenthau, Jr., the governor of the Farm Credit Administration.

William F. Stevenson, the chairman of the board of Home Owners' Loan Corp.

Hugh S. Johnson, the administrator of the industrial recovery act.

George Peek, the special assistant on agricultural exports.

Harry L. Hopkins, the Federal relief administrator.

Arthur E. Morgan, the chairman of the board of the Tennessee Valley Authority.

Joseph B. Eastman, the Federal railroad co-ordinator.

Robert Fechner, the director of the civilian conservation corps.

"Brain Trust"

The group of special economic advisers popularly known as the *"Brain Trust"* includes the following: Prof. Rexford G. Tugwell, Prof. Adolph A. Berle, Jr., Prof. Mordecai Ezekiel, Prof. John Dickinson, William C. Bullitt, Lewis Douglas, Prof. Felix Frankfurter, Prof. George F. Warren, Prof. James H. Rogers, Dr. Isadore Lubin, Prof. Milburn L. Wilson, James P. Warburg, Charles W. Taussig, Dr. Leo Wolman, Prof. Leverett S. Lyon.

Reconstruction Finance Corporation

Board of Directors: Jesse H. Jones (chairman), Harvey Couch, Wilson McCarthy, William H. Woodin, John J. Blaine, C. B. Merriam, Frederick H. Taber.

Secretary: G. R. Cooksey.

Treasurer: H. A. Mulligan.

Employment Administration

Director of Civilian Conservation Corps: Robert Fechner, Dept. of Labor.

Director: W. Frank Persons.

Advisory Council: Robert M. Hutchins, Chairman.

State Directors:
Alabama—A. J. Speer, Birmingham.
Arizona—Ray Gilbert, Phoenix.
Arkansas—W. A. Rooksbery, Little Rock.
California—Jack Stellern, Los Angeles.
Colorado—Craig S. Vincent, Denver.
Connecticut—Miss Millicent Pond, Hartford.
Delaware—Howard P. Young, Wilmington.
Florida—Dr. Edward M. L'Engle, Jacksonville.
Georgia—Cator Woolford, Atlanta.
District of Columbia—David Roml, Washington.
Idaho—John Foreman, Pocatello.
Illinois—Roy Jacobsen, Chicago.
Indiana—Eugene C. Foster, Indianapolis.
Iowa—Hans C. Pfund, Des Moines.
Kansas—Samuel Wilson, Topeka.
Kentucky—Edward F. Seiller, Louisville.
Louisiana—Judge Rufus Foster, New Orleans.
Maine—Eugene I. Cummings, Westbrook.
Maryland—Oliver C. Short, Baltimore.
Massachusetts—Robert S. Quimby, Watertown.
Michigan—Clarence E. Weiss, Detroit.
Minnesota—O. D. Hollenbeck, Minneapolis.
Mississippi—George R. Nobles, Jackson.
Missouri—Martin A. Lewis, Jefferson City.
Montana—R. R. Purcell, Helena.
Nebraska—George Hodge, Lincoln.

Nevada—David E. Ericson, Reno.

New Hampshire—Harold M. Davis, Nashua.

New Jersey—Harry Hunter Tukey, Madison.

New Mexico—Waite J. Keener, Belen.

New York—Wilfred H. Winans, New York City.

North Carolina—Capus M. Waynick, High Point.

North Dakota—James Taylor, Bismarck.

Ohio—Stanley B. Matthewson, Columbus.

Oklahoma—Edward G. Burke, Oklahoma City.

Oregon—E. L. Mersereau, Portland.

Pennsylvania—John McCune, Jr., Grove City.

Rhode Island—Percival De St. Aubin, Providence.

South Carolina—Thomas K. Johnstone, Columbia.

South Dakota—S. H. Collins, Aberdeen.

Tennessee—Green Benton, Nashville.

Texas—Byron Mitchell, Austin.

Utah—George A. Yager, Salt Lake City.

Vermont—H. R. Pierce, Montpelier.

Virginia—George W. Guy, Richmond.

Washington—Paul Pigott, Seattle.

West Virginia—James H. McGinnis, Beckley.

Wisconsin—Paul C. Winner, Madison.

Wyoming—James Morgan, Cheyenne.

Farm Administration

Administrator: George N. Peek. *Co-Administrator:* Charles Brand.

Frederic Claxton and Frederic Clemson Howe, representatives of *consumers' interests.*

Cotton Production Administrator: C. A. Cobb.

Robert Stevens, of J. P. Stevens & Co., liaison officer at Washington between Secretary of Agriculture Henry A. Wallace and National Recovery Administrator Hugh S. Johnson.

M. L. Wilson, chief of wheat production section of Agricultural Adjustment Administration.

Smith W. Brookhart, special adviser to the Agricultural Adjustment Administration.

Farm Loans

Henry Morgenthau, Jr., *Governor of the Farm Credit Administration.*

Application blanks may be obtained by addressing C. W. Carson (formerly of Amarillo, Texas), Federal Farm Board, 1300 E St., Washington, D. C.

Home Loans Administration

Chairman of Federal Home Loan Bank Board: William F. Stevenson.

Secretary: A. E. Hutchison.

Field Director: Frank A. Chase.

General Counsel of the Federal Home Loan Bank Board and the Home Owners' Loan Corp.: Horace Russell; Gus C. Edwards, associate counsel.

Treasurer of the Home Owners' Loan Corp.: James G. Strong.

Assistant General Managers: W. P. Goodman and James A. Hoyt.

State administrators are as follows: *Alabama*—E. H. Wrenn, Jr., Birmingham. *Arizona*—William R. Wayland, Phoenix. *Arkansas*—Frank Milwee, Little Rock. *California*—Monroe Butler, Los Angeles. *Colorado*—John Lynch, Denver. *Connecticut*—Peter M. Kennedy, New Haven. *Delaware*—Thomas B. Young, Wilmington. *District of Columbia*—Charles A. Jones, Washington. *Florida*—James R. Stockton, Jacksonville. *Georgia*—Frank Holden, Atlanta; general attorneys for the assistant state managers, Charles J. Bloch, Macon, and David S. Atkinson, Savannah. *Idaho*—C. C. Wilburn, Boise City. *Illinois*—William G. Donne, Chicago. *In-*

diana—E. Kirk McKinney, Indianapolis. *Iowa*—Geis Botsford, Des Moines. *Kansas*—W. M. Price, Topeka. *Kentucky* —W. T. Beckham, Louisville. *Louisiana*—Paul B. Habans, New Orleans. *Maine*—F. Harold Dubord, Portland. *Maryland*—David I. Stiefel, Baltimore. *Massachusetts*—Charles F. Cotter, Boston. *Michigan*—John F. Hamilton, Detroit. *Minnesota*—Otto Bremer, St. Paul. *Mississippi*—Wiley A. Blair, Jackson. *Missouri*—G. C. Vandover, St. Louis. *Montana*— E. C. Carruth, Great Falls. *Nebraska*—Charles Smrha, Grand Island. *Nevada*—George W. Friedhoof, Reno. *New Jersey*— G. Frank Shanley, Trenton. *New Hampshire*—Charles E. Bartlett, Manchester. *New Mexico*—E. C. Robertson, Albuquerque. *New York*—Vincent Dailey, New York City. *North Carolina*—Alan S. O'Neal, Salisbury. *North Dakota*—Fred W. McLean, Fargo. *Ohio*—Henry G. Brunner, Columbus. *Oklahoma*—John F. Mahr, Tulsa. *Oregon*—J. P. Lipscomb, Portland. *Pennsylvania*—Jacob H. Mays, Philadelphia. *South Carolina*—Donald S. Matheson, Columbia; Greenville branch, T. P. P. Carson. *South Dakota*—Almer C. Steensland, Sioux Falls. *Tennessee*—Charles H. Litterer, Nashville. *Texas*— James Shaw, Dallas. *Utah*—J. F. Fowles, Salt Like City. *Vermont*—Park H. Pollard, Rutland. *Virginia*—John J. Wicker, Jr., Richmond. *Washington*—W. E. McCroskey, Seattle. *West Virginia*—Walter V. Ross, Charleston. *Wisconsin*—J. R. McQuillan, Madison. *Wyoming*—Bayard Wilson, Casper.

National Recovery Administration

Administrator: Gen. Hugh S. Johnson. *Assistant for Industry:* Robert W. Lea. *Assistant for Labor:* Edward F. McGrady of Washington, D. C., legislative representative for many years of the American Federation of Labor. *Chief of Legal Division:* Donald R. Richberg, of Chicago, attorney for railroad brotherhoods and recognized authority in public utility rate litigation. *Chief of Research and Planning Division:*

Dr. Alexander Sachs, economist and director of the Lehman Corp. *Deputy Administrators:* W. L. Allen, Prof. Earl D. Howard, Arthur D. Whiteside, Maj.-Gen. C. C. Williams, K. M. Simpson, Nelson Slater, Malcolm Muir, Philip C. Kemp, Harry O. King, Major R. B. Paddock, W. W. Pickard, Dr. Lindsay Rogers, Sol Rosenblatt.

Assistants: Robert K. Strauss, F. M. Robinson. *Chief of Administrative Division:* John W. Power. *Chief of Public Relations Division:* Boaz Long.

Special Industrial Recovery Board will include in addition to Gen. Hugh S. Johnson the following: Chairman, Secretary of Commerce Daniel C. Roper; Attorney General Homer S. Cummings; Secretary of Labor Miss Frances Perkins; Secretary of Agriculture Henry A. Wallace; Secretary of the Interior Harold L. Ickes; Budget Director Lewis W. Douglas; Chairman Charles H. March of the Trade Commission.

Executive Committee of Industrial Control: Chairman, John H. Fahey, Vice Chairman, Robert E. Wood, Secretary, Henry H. Heimann.

LABOR ADVISORY BOARD

Dr. Leo Wolman, chairman, John Frey, Joseph Franklin, William H. Green, Sidney Hillman, Father Francis Haas, Rose Schneiderman.

INDUSTRIAL ADVISORY BOARD

Walter C. Teagle, chairman, Austin Finch, Edward N. Hurley, Louis Kirstein, Alfred P. Sloan, Jr., Gerard Swope, William J. Vereen, John B. Elliott, Henry H. Heimann, David R. Coker, E. Kent Swift.

CONSUMERS' ADVISORY BOARD

Mrs. C. C. Rumsey, chairman, Prof. Frank Graham, Mrs. Joseph J. Daniels, Miss Belle Sherwin, Prof. Alonzo E. Taylor, Lucius R. Eastman.

Senator Robert F. Wagner, chairman; William H. Green, president of the American Federation of Labor; Dr. Leo Wolman, professor of economics of Columbia University; John L. Lewis, president of the United Mine Workers of Ameri a; Walter C. Teagle, president of the Standard Oil Company of New Jersey; Gerard Swope, president of the General Electric Company; Louis E. Kirstein, general manager of William Filene's Sons Company of Boston.

EMERGENCY RE-EMPLOYMENT PROGRAM

Executive Director: Gen. Thomas H. Hammond.
District Recovery Boards:

New England—Robert Shepard, Providence; Redfield Proctor, Proctorville, Vt.; James P. Moriarty, Boston; Roy D. Hunter, West Farmington, N. H.; Joseph Alsop, Hartford, Conn.; James F. Carberry and Walter S. Bucklin, Boston.

Eastern District (parts of New York, New Jersey and Connecticut)—John L. Hartnett, Troy, N. Y.; John Vanneck, New York, N. Y.; Pauline M. Sabin, Southampton, L. I.; Dr. Nicholas Murray Butler, Columbia University; Charles A. Beard, New Milford, Conn.; John R. Hardin, Newark, N. J.; John Milton, Jersey City.

Buffalo District (western New York)—Dr. Francis E. Fronczak, Buffalo; Bernard E. Finucane, Rochester; Mrs. C. Leonard O'Connor, Portland; Alexis N. Muench, Syracuse; Clarence H. Kennedy, Elmira; John H. Wright, Jamestown; E. J. Williams, Pinsdale.

Philadelphia District (eastern Pennsylvania and Delaware) —Samuel S. Fels, Philadelphia; J. T. Skelly, Wilmington, Del.; I. B. Finkelstein, Wilmington; Fred A. Heim, Bethlehem, Pa.; George W. Hensel, Jr., Quarryville, Pa.; Thomas Kennedy, Hazleton, Pa.; Karl De Schweinitz, Philadelphia.

Pittsburgh District (western Pennsylvania and West Vir-

ginia)—Ernest T. Weir, Weirton, W. Va.; George B. Sprowls, Claysville, Pa.; J. C. Chaplin, Pittsburgh; Gray Silver, Martinsburg, W. Va.; Patrick T. Fagan, Pittsburgh; Arthur Colgrove, Corry, Pa.; George L. Coyle, Charleston, W. Va.

Charleston District (South Carolina)—R. M. Jefferies, Walterboro; Sheppard Nash, Sumter; A. L. M. Wiggin, Hartsville; Alfred Moore, Wellford; John T. Stevens, Kershaw; Earl Britton, Columbia; Wilton Hall, Anderson.

STATE RECOVERY BOARDS

Maine—Edward P. Murray of Bangor, Elmon O. Tibbetts of Waterville, Luther Dana of Westbrook, Henri Benoit of Portland, John B. Michaud of Van Buren, Charles Blood of Dover-Foxcroft, Wallace Mabee of Eastport, George Desjardins of Oldtown, Robert E. Daggett of Waterville.

New Hampshire—Ernest M. Hopkins of Hanover, John B. Jameson of Concord, Huntley M. Spaulding of Rochester, Andrew Jackson of Middletown, John L. Barry of Manchester, Ovide J. Coulombe of Berlin, Dana J. Brown of Ossipee, Albert Hyslop of Portsmouth, Alfred J. Pierce of Bennington.

Vermont—Newman K. Chaffee of Rutland, A. Vail Allen of Fairhaven, T. B. Wright of Burlington, Dr. W. H. Beardsley of Springfield, Harold Mason of Brattleboro, J. E. Athol of Hardwick, J. E. O'Donnell of St. Albans, H. E. Raymond of Sheldon, Harry W. Witters of St. Johnsbury.

Massachusetts—P. A. O'Connell of Boston, Stanley King of Amherst College, Allan Forbes of State Steel Trust Co., Boston, Charles J. Mahoney of Boston, E. Kent Swift of Whitinsville, James Wall of North Adams, Edward Filene of Boston, Edward A. French of Boston & Maine R. R., Miss Margaret Weisman of Massachusetts Consumers League, John J. Power of Worcester.

Connecticut—Frank Bergin of New Haven, Edward G.

Dolan of Manchester, Fanny D. Welch of Columbia, Don A. Costor of Bridgeport, E. Kent Hubbard of Middletown, William Fitzgerald of Norwich, Joseph Holloran of New Britain, John J. Walsh of Stamford, Milton McDonalruk of Bridgeport.

Rhode Island—James E. Smith of Providence, Archie W. Merchant of Providence, Dr. Horace P. Beck of Newport, John J. Dunn of Westerly, Myles Johnson of Newport, Albert Lamarre of Pawtucket, William A. Shawcross of Providence, Louis W. Cappelli of Cranston, Edmond H. Guerine of Woonsocket.

New York—W. Averell Harriman of New York City, Chairman, James F. Conway of Plattsburg, Peter D. Kierman of Albany, Albert Kessinger of Rome, Perley Morse of Suffern, William A. Denison of Rochester, Moses Symington of Long Island City, David J. McLean of Brooklyn, Julia D. Hanson of Schenectady, P. Sherwin Haxton of Oakfield.

New Jersey—Theodore Boettcher of Paterson, Ferdinand Roebling of Trenton, Charles J. Roh of Newark, H. C. Beaver of Harrison, Thomas N. McCarter of Newark, Clinton L. Bardo of Camden, Charles Edison of West Orange, Lester Collins of Morristown, Percy Stewart of Bloomfield.

Pennsylvania—W. M. Jacoby of Pittsburgh, John Phillips of Harrisburg, Warren W. Bailey, Jr., of Johnstown, Charles Lynch of Greensburg, J. David Stern of Philadelphia, Matthew H. McClockey, Jr., of Philadelphia, Louis C. Emmons of Swarthmore, M. E. Comerford of Scranton, S. Forry Laucks of York.

Public Works Administration

Administrator: Secretary of the Interior Harold L. Ickes.
Public Works Board: Secretary Harold L. Ickes, Secretary of Commerce Daniel C. Roper, Secretary of Agriculture Henry

A. Wallace, Secretary of War George H. Dern, Secretary of Labor Miss Frances Perkins, Attorney General Homer S. Cummings, Budget Director Lewis W. Douglas, L. W. Robert, Jr., Assistant Secretary of the Treasury in charge of Public Buildings and Purchases, Oscar Chapman, second assistant. Executive Assistant: Emil Hurja.

Deputy Administrator: Col. Waite.

Regional advisers:

Region 1—Maine, Vermont, New Hampshire, Massachusetts, Rhode Island and Connecticut; headquarters, Boston; adviser, Ralph L. Cooper of Belfast, Me.

Region 2—New York, Pennsylvania and New Jersey; headquarters, New York City; adviser, Edward J. Flynn, present Secretary of State of New York.

Region 3—Illinois, Indiana, Michigan, Ohio and Wisconsin; headquarters, Chicago; adviser, Daniel J. Tobin of Indianapolis.

Region 4—North Dakota, South Dakota, Nebraska, Minnesota, Iowa and Wyoming; headquarters, Omaha; adviser, Frank Murphy, Wheaton, Minn.

Region 5—Montana, Idaho, Washington and Oregon; headquarters, Portland; adviser, Dana Marshall of Portland, Ore.

Region 6—California, Nevada, Utah, Arizona; headquarters, San Francisco; adviser, Justis S. Wardell of San Francisco.

Region 7—Texas, Louisiana, New Mexico; headquarters, Fort Worth; adviser, Clifford Jones, Spur, Texas.

Region 8—Colorado, Kansas, Oklahoma, Missouri and Arkansas; headquarters, Kansas City; adviser, Vincent M. Miles, Fort Smith, Ark.

Region 9—Mississippi, Alabama, Georgia, South Carolina, Florida; headquarters, Atlanta; adviser, Monroe Johnson, Marion, S. C.

Region 10—Tennessee, Kentucky, West Virginia, Maryland, Delaware, Virginia and North Carolina; headquarters, Richmond; adviser, George L. Radcliffe, Baltimore.

State Boards:

Alabama—Milton H. Fies of Birmingham, Mayer W. Aldridge of Montgomery, and Fred Thompson of Mobile.

Arizona—William W. Lane of Phoenix, Leslie G. Hardy of Tucson, and Moses B. Hazeltine of Prescott.

Arkansas—E. C. Horner of Helena, Haley M. Bennett of Little Rock, and John S. Parks of Fort Smith.

California—Hamilton H. Cotton of San Clemente, Franck Havenner of San Francisco, and E. F. Scattergood of Los Angeles.

Colorado—Thomas A. Duke of Pueblo, Morrison Shafroth of Denver, and Miss Josephine Roche of Denver.

Connecticut—John J. Pelley of New Haven, Archibald McNeil of Bridgeport, and Harvey L. Thompson of Middletown.

Delaware—Lee Layton of Dover, Will P. Truit of Milford, and William Speakman of Wilmington.

Florida—C. B. Treadway of Tallahassee, W. H. Burwell of Miami, and T. L. Buckner of Jacksonville.

Georgia—Thomas J. Hamilton of Augusta, Arthur Lucas of Atlanta, and Ryburn Clay of Atlanta.

Idaho—Beecher Hitchcock of Sandpoint, Frank E. Johnesse of Boise, and Edward C. Rich of Boise.

Illinois—Carter H. Harrison of Chicago, James L. Houghteling of Chicago, and James H. Andrews of Kewanee.

Indiana—Lewis G. Ellingham of Fort Wayne, Charles B. Somers of Indianapolis, and John N. Dyer of Vincennes.

Iowa—Harold M. Cooper of Marshalltown, W. F. Riley of Des Moines, and W. P. Adler of Davenport.

Kansas—R. J. Paulette of Salina, Martin Miller of Fort Scott, and Ralph Snyder of Manhattan.

Kentucky—Wylie B. Bryan of Louisville, N. St. G. T. Carmichael of Kyrock, and James C. Stone of Lexington.

Louisiana—James E. Smitherman of Shreveport, Edward Rightor of New Orleans and James W. Thomson of New Orleans.

Maine—James M. Shea of Bar Harbor, John C. Scates of Westbrook, and William H. Ingraham of Portland.

Maryland—J. Vincent Jamison of Hagerstown, W. C. Stettinius of Baltimore, and Charles E. Bryan of Havre de Grace.

Massachusetts—Alvan T. Fuller of Boston, John J. Prindiville of Framingham, and James P. Doran of New Bedford.

Michigan—Murray D. Van Wagoner of Pontiac, Frank H. Alford of Detroit, and Leo J. Nowicki of Detroit.

Minnesota—John F. D. Meighen of Albert Lea, Fred Schilplin of St. Cloud, and W. N. Ellsberg of Minneapolis.

Mississippi—Hugh L. White of Columbia, Horace Stansell of Ruleville, and Birney Imes of Columbus.

Missouri—William Hirth of Columbia, Harry Scullin of St. Louis, and Henry S. Caulfield of St. Louis.

Montana—James E. Murray of Butte, Raymond M. Hart of Billings, and Peter Peterson of Glasgow.

Nebraska—John Latenser, Jr., of Omaha, John G. Maher of Lincoln, and Dan V. Stevens of Fremont.

Nevada—Robert A. Allen of Carson City, William Settlemeyer of Elko, and Edward Clark of Las Vegas.

New Hampshire—Harold G. Lockwood of Dartmouth College, Robert C. Murchie of Concord and Stanton Owen of Laconia.

New Jersey—Edward J. Duffy of Temack, William E. White of Red Bank, and Walter Kidde of Montclair.

New Mexico—J. D. Atwood of Roswell, Henry G. Coors of Albuquerque, and Felipe Sanchez y Baca of Tucumcari.

New York—Peter G. Ten Eyck of Albany, John T. Dillon of Buffalo, and Paul M. Mazur of New York.

North Carolina—Dr. Herman G. Baity of Chapel Hill, John Devane of Fayetteville, and Frank Page of Raleigh.

North Dakota—Henry Holt of Grand Forks, Stephen J. Doyle of Fargo, and Thomas Moody of Williston.

Ohio—William A. Stinchcomb of Cleveland, Rufus Miles of Columbus, and Henry Bentley of Cincinnati.

Oklahoma—John H. Carlock of Ardmore, Frank C. Higginbotham of Norman, and Walter A. Lybrand of Oklahoma City.

Oregon—Bert Haney of Portland, C. C. Hockley of Portland, and Robert N. Stanfield of Baker.

Pennsylvania—Joseph C. Trees of Pittsburgh, A. E. Malmer of Philadelphia, and J. Hale Steinman of Lancaster.

Rhode Island—William S. Flynn of Providence, John Nicholas Brown of Newport, and William E. Laford of Woonsocket.

South Carolina—L. P. Slattery of Greenville, Burnet R. Maybank of Charleston, and Thomas B. Pearce of Columbia.

South Dakota—Leon P. Wells of Aberdeen, Herbert E. Hitchcock of Mitchell, and S. H. Collins of Aberdeen.

Tennessee—Col. Harry S. Berry of Nashville, Roane Waring of Memphis, and W. Baxter Lee of Knoxville.

Texas—Col. Ike Ashburn of Houston, S. A. Goeth of San Antonio, John Shary of Mission, and R. M. Kelly of Long View.

Utah—William J. Halloran of Salt Lake City, Ora Bundy of Ogden, and Sylvester Q. Cannon of Salt Lake City.

Vermont—Frank H. Duffy of Rutland, P. E. Sullivan of St. Albans, and Lee C. Warner of Bennington.

Virginia—Henry G. Shirley of Richmond, J. Winston Johns of Charlottesville, and Richard Crane of Westover.

Washington—William A. Thompson of Vancouver, C. W. Greenough of Spokane, and Roy Lafollette of Colfax.

West Virginia—D. H. Stephenson of Charleston, William P. Wilson of Wheeling, and Van A. Bittner of Fairmont.

Wisconsin—Walter G. Caldwell of Waukesha, William G. Bruce of Milwaukee, and John Donaghey of Madison.

Wyoming—Patrick J. O'Connor of Casper, Leroy E. Laird of Worland and John W. Hay of Rock Springs.

Railroads Administration

Federal Co-ordinator of Railroads: Joseph B. Eastman.

Director, Freight Service Section: J. R. Turney of St. Louis, Mo., a vice president of the St. Louis Southwestern Railway Co.

Director, Car Pooling Section: O. C. Castle of Houston, Texas, superintendent of transportation for the Southern Pacific Company in Louisiana and Texas.

Purchasing Specialist: R. L. Lockwood of Washington, D. C., formerly with the Commerce Department.

Eastern Regional Director: N. J. German, Pittsburgh, Pa., president of the Montour Railroad.

Western Regional Director: V. V. Boatner, Chicago, Ill., former president of the Chicago Great Western Railroad.

Southern Regional Director: C. E. Weaver, Savannah, Ga., general manager of the Central of Georgia Railway.

Eastern Traffic Assistant: W. H. Chandler, of New York, chairman of the executive committee of the Shippers' Conference of Greater New York.

Western Traffic Assistant: C. E. Hochstedler, Chicago, Ill., traffic director of the Chicago Association of Commerce.

Southern Traffic Assistant: M. M. Caskie, Mobile, Ala., general manager of the Alabama State Docks and general manager of the Terminal Railway at Mobile.

Executive and Legal Assistant: J. W. Carmalt, Washington, D. C.

Executive Assistant: J. L. Rogers, special examiner for the Interstate Commerce Commission.

Research Staff: O. S. Beyer, Washington, D. C., labor

specialist; Leslie Craven, Durham, N. C., professor of law at Duke University; W. B. Poland, New York, consulting engineer; Fred W. Powell, editor of the Institute for Government Research, Washington, D. C.

Eastern Regional Co-ordinating Committee: F. E. Williamson, New York Central; W. W. Atterbury, Pennsylvania; Daniel Willard, Baltimore & Ohio; J. R. Bernet, Chesapeake & Ohio, and J. J. Pelley, New York, New Haven & Hartford; M. C. Kennedy, Executive Secretary, 143 Liberty St., New York, N. Y.

Southern Co-ordinating Committee: Fairfax Harrison, Southern Ry. System; L. A. Downs, Illinois Central System; L. R. Powell, Jr., Seaboard Air Line Ry.; George B. Elliott, Atlantic Coast Line R. R. Co.; W. R. Cole, Louisville & Nashville R. R.; Charles A. Wickersham, Executive Secretary, 4 Hunter St. S. E., Atlanta, Ga.

Western Co-ordinating Committee: Carl R. Gray, Union Pacific System; Ralph Budd, Chicago, Burlington & Quincy R. R.; S. T. Bledsoe, Atchinson, Topeka & Santa Fe Ry. Co.; H. A. Scandrett, Chicago, Milwaukee, St. Paul & Pacific R. R. Co.; Hale Holden, Southern Pacific Co.; E. C. Webster, Executive Secretary, 468 Union Station Bldg., Chicago, Ill.

Miscellaneous Boards

Securities Act

Will be administered by the following members of the *Federal Trade Commission:* Charles H. March, chairman; Garland S. Ferguson; William E. Humphrey; Ewin L. Davis. Acting chairman of committee preparing forms and writing regulations: B. B. Bane, commission attorney.

TENNESSEE RIVER VALLEY

The "Mussolini of Muscle Shoals" is Arthur E. Morgan, president of Antioch College (Ohio). *Directors:* John Harcourt, Alexander Morgan, from Tennessee; David F. Lilienthal, from Wisconsin.

Controller: F. J. Carr, president of Controllers' Assn. of America.

EMERGENCY RELIEF ADMINISTRATION

Administrator: Harry L. Hopkins.

Chapter XVI

DEFLATION AND THE REVOLUTIONISTS

BUSINESS men and investors who will personally visit Washington and talk with administration leaders will learn that there is at least a statistical basis for revolutionary actions. I refer to two sets of figures and charts relative to debts which the Brain Trust watches.

The first set of tables and charts shows that debt is increasing more rapidly than assets. Frankly, compound interest at 6 per cent is one basic cause of the present revolution. Statistics clearly show that the world as set up today cannot stand the present increase in debt as it is now accumulating under compound interest at its present rate.[1]

The second set of tables and charts is not so convincing, but they indicate that there is not enough net income in the terms of goods to pay 3 per cent interest on the total world's investment. If one of us owned all the wealth of the world and had all the annual income we could get only about 2 per cent on our investment. To put it another way, if three persons should invest at random $1,000 each, it would be necessary for two

[1] Those interested in a further study of this angle should read the book entitled *Debt and Production*, by Bassett Jones. New York: John Day Company, 1933.

to go without any interest payment in order for one to secure 6 per cent!

These theorems cannot be proved owing to the great dispute as to the figures involved. But those interested in further study of this problem should read *The Internal Debts of the United States,* by Evans Clark, published by The Macmillan Company, New York (1933). This book is one of the splendid products of the Twentieth Century Fund sponsored by Mr. Edward A. Filene. Mr. John Maynard Keynes of London has also written on this subject. The reasons for the above two beliefs are found in the word *waste.*

METHODS OF SOLVING THE DEBT PROBLEM

I feel that the above two factors have been potent in bringing about the revolution now in progress and as yet little has been done to solve the problems they present. The administration has considered the following six methods of approach:

1. The laissez-faire method of "letting nature take its course" through bankruptcies and reorganizations. The real question here is whether or not people will stand for this today. This method has been possible up to this time, but there is grave question whether it can indefinitely continue.

2. A compulsory cutting of interest rates. This may be accomplished through an amendment to the Federal Bankruptcy Law or it may require an amendment to the Constitution. Even granted that proper legislation for this could be secured in this country, the administration would then face the problem of preventing capi-

tal from being exported to other countries, where it could get higher rates of interest. This means that any legislation for lower interest rates in this country would either need to be followed by international legislation or else by legislation forbidding the export of capital. Of course, the more legislation that is enacted and the more complicated the situation becomes, the more are its disadvantages liable to exceed its advantages.

3. The radical cutting of all indebtedness by 25 or 50 per cent. From the legislative point of view this seems to be the most practical method of approach. It could be accomplished by federal legislation without international legislation and after the job is once done capital might be attracted to this country instead of exported from this country.[1]

4. There also is a proposed method of debt elimination by turning all indebtedness into income bonds or preferred stocks with a minimum rate of say 2 per cent. The plan in this case would be to have the excess rate determined by business conditions of the nation as a whole, as indicated by some such barometer as the Babson chart. If such a housecleaning should take place, it should be accompanied by legislation that would prevent future debt and confine capital investments to stocks and income bonds.

5. The most unpopular method would be the forced payment of these debts through thrift.[2] The citizens

[1] Those desiring more information on this subject are referred to *Sacrifice or Chaos?* by R. R. Schweitzer. Norfolk, Va.: Printcraft Publishing Company.

[2] Statistics indicate that about one-half of the total annual income of the United States is wasted on the following fifteen items:

of the United States could pay off all their debts which aggregate only $200,000,000,000 in eight years by the mere elimination of waste. 6. The most popular method of solving the problem is through either inflation or cheapening the money of the country. This has the advantage of being painless in the early stages and the disadvantage of being painful in the final stages. However, of all the six methods this is the one that has been most talked about in Washington. Therefore, we will discuss it in detail.

Let me first say that it (inflation) is a great bugbear to the Roosevelt administration. The President

---

Harmful or useless speculation; fire losses and auto accidents; unnecessary sickness and industrial accidents; *excess* drinking and smoking; harmful foods, patent medicines and quackery; destructive movies, books and magazines; needless noise and nervous fatigue; adulterations in food and clothing; dumping to uphold present price system; cosmetics and perfumery; joy riding and harmful recreation; waste of light and fuel; unnecessary selling expenses; coffins and funeral expenses; and miscellaneous items. This waste of one-half of our income does not include expenditures of the army and navy, nor the super-expenditures of the rich. Furthermore, they do not give consideration to the further possibility for saving by the substitution of efficient for antiquated machinery, the relocation of plants, the scientific management of factories, farms, and forests, and, most important of all, the sterilization of criminals, insane, and unfit. The waste through the above items exceeds $25,000,000,000 annually in the United States alone.

By employing the people now engaged in these wasteful industries to work in improving the nation's homes would result in raising 100 per cent the nation's standard of living. It would enable everyone to have double in useful food, clothing, shelter and comforts, what they now are forced to be content with. It would be equivalent to a 100 per cent raise in wages.

and his advisers know that a reasonable dose of this drug may help their cause; but they likewise know that an overdose will surely kill their cause. Furthermore, inflation, like most drugs, demands constantly larger doses. When once started the inflation habit develops like the morphine habit. Hence, this entire question of inflation is of tremendous importance to the revolutionists. It may make or break their entire program.

THEORY OF REDUCING DEBTS THROUGH CHEAP MONEY

As this question of inflation is one of the most vital to the revolutionists, the reader should first make sure that he and I are talking the same language when we speak of inflation. There are probably as many definitions of the word as there are economists. Nevertheless, nearly all appreciate that one has the same vague idea as another. Among the soundest definitions of inflation is the following: "The coming into action of increasing amounts of purchasing power relative to the physical volume of business being carried on." In still simpler language: "Increasing quantities of money or checks in circulation as compared with the volume of production and services."

Let us see how inflation fits into our monetary system today. Most unfortunately, this requires a few paragraphs of review of our present system.

Passing from the barter stage, which everyone understands, to the period when precious metals came to be used as money, we find that gold and silver became of great importance. These became the tools with which to exchange goods of different types. As shipping made

forward strides, sudden discoveries of large supplies of
the precious metals came into the civilized world from
distant parts. Such supplies were inflationary. When
business had advanced and the new sources of metal
gave out, prices would drop and business would decrease.

Let us assume that gold and silver alone were to be
used as money: With increasing population and production of goods, business would require increasing
quantities of the exchange tools. Gold and silver mining, therefore, would require a horde of miners busily
extracting the metals. But even then the supply might
not increase as fast as population and business. The
result would be gradually declining prices because for
each unit of gold more and more of the products of
agriculture and industry would have to be exchanged.
Thus, with a general expectation of gradually declining
prices in the course of years, those who held coins
would see fit to hoard such precious metals. This would
decrease still further the supply of tools for exchange
of business and would slow up progress.

Those who had ideas for new business, making new
goods and so forth, would find no supply of money to
put the idea into action. The force of human progress
was so great and the supply of coins increased so
slowly that many cases of inflation or debasement of
the coinage were a natural necessity in order to increase
the quantity of money. *Most often, however, such instances of inflation took place when government
budgets were out of balance and severe hardships were
being experienced in the nations concerned.* Perhaps
even in those cases the immediate plight of things

dimmed the fundamental cause outlined above. Inflation in such instances was a simple process of using less of the precious metals in the coins, thereby making it possible to issue more coins.

It is noteworthy that such debasement of the coinage resulted in the good coins previously in existence being hoarded, because merchants have been well aware for thousands of years that metal is safer than any government. Because of this universal experience in past history, President Roosevelt wisely—if not legally—endeavored to collect all gold in 1933 before announcing any inflationary program.

BEGINNING THE USE OF CHECKS

A further method of inflation developed gradually as moneylenders became sufficiently wealthy to require large safety vaults. Among such moneylenders there were some who had the confidence of other wealthy people whose coins were deposited in the moneylenders' vaults. This concentrated the supply of money. The sum of these quantities grouped together made it possible to lend from the amount in the vaults, thereby increasing what we call the efficiency of the currency system. This was inflation in the sense that the coins were working better—the purchasing power as against business being done was increased. Still later it was found more convenient for the borrower not to withdraw the money borrowed from the safety deposit vault, but to leave it there and use a check which he turned over to the payee in spending such borrowings.

As this checking process came into more general

use, it was soon discovered that since the money lent and the depositors' money stayed in the vaults, the moneylenders could perhaps *overlend*. That is, if the money was to be spent in the vicinity and no one would come to take it out of the vault, but would use checks instead, the moneylenders could lend more than they had in the vault. A sufficient percentage was kept on hand to satisfy the few who might come to take out money represented by their deposit or by a check. The peculiar thing about this excess lending is that the borrower owes real money definitely to the bank; but the bank does not have this excess amount lent, nor do the depositors. Many complications would have developed if the system, once started, had been abolished. In any event, the idea proved so beneficial to trade that it was soon legalized and banks were established with government sanction to lend in greater amounts than the currencies in their vaults. The establishment of this banking system was, therefore, an inflation.

The major justification for the system rests in the saving of mining costs since the checks thus artificially created by excess lending function as a tool of exchange. The difficulty mentioned at the outset with respect to the declining trend of prices if coins alone were to be used and the consequent increase in hoarding was thereby eliminated. Different tendencies were created: As business and the efficiency of the banking system increased, the quantity of checks could increase. So that, instead of declining, prices might actually hold steady or advance; and hoarding, instead of increasing, might actually decrease. This use of credit was an ideal set of forces to boost business and trade, to put into action every possible idea that might benefit civilization. The only necessity was a safety brake. This, governments thought, was effectively had in the requirement of a certain percentage of reserves in currency against the deposits in the bank.

Later, as in 1914 and 1917 after the establishment of the Federal Reserve System in the United States, these reserve requirements were sharply reduced. This permitted much more check money and was still further inflation, leading to the high prices of 1920. After the speculative crash of 1920, the forward surge of progress continued, business increased and prices gradually declined. Therefore, it should be remembered that inflation is nothing new. Governments have always been inflating. Our own Federal Reserve System was an inflation scheme which was partly responsible for the 1929-33 depression and the present silent revolution.

Of course, since checks are claims against the currency in the vaults of the banks, and many of these checks had been allowed to be made in excess of the currency, there would come in hard times mass attempts to collect the nonexistent cash. Banks would fail, and the failure would wipe out the checks, thus reducing the tools with which to carry on the exchange of business. Such are modern periods of deflation in the United States. Prices would tend to remain low until such a time as bankers again became confident that they could overlend without people attempting to collect.

The general knowledge that the banking system creates nonexistent funds, and thereby a rather inflated price level is acknowledged in the fact that savings banks are allowed to invest only in securities where the coverage in dollar value is far greater than the amount invested or lent. Moreover, banks themselves confirm the normally inflated level of prices in a banking community since they always require far greater value of a security than the amount they lend.

BANKING VS. DEBT

During depressions epidemics of failures are more or less severe. In the United States, the epidemic from 1929 to 1933 reached the greatest proportion in the history of the country. In fact, throughout large sections of the country the judicial system of enforcing debt contracts, through the transfer of property by foreclosure or bankruptcy, broke down entirely. Respect for law turned into scorn. Debts entered into with good intentions were ignored with a contempt which felt itself justified because of the extremely unusual and apparently unfair circumstances which made the payment of interest and the entire debt impossible.

That is easily understood in this fashion: If a farmer's debt is made when prices are high, say, $1.50 a bushel for wheat, the interest requirement at 6 per cent of $1.50 is expected to be 6 per cent or 1/16 of a bushel. If the price of wheat goes down to 40 cents, the interest requirement at 6 per cent of the $1.50 (9 cents) is said to become unfair, being nearly 25 per cent of a bushel! So it is with the debts of other individuals performing other jobs, such as owning mortgaged apartment houses, etc. Of course, the borrower never thinks of what happens when prices turn in the other direction and the lender loses.

Following 1929 were five years of unemployment and curtailment of production. By 1933 the ability of the nation to produce goods and to increase business had not yet improved materially. Yet these five years of hard times have cost the United States government perhaps as much as ten billion dollars over and above receipts from taxation. This, mind you, in case you are likely to treat billions as lightly as do Congressmen, is an increase of 50 per cent in the national debt in the space of only five years! And with nothing to show for it but plowed-under cotton fields and dilapidated tenement houses! It is not strange, therefore, that merchants remember that metal is safer than governments. The government's ability to pay, in terms of metal, became only from two-thirds to three-fourths of what it formerly was, which made foreigners and our own merchants willing to give only about 65 to 75 cents' worth of metal for our dollar.

CHEAPENING MONEY

Thus inflation through cheapening money generally comes as a result of economic forces and of unbalanced government budgets; and so it did in this country. But there were other events far more important to the individual taking place simultaneously with deterioration in the earning power of the government. These were an epidemic of failures, the severe decline in security prices, the growing disregard for law, and the fact that insurance companies, savings banks and building and loan associations were insolvent at the quoted values of their assets. Some kind of inflation seemed necessary to raise these dollar values and prevent complete collapse in social faith. This need was emphasized more than any other as the reason for abandoning the gold standard.

Of course, when the quantity of gold in each dollar is reduced, it is possible to make so many more dollars out of the gold that we have. With the banking system outlined above, the increase of a few billions in currency can result in a potential increase of many billions of excess lending ability, or check money. This was the argument of the revolutionists in their endeavor to make their revolution as painless as possible.

To appreciate the niceties of debt readjustment by thus cheapening money, the method must be contrasted to other debt adjustment alternatives. In a word, inflation after a while tends to affect all prices and salaries in one full sweep. Higher prices and the greater quantity of money floating around make it easier for all to pay their debts. The honest man, who would make his best efforts to pay in full in any case, is not faced with the competition that he would have had from the shirker, who would go bankrupt and start anew with a clean slate if there were no inflation to ease the way out.

By inflation creditor and debtor have no disagreement to iron out. Their relations are not impaired as individuals to each other. Future good relations are thereby insured. In fact, by debasement of the coinage or devaluation of the dollar only one institution defaults, and that is the government! It must be remem-

bered that the foundation of progress rests in business
or exchange of ideas and services. Such exchange would
not be possible without the all-important moral force
of faith in one another's word. Thus, when the failure
epidemic becomes too great, inflation comes in as a
protector of faith among individuals. Usually the nation soon comes to a new understanding as to the expected permanent future value of its coinage. Those
who have funds to invest gradually abandon their fears
and make the best of a new situation.

IMPORTANCE OF STABILIZATION

Those who are hit hardest or gain least by inflation
and the subsequent rise in prices of goods or the cost
of living are investors whose funds were placed in
high-grade securities or with strong honorable debtors.
The interest rates on such loans are low, the market
value of the loan near par, and inflation reduces the
purchasing power of the creditor's fixed income (as
prices rise). Such investors are the millions whose
funds are invested in savings banks or insurance companies. They are those whose savings are moderate and
who usually are not acquainted with business and investment procedure as well as those who have large
wealth. True, most of these are also wage and salary
earners or closely related to persons who will benefit
by increased employment if business improves as a result of rising prices.

In considering depositors in savings banks and insurance companies, it must not be overlooked that the
value of the assets of these institutions had declined so

much in 1933 that the depositors were faced with the
alternative of receiving about 70 cents on the dollar if
no inflation were to take place, or to receive 100 cents
in a cheaper dollar worth 70 cents in metal on the old
basis. But the purchasing power of the cheaper dollar
for other commodities than the precious metals need
not be less than it was in 1913, twenty years before—
at least that has been the claim of the inflationists.

Of course, business moves ahead when new purchasing power is put into action. (Do not overlook the
fact that the mere buying of commodities as many have
done to protect themselves against inflation does not
by itself increase business.) New purchasing power
comes into effect and business moves forward when
those in charge of such operations see gain in the action. When is there likely to be a gain? Certainly not
if selling prices will be lower than costs—*and again certainly not if selling prices, though higher, were to be in
money which threatened to become worthless soon.*
Many people in discussing inflation overlook this latter
aspect of the subject. They are not aware that beyond
a certain point, which may be impossible to determine,
there would be a tendency for business to stop entirely
and to hoard the available supply of goods in warehouses and in process. In such a case inflation would
destroy its present objective. *Here is the need for stabilization.*

Any debasement of coinage by more than 50 per cent
is likely to lead to dire results. It would appear that
at the present stage of civilization the average citizen
can adjust himself to a 50 per cent change in the purchasing power of his tool used for exchange of goods,

but that a depreciation greater than about 50 per cent results in complete dislocation of the different parts of the social organization. Thus inflation is a dangerous drug with which to play and—although it has a legitimate use at times—can do irreparable damage.

FIAT MONEY UNNECESSARY

This nation is a check-using country by habit. Large increases in the circulation of paper money which occurred during the banking difficulties were, to a great extent, returned to the banks. Some people would like to see the government issue more fiat money, or, in other words, run the printing presses for a while. That always has a bad effect on sentiment and instills only more fears among those who have funds to invest. With present banking legislation, it is absolutely unnecessary. We have, to all practical purposes, the very system of fiat money operating at present in a disguised form. This country uses principally Federal Reserve notes. The Federal Reserve banks in turn have been buying government bonds by the billions in this depression, against which they can issue Federal Reserve notes and place them in circulation.

Why have not these Federal Reserve notes circulated? Because up to about September, 1933, such government bonds purchased were principally not new bonds and the seller merely directed the Federal Reserve banks to credit the seller's account at the bank instead of giving him money. Thus in the United States the equivalent of running printing presses could be reflected by increasing excess reserves of the member banks. Beginning in the fall of 1933, however, the government's business reviving programs were running into substantial expenditures, with the result that new bond issues sold to the Federal Reserve banks for such purposes actually put to work considerable sums of new credit.

When a depression has spent the greater part of its force, and the dollar has reached a quotation of about 65 to 70 cents of its former value, in terms of gold, a peculiar question arises. It is, what will be done with the gold in the vaults of the Federal Reserve banks and other banks when stabilization takes place? The quantity of gold then becomes suddenly about 50 per cent more dollars than it formerly was. It must not be overlooked that the Federal Reserve banks are owned by the member banks, which in turn are owned by stockholders. The government required the citizens of the nation in 1933 to yield up their gold. The government could require the Federal Reserve to do likewise. Then the Treasury would have sufficient free gold of its own to issue billions of new treasury notes having the same gold backing as the Federal Reserve notes might then have.

Thus, the credit inflation possibilities under the present set-up are tremendous. Credit inflation such as we had in 1920, and at other periods, is also a cheap money program. Even though under such circumstances interest rates may be high, the fundamental fact remains that credit inflation is a cheap money program until such time as attempts are made to collect debts wholesale. Some may have fears with respect to the potential inflationary possibilities that are developing. For instance, the member banks have been buying tremendous quantities of government bonds during the course of the depression, and now the Federal Reserve banks may buy these and issue Federal Reserve notes against them, or credit the account of the member banks. Thus, for each $1,000 bond sold by the member banks to the Federal Reserve banks, potentially something like $8,000 of credit could be extended by commercial banks under present reserve requirements. As a safety brake on credit inflation, one of the last paragraphs of the Farm Adjustment Act, passed in May, 1933, stipulates that the authorities of the Federal Reserve banks and the government have the power to increase the reserve requirement which, in other words, would mean decrease the excess lending ability of the banks per dollar of currency. As an incentive to inflation, is the power of the Reconstruction Finance Corporation to bid up the price of gold. In closing let me give the reasons for and against inflation.

REASONS FOR INFLATION

1. To raise the general price level of commodities and services back to the average at the time when the bulk of long-term debts were contracted. Thus the greater dollar income would ease the burden of interest and settlement of debts to about the point which both debtor and creditor counted on when the debt was made.

2. To assure dollar profits to business men, and incite productive activity.

3. To restore the savings banks and insurance companies to a solvent position.

4. To induce owners of cash and credit to put it to use.

5. To raise the government's revenue to balance budgets.

REASONS AGAINST INFLATION

1. If a change in gold redemption against currency is part of the inflation program, it means default on the government's promise to pay such gold.

2. Creditors will be wary of lending more to others, preferring to reap benefits of inflation for themselves, especially in view of the severe losses they would have on existing bonds and mortgages which they hold.

3. Creditors will lend to others only after prices have advanced considerably, resulting in a new debtor class at peak prices, and so not changing the social problem from what it was previous to the depression.

4. Unless payrolls are advanced simultaneously with rising prices, the worker faces a declining purchasing power.

5. By the time inflationary methods are finally decided upon and put into effect, a large percentage of debtors have already lost their properties to the creditors. A great part of the benefits, therefore, go to those who obtained properties and other good assets by foreclosure at fractions of their values. Thus, many debtors and business men who pleaded for inflation in the first half of the depression find themselves left out when the advancing trend finally takes place.

Hence even the revolutionists themselves are in a quandary as to what to do.

CHAPTER XVII

WHAT OF THE FUTURE?

IN CONCLUSION let me return to my life work as a statistician. Let me attempt to answer honestly what will follow these great revolutionary policies started on March 4, 1933. Will the United States continue to grow more and more radical as has Russia, or will it experience a reaction toward conservatism as has England?

Without doubt the "prosperity" of the "twenties" (1924-29) was as false as that of the "gay nineties" (1890-93). It was based on glaring injustice and bad economics. President Roosevelt and his advisers stand for a new morality which is sure to bear fruit, whatever happens to his party in years to come. Therefore, every good citizen should stand for the ideals and goals of this revolutionary group, whether or not we believe in the methods.

As the Central Conference of Jewish Rabbis[1] declared in September, 1933, the new morality is merely based upon the incontrovertible principle that social good is to be determined not by the welfare of the few but by that of the many. It frowns upon the exploitation of labor-saving machinery without ample provision by a limitation of hours of labor to prevent

[1] Obtainable from Rabbi Edward L. Israel, Har Sinai Temple, Bolton and Wilson Streets, Baltimore, Maryland.

wholesale unemployment. It seeks to prevent the greed which would deny the masses the means of buying in decent measure for their sustenance the products of their toil. It abhors any effort to construe economic planning in terms of economic fascism which would spell the doom of all true industrial democracy and would bring only oppression and violence. It recognizes that sound economic planning necessitates not only closely knit organization among employers but also among employes. There can be no economic wisdom which fails to reckon with labor as an integrated portion of industry, organized under its own leaders selected by a truly free choice.

These are the chief angles of the newly accepted economic morality. They are, however, only the beginnings of an expanding social conscience. Unemployment insurance, old age security, adequate accident and health insurance, complete abolition of all forms of child labor—these are some additional features of a program which organized religion has long advocated through its social creeds. If we really achieve the ethical attitude toward economic life which is the chief aim of the new order, the official acceptance of these additional features will be speedy and complete.

The testimony of history is invoked to show that a civilization such as ours, which sets all its goals and places all its incentives upon the individual power of accumulating material riches, cannot long endure. Society, by orderly and democratic means, must follow further the steps it has already begun to take and exercise increasing control over the forces of production and distribution as well as the system of profits. Not only must the economic well-being of all be insured, but the great spiritual qualities of human society must be freed from a bitter all-engrossing struggle for bread —freed for the finer potentialities of which humanity is capable. It means that the test of man's wits in that struggle will be with the forces of nature and not with the connivings of his fellow man. It means that humanity will be partners instead of enemies in the great task of living.

Both the Catholics—through Pope Pius XI's famous Encyclical on "Reconstructing the Social Order"—and the Protestants by many books[1] of their leaders, have emphasized these same pertinent facts. Furthermore, business men themselves realize that it was the general lack of sane religion which caused the vicious downward circle of 1929-33; viz., less employment developed less payrolls; less payrolls developed less purchasing power; less purchasing power developed less business; while less business resulted in even less employment. They further recognize that only a spiritual revival can cause this circle to reverse itself so that more confidence will create more employment; more employment will create more purchasing power; more purchasing power will create more business; while better business will result in even more employment. Therefore, the Roosevelt program has the best of backgrounds. In fact,

---

[1] *The Third American Revolution*, by Dr. Bensen Y. Landis, published by the Y.M.C.A. Association Press, New York City; "The Protestant Churches and the Social Crises," by Edmund R. Chaffie, published by Mae Williams; and *The Social Gospel and Christian Culture*, by Charles C. Morrison, published by Harpers.

the churches would probably be with the President en masse if he had not split with them on the liquor question.

THE REVOLUTIONARY PROGRAM

During the presidential campaign of 1932 and the months following Roosevelt's victory, he and his friends worked on twelve lines of action. They looked upon the enemy "Depression" as an army to conquer and they planned twelve different lines of attack. These have been treated by various writers approximately as follows:

1. Special interests must be sacrificed to general interests. This is the basic principle of the revolution in connection with the redistribution of income.

2. The adoption of a system of economic planning in the interests of the entire country.

3. Protection of the credit of the federal government by a policy of economy and the balancing of the budget.

4. Balancing farm and industrial prices and getting the prices of raw materials back to the 1926-28 level.

5. Inaugurating the large public works program and other features to create employment.

6. Entering into the ownership and operation of great public works such as Muscle Shoals, Columbia River, St. Lawrence development, Boulder Dam and the Mississippi River in the interests of undeveloped sections and handicapped people.

7. Protecting the people's savings by strengthening the banking situation and safeguarding the issuance and sale of securities.

8. Coordinating of transportation systems to eliminate waste and increase efficiency, the purpose being both to reduce rates and to protect investors.

9. Take a vigorous part in world affairs on the theory that one nation cannot prosper in the long run unless other nations prosper likewise.

10. Reduce working hours, both to spread employment and to create more leisure for spiritual and cultural development. ·

11. Protect legitimate debtors from losing their homes and farms by the creation of the Farm Credit Administration and the Home Loan Corporation.

12. Embark upon federal relief to assure every worthy person who is able to work a position, and those who are not able to work, aid.

Surely the above lines of action are worthy goals. The question is whether they can be quickly given effect by the American people. Can these changes be brought about merely by legislation or must they come gradually through spiritual awakening and education? May not Roosevelt fall through a "noble experiment" with business as Hoover fell through a "noble experiment" with prohibition? Are not the arguments for and against both causes similar?

DEMOCRACY'S DIFFICULTY

I believe in the goal for which President Roosevelt is striving: a more equal distribution of the nation's products with a retention of individual liberty, initiative and reward. I sincerely hope his great experiments to accomplish this end will be successful. I am helping in every possible way and am urging others to do so. But the desired result cannot be reached through killing millions of hogs and destroying millions of acres of cotton, *merely to protect an antiquated price system and an existing debt structure.* Nor can it be attained by permitting veterans, labor leaders, bankers or industrialists to bulldoze the government.

The real difficulty is that democracy has become too complicated. Unless there is a spiritual revival and a change in the *motives, purposes* and *ambitions* of the people, it may take a housecleaning to get us out of the jam. The whole process has become so involved that there may be only one solution; namely, clean it all out and start over again depending upon a righteous dictator in the meantime.

Certain city governments are flagrant illustrations. Some cities surely have shown that they cannot govern themselves. As an ardent exponent of liberty and democracy I would contend that when a city fails in honest government it should be ruled by a dictator appointed by Washington. "Reform" governments last only a short time. When the majority of people of a city have the right spirit, local government is practical; but many cities do not seem to be ready for it.

The same principle applies to organized labor. President Roosevelt is right in insisting that wage workers have a right to organize and bargain collectively, but when labor unions become too intrenched they are likely to be ruled by irresponsible leaders. This is one reason for the "company union." When honestly operated it corresponds with town government, which has always done well. I want to see labor get higher wages and better working conditions; but if their leaders over-reach, they surely will bring about a dictatorship, and that will be their downfall.

Mind you, I am not now suggesting government ownership or even government operation. A river cannot rise higher than its source. If a majority of the people have not the right spirit *individually*, they can be no better *collectively*. Putting several bad eggs together does not make a good omelet. My point simply is that the securing of justice, the punishment of crime, the operation of our cities, the methods of labor unions, the action of veterans, and many other things have become so complicated or arbitrary that they no longer serve their purpose. If they do not reform themselves quickly, the American people may lose their patience and wipe out each system and start over again. This would mean temporarily a dictatorship until the United States Constitution is revised to provide for the new conditions which our forefathers never contemplated.

Perhaps industry does not need a dictator; but can there be any more flagrant illustrations of waste and inefficiency than are exhibited in business? The useless duplication of everything from chain stores to gasoline filling stations, coupled with much misdirected advertising helps to explain why goods cost consumers so much. This cost of distribution is blocking production and causing unemployment. Manufacturing could perhaps be let alone for another generation; but a dictator of distribution would seem to be needed at once. Many claim such a change would reduce living-costs 50 per cent and increase volume of sales correspondingly to the advantage of all. Advertising has an important function; but it should be properly directed and not left to unprincipled men or devoted chiefly to increasing the use of cigarettes, beer and cosmetics. The advertising pages of the press have far greater possibilities.

BANKERS AND CHURCHES

The bankers are already "getting theirs," so we will not jump on men who are down; but it would appear that they deserve what has come to them. The farmers, through class legislation, are tying themselves into a knot which I fear only a benevolent dictator can cut. The railroads and public utilities are in disfavor because of lawyers, bankers and labor leaders. The amusement industry is undermining the morals and motives of our people. Its commercialism and wretched leadership surely needs a housecleaning. Movies, radio and other great inventions cannot long be permitted to operate merely to benefit a few people at the expense of American manhood.

Even the churches, colleges and charitable organizations need overhauling. These all started in a simple way and with the purest motives. They have become so unwieldy, however, as often to forget the purposes for which they were founded. I can speak with authority on this subject. It is more evident every year that those at the head of our great Protestant denominations are more interested in their own jobs than in the welfare of their ministers and church members. The same tends to be true of our large educational institutions and charitable organizations. I firmly believe in the great need and usefulness of these religious and

other bodies; but if they will not reform themselves, a
housecleaning may be necessary. In the interim, they
must not be surprised if they are ruled by a dictator.
*A palliative such as inflation or price fixing will merely
delay the evil day.*

No sane person believes in a dictatorship as a permanent solution of the present wretched situation. A dictator would serve only to clean house and hold things
together until our federal constitution is revised in a
legal manner. We must, however, raise a new generation of young people, to be actuated by the spirit of
service, rather than by greed, dishonesty and incompetence. This must be done through the homes, schools
and churches, after the present débris is cleared away.
In the last analysis, government, industry and welfare
are spiritual issues. Life, liberty and happiness depend
upon us as individuals and must be secured through
less, rather than merely through *more*, legislation.
Whether or not this change can now be brought about
without what is equivalent to a temporary dictatorship
is a question.

AN HONEST REVOLUTIONARY PROGRAM

If a dictatorship should take place, the dictator
would probably work along three lines, as follows:
(1) He would stop the present sniping between employers and wage workers, between bankers and depositors, between public utilities and communities,
between the government and its tax payers, between
the cities and the rural districts, between the farmers

and the industrials, the veterans and the non-veterans, the North and the South, the East and the West.

(2) He would outline a definite plan, extending over about twenty years, for *gradually* taking over the essential industries from private to public control, and giving the owners thereof a just recompense. (3) In the meantime, such a dictator would unshackle industry, and give it full opportunity of freedom—unhandicapped by uneconomic legislation, such as sur-taxes, processing taxes, and the like.

Such a twenty-year plan would permit the present generation, who have been educated, trained and developed under the capitalistic system, to continue thereunder; but would train those born after the dictatorship to work and depend upon the new system. This would be just, both to those now living and those to be born in the future. The real crime of the socialist program is to wipe out the savings of people whom the state itself educated and trained to depend upon the present system. If, however, a new generation from birth were educated, trained, and understood that they must get their living through some new technological system, they would have nothing to complain about.

Of course, the present system of using inheritance taxes or capital taxes for the operating expenses of government is very wrong. It, however, would be reasonable to have a small annual capital tax, which would be used for taking over industry gradually during the twenty years ahead. Such a capital tax would enable the government ultimately to secure these industries *without being burdened by debt,* and at the same time, to reimburse at a fair price, those who now own the industries which would be taken over. The difficulty today is that a guerrilla warfare exists between the conservative and radical groups, each sniping at the other without rhyme or reason.

Without doubt, the capitalistic system will some day be substituted by something more just and more sensible. Personal profit cannot always be the motive for industry and commerce. When such a change takes place, however, the change should carefully be planned to extend over a generation. This would protect those who have been brought up under the present system, and would give the time to train properly those who are to operate under the new system. In the meantime, as above indicated, the dictator would remove the present shackles from business, using all forms of sur-taxes to flatten the business cycle, rather than to extend it. This means that he would put on sur-taxes during periods of prosperity and high prices, but would entirely eliminate such taxes during periods of depression and unemployment.

LESSON OF HISTORY

A study of history shows the following four facts: (1) Every nation passes through much the same stages. The histories of individual nations differ as to details, but not as to their basic struggles. (2) The world cannot be judged as an entirety. Although each nation develops from primitive tribal conditions to a complex civilization, yet nations are at different stages at one time. (3) The great progress in nations is brought about neither by the conservatives nor by the radicals, but rather by the great middle class. This middle class puts up with the conflict between the other two classes for a certain time, and then loses its patience and takes control in the form of a dictatorship. (4) In the case of the Anglo-Saxon race, these changes have occurred about every 150 years. For instance, the religious conflict was supreme until 1492, when we entered the era of reform and discovery, lasting 156 years. In 1648 we entered the period of struggle for political freedom, which continued 139 years; and in 1787 we entered the democratic period of rugged individualism which continued up to the present, namely, 146 years. Another great era is now due. What will it be?

A study of history further shows that the world has continually been growing better, but that it can advance only so far materially, politically and intellectually as that advance is backed up by corresponding spiritual development. When the political, material or scientific advance gets too far ahead of the spiritual advance, civilization temporarily gets out of balance. The inevitable result has been a dictatorship. This dictatorship continues until things again get in balance and another new era begins. In 1928 and 1929, when my Wall Street friends were hailing "A New Era of Prosperity," Wellesley, Massachusetts, was looked upon as a hotbed of Jeremiahs! I did not believe in that "New Era," and constantly asserted that it was false and would fail. I feel differently, however, regarding the present New Era which is set upon a more equal distribution of the nation's annual income. This is now just beginning. I believe this new goal will determine the program for the next 150 years, *although it will soon be found necessary also to redistribute and foster judgment, initiative, industry, courage and those other rugged traits which made America.*

CONCLUSIONS

Previous eras were brought about by conflicts over religion, government, or science. This "New Era" which we are now entering is being brought about by a conflict over the *distribution of the nation's annual income.* It is being crystallized by the immediate conflicts between capital and labor, between private and government control. No one group will be victorious. The middle classes will stand this conflict only for a limited period. Then, as the result of depreciated currency and high prices or some other cause, they may take charge of the situation with a temporary dictatorship. Then would follow a Constitutional convention to provide for new conditions which the makers of the Constitution did not foresee.

Who the dictator would be, if any, no one knows. Dictators are self-made and usually are men who have suffered persecution rather than men who are elected by popular vote. The important thing is that a dictator shall be spiritually minded and absolutely unselfish, with good judgment and indomitable courage. In short, I do not worry about communism, socialism, capitalism, or labor-unionism. The American people will stand these selfish class groups for only a reasonable time. Then they will rise in their wrath, clean out all class leaders, and substitute *temporarily* an impartial dictator who would give each group its proper place in the de-

velopment of the nation. That is, this will happen *if
these class conflicts become too severe*. This dictator
would continue in power until people again come to
their senses and catch up spiritually and intellectually
with the progress they had theretofore made along
other lines. Those of us who love democracy naturally
hope such a dictator will never be necessary.

Statistics clearly indicate that we now are in an economic revolution of which the Blue Eagle may become
the symbol of such a dictator. On the other hand, the
revolutionists may make such a mess of things that
there will follow a Republican landslide and a popular
reaction toward conservatism without any resort to a
dictatorship. Meanwhile the government, through the
R.F.C. and other bodies, is rapidly becoming the largest
investor in American railroads, banks, and other corporations. This of itself will tend for conservatism
rather than for revolution. In addition, the conservatives now have in their favor the working of Newton's
Law of Action and Reaction, which law favored the
liberals during the years directly following 1928.

INDEX

AAA, 11, 134
Abbott, Grace, 106
Addams, Jane, 92, 98
Administrative Justice and the Supremacy of Law, 214
Aeronautical Board, 194
American Academy of Political and Social Science, 100
American Agriculturist, The, 233, 234
American Federation of Labor, 83, 101, 102, 108, 109
American Statistical Association, 106
Annals, 101
Appropriations Committees, 266, 269
of the Senate, 203
Attorney-General's Department, 203

Baruch, Bernard M., 37
Berle, Adolph A., Jr., 34, 35, 283
Brandeis, Louis D., 35
Bryan, William J., 204, 220, 254
Buchanan, James P., 36, 268
Bullitt, William C., 33, 283
Bureau of Foreign and Domestic Commerce, 200, 216
Bureau of Labor Statistics, 20, 106

Bureau of Ordnance, 192
Bureau of Supplies and Accounts, 193
Bureau of Yards and Docks, 192
Burleson, Albert Sidney, 200
Byrns, Joseph W., 36

CCC, 134, 177, 179
Census Bureau, 199
Chapin, Roy D., 206
Children's Bureau, 106
Clark, Champ, 75, 76
Commissioner of Internal Revenue, 202, 204, 208
Commodity Price Index, 112
Compensation Board, 194
Congregationalist, 55
Congressional Directory, 261, 266, 270
Connery, William P., Jr., 109, 268
Coolidge, Calvin, 1, 28, 35, 52, 57, 123, 153, 162, 172, 186, 204, 206, 258
Copeland, Royal S., 267
Cost-of-Living Index, 112
Cox, James M., 120, 204
Cummings, Homer S., 24, 218-229, 288, 292
a good speaker, 220
background, 224
clubs, 228

331